BAD HAND

A Biography of General
Ranald S. Mackenzie

Ranald S. Mackenzie in dress uniform in the mid-1870s
(Amon Carter Museum of Western Art)

BAD HAND

A Biography of General Ranald S. Mackenzie

by Charles M. Robinson III

Foreword by Stan Hoig

STATE HOUSE PRESS
McMurry University
Abilene, Texas
2005

Library of Congress Cataloging-in-Publication Data

Robinson, Charles M., 1949-
    Bad Hand: a biography of General Ranald S. Mackenzie/by
Charles M. Robinson III.—rpt. 2005

    p. cm.
    Includes bibliographical references and index.
    1. Mackenzie, Ranald Slidell, 1840-1889. 2. Indians of North
America—Wars—1866-1895. 3. Generals—United States—Biography.
4. United States. Army. Cavalry, 4th—History. I. Title.

E83.866.M33R63   1993   973.8'092—dc20 [B]   93-530

ISBN-13: 978-1-880510-02-5
ISBN-10: 1-880510-02-2

Printed in the United States of America

State House Press
McMurry Station, Box 637
Abilene, Texas 79697-0637

Distributed by Texas A&M University Press Consortium
www.tamu.edu/upress • 1-800-826-8911

Cover design by Rosenbohm Graphic Design

To My Mother

ROSALYN C. ROBINSON

TABLE OF CONTENTS

LIST OF ILLUSTRATIONS

LIST OF ILLUSTRATIONS

Acknowledgments

For my theories regarding Mackenzie's insanity, sole credit belongs to my brother, Ross C. Robinson of the Texas Department of Mental Health and Mental Retardation in Tyler and Athens, Texas. He first raised the possibility of a cause other than venereal disease, based on his own work with military psychosis, and referred me to the relevant sections of DSM-III. Franklin Smith, director of El Chamizal National Memorial in El Paso, put Mackenzie's illness into historical perspective for me. John Joershke, editor, Western Publications, Stillwater, Oklahoma, encouraged my initial article on the subject, "Mackenzie's Madness."

Thanks also go to J'Nell Pate for pointing out the need to emphasize Mackenzie's accomplishments in ending the Ute War, and to the Newberry Library of Chicago for permission to reprint portions of Richard I. Dodge's diary of the Powder River Campaign.

I wish to acknowledge the assistance of the Library of Congress and National Archives, Washington, D.C.; Williams College, Williamstown, Massachusetts; U.S. Military Academy, West Point, New York; Arnulfo Oliveira Library, Fort Brown, Brownsville, Texas; Oklahoma State Historical Society, Oklahoma City; Thomas Gilcrease Institute, Tulsa, Oklahoma; University of New Mexico, Albuquerque; Eugene C. Barker Texas History Center, University of Texas, Austin; Amon Carter Museum of Western Art, Fort Worth; Wilton Jordan, San Benito, Texas; Greater Slidell Area Chamber of Commerce, Slidell, Louisiana; Southwestern Collection, Texas Tech University, Lubbock; Claire Kuhn, Panhandle-

Plains Historical Society, Canyon, Texas, and the U.S. Army
Military History Institute at Carlisle Barracks, Pennsylvania.

This was an expensive project, and I received no grants.
Had it not been for a group of understanding bankers, who
trusted me and believed in this work, it would never have been
completed. Thanks to L. Nathan Winters, Ernest Taubert and
Frank Sanchez, of the San Benito Bank and Trust Co., and to
Robert B. Dunkin of the First National Bank of San Benito.

There are some special people who deserve acknow-
ledgment: my eighth grade history teacher, Mrs. Menton J.
(Betty) Murray; my long-suffering and ill-rewarded agent,
Bertha Klausner, New York; James L. Haley of Austin for the
loan of reference materials, for his comments and, most of all,
for his friendship; the San Benito, Texas, Public Library,
particularly Rosie Mares and Lupita Flores of Interlibrary
Loan; Tom Munnerlyn and Debbie Brothers of State House
Press, my publishers, and Erik J. Mason, my editor; and
finally, my wife, Perla, and daughter, Rita.

Foreword

With more than a century having passed since the last of its Indian wars, Americans are still sorting out the truths and non-truths, the rights and wrongs, the heroes and the non-heroes. The task is not a simple one, largely because much of Western military history has been written to satisfy the yearning of the American public for the exemplar warrior to idolize and hold up as a symbol for the body politic. All too often publicity, imagery and sheer luck, more than martial performance, are key factors in the creation of this *beau idéal* soldier.

The ghost of George Armstrong Custer, which still commands a legion of ardent admirers, well illustrates the fact that good public relations and good fortune are sometimes more effective than accomplishments in building reputation. Custer is still seen by many Americans as *the* great Indian fighter. In truth, as Charles Robinson has pointed out in this work, Custer fought only two engagements of any prominence with the Indians. Despite whatever bravery and military acumen Custer may have possessed, his only victory over Indians (which he proclaimed to be a larger conquest than it really was) was to overrun a small village of Cheyennes on the Washita River in present Oklahoma in 1868. His other engagement, of course, was the tragic defeat at the Little Bighorn of present Montana in 1876.

If such a title as *the* great Indian fighter is to be conferred, Ranald S. Mackenzie is a far more creditable candidate. Some historians might place Nelson A. Miles or George Crook in contention, but it would be difficult to sustain either of them against Mackenzie's record, either in the number of their major engagements or in their battle successes.

The military leaders who formed the Indian-fighting army following the Civil War soon learned that chasing warriors on the Western plains was a hopeless undertaking. The Plains Indians seldom stood their ground to fight pitched battles and their grass-fed ponies could easily outrun and outmaneuver the heavier, grain-fed army mounts. If the Indians saw they were outnumbered or couldn't win, they simply faded away to fight another day. Indeed, it was probably Custer's frustration in not being able to pin down the Indians for a fight that, in part, prompted him to charge impetuously into the Sioux-Cheyenne camp on the Little Bighorn.

As a result of the army's failure to engage and defeat warriors in the field, it adopted a more severe technique of warfare—to march on the Indians' home villages, to attack without warning or offering a chance for surrender, and to kill whoever happened to get in the way. It was precisely this military tactic of striking the Indians' homes and families that, as the movies like to say, "won the West." Without question, Mackenzie was more effective at this than were Custer, Crook, or Miles.

Mackenzie was a hard-fighting cavalry officer whose attention was directed mainly toward defeating the enemy rather than embellishing the results. Still, as we see in this life story of him, he was a man of both personal strengths and weaknesses, one who fought great personal battles as well as battles on the fields of combat. Here, too, we gain insight into the rancorous contests for recognition and rank in which military personalities sometimes became embroiled.

Because he died pathetically insane, history has treated

Mackenzie as a tragic figure rather than a heroic one. Such an end contains none of the glamour of the paintings of Custer atop a windswept Montana hill—the last man, pistol in hand, grandly facing a horde of Indian warriors and a glorious death.

Perhaps if Mackenzie had died in battle, if he had let his hair grow long and had worn fringed buckskins, if he had spent more effort on self-publicity, if he had wed a wife who was a prolific writer and defended him long after death, if he had not lost two fingers in battle, if he had not suffered his mental illness at the end—well, perhaps then history would have given him more recognition as the brilliantly successful cavalry commander he was. This book is a major step forward in gaining Mackenzie the recognition he so rightfully deserves.

STAN HOIG
Professor Emeritus
University of Central Oklahoma

PROLOGUE

On January 19, 1889, Brigadier General Ranald Slidell Mackenzie died in the home of a cousin on Staten Island. Mackenzie had been retired nearly five years earlier, subsequent to an army board which found him insane. After his involuntary retirement he lived in growing isolation and increasing debility, regressing into childishness and eventual obliviousness. His death passed almost unnoticed except by family and friends, yet there was nothing else that day to command the public's attention to any large degree. Europe was reasonably quiet. The Balkans were between spats, and nothing of import was happening in the Far East. There may have been unrest somewhere in Central or South America, but disputes there were common. In the American West, where the great drama of the Indian Wars was in the last act after a quarter century of continual fighting, the army was engaged in the final phase of its operations against scattered bands of the once-powerful Indian tribes. The death of one of the country's greatest Indian fighters should have attracted more attention.

Clockwise from top: Crook, Custer, Mackenzie, Miles
(Contemporary engraving, Author's collection)

But even if Mackenzie died in relative obscurity, his achievements stand. On the plains where five nations—Spain, Mexico, Texas, the Confederacy and the United States—had struggled for 150 years to resolve the Kiowa-Comanche problem, Mackenzie resolved it in five. He pacified the Sioux at the Red Cloud Agency by deposing Red Cloud himself. He averted a war with the Utes by ordering them to pack and move to their reservation, and he headed off a potential Apache crisis in Arizona and New Mexico.

Lesser military men have commanded greater attention—Custer for example. With a great deal of panache but little actual campaigning, Custer has held center stage in the Indian Wars for over 120 years; yet his greatest single achievement seems to have been the useless slaughter of five companies of Seventh Cavalry, including himself, at the Little Bighorn. He has been praised and he has been damned, but people know who he is. Mention Mackenzie and one often receives a blank stare.

Part of the recognition problem lies with the man himself. Mackenzie's career came to an abrupt end when he was forty-three, and his life ended at forty-eight. He lived and died a bachelor. His romantic interests rested on only one woman, and she was married to someone else. He had few friends. Early in his career he lost part of his right hand, which made writing difficult, and there are no personal diaries or letters to give insight into his private thoughts. This irritated his former classmates at Williams College in his own lifetime, and has frustrated historians ever since. Any personal correspondence that once existed has been lost.[2] His only efforts at publicity were occasional letters to the New York *Times* defending the morals and conduct of his troops.

Ironically, for a man who is so little known, Mackenzie's

life and career have served as the basis of several Western films, most notably John Ford's *Rio Grande*. Based on Mackenzie's raid into Mexico, the film goes so far in historical accuracy as to bring in Phil Sheridan (J. Carroll Naish), who tells the Mackenzie character, named Colonel York (John Wayne), that he must cross the border into Mexico and settle the Indian problem. The audience also learns that York's association with Sheridan dates back to the Shenandoah Campaign, as did Mackenzie's. The raid was also the subject of a historical novel, *The Mackenzie Raid* by Colonel Red Reeder, which was published by Ballantine Books of New York in 1955.

Why was Mackenzie portrayed under a pseudonym in the John Wayne film? Perhaps because of the nature of the man himself. Western literature and films of the 1950s required some sort of romantic interest, and Mackenzie simply did not fit the bill. It is difficult, if not impossible, to imagine him in a love-hate relationship with the likes of Maureen O'Hara.

It remained finally for television to give Mackenzie his own billing. In the late 1950s and early '60s, when the TV western was at its height, a series called "Mackenzie's Raiders" attempted to tell the story of the Fourth Cavalry. The program was full of inaccuracies, the hazard of any series which must produce half-hour dramatic stories every week for several seasons. Fort Clark, Texas, in actuality an open stone cantonment on top of a hill, was transformed by Hollywood into a stereotypical stockade, with rifle stands and blockhouses. The historical account of Secretary of War W.W. Belknap's visit was rewritten to have him send Mackenzie after white outlaws hidden in Mexico, rather than hostile Indians. Rugged Richard Carlson was hardly a look-alike for the delicate features of the real Mackenzie. Still, the television show and the comic books it inspired found their following

Dell Comic book of TV's Richard Carlson as Ranald S. Mackenzie
(Author's Collection)

in a generation of youngsters, most of whom had grown up on a steady diet of John Wayne.

What of the real Mackenzie—the soldier? His battles were not spectacular, but they were victories. He possibly could have achieved greater numbers of Indian casualties by dividing his forces and attacking hostile villages from several sides simultaneously—and he was advised to do so at least once—but he knew that a command divided was a command exposed. A full frontal attack might allow more of the enemy to escape through the rear, but it also kept the troops together in a single mass of military strength. Had Custer followed this example on June 25, 1876, he might have lived to draw his retirement pay.

Mackenzie, aware that an enemy without a base or mobility is a defeated enemy, was content to terrorize the Indians and destroy their villages, supplies and horses. Mackenzie's battles added up to total defeat for the Southern Plains tribes.

In *Son of the Morning Star*, Evan S. Connell wrote that Custer "could be likened more to an actor than a playwright."[3] Mackenzie, no actor like Custer, was nevertheless both playwright and director, the author with the inspiration for the drama and the technician who made it work. Like Custer, he was egoistical; but his egoism led him to do his job—to be the best soldier in the army. He did not share Custer's flair for theatrics, nor did he have Custer's thirst for casualties. To him, a superbly executed military action was one which achieved maximum results with minimal losses on either side. Custer played for history; Mackenzie played for results. Custer lost more men of the Seventh in a single afternoon than Mackenzie lost during his entire career as colonel of the Fourth. Glamour and glory were the hallmarks of Custer's Seventh; victory and survival were the hallmarks of Mackenzie's Fourth.

Despite his successes, there is no indication of comraderie or even much affection in the memoirs of those who served under Mackenzie. Troops often give pet names to beloved commanders. Thus Eisenhower was "Ike," Lee was "Marse Robert," and Stilwell was "Uncle Joe." The only nickname used for Mackenzie by his soldiers was "Three-Finger Jack," an unkind reference to his mutilated hand for which he was known by the Indians as "Bad Hand." Occasionally, with memory dimmed by time, former subordinates called him "the Old Man." He was nervous, impatient and irritable. Years later, a sergeant of the Fourth recalled to a former officer one occasion when two officers protested a raid against Indian villages in Mexico, which was clearly illegal even though it was successful:

> Not that I think he was wrong in doing so, but I'll confess to you, Captain, that some where inside of me there has always been an ungratified longing to know that someone dared to do what I many times wanted to do, *talk back to the "Old Man."* This feeling is unsoldierly but human. I respected him as a great and successful Indian fighter, a brilliant soldier and an officer under whose command I served, but all the same he got on my nerves terribly at times and I would leave his presence biting my tongue and nearly exploding with a desire to kick over the traces.[4]

Mackenzie was an autocrat who was feared, and at times perhaps even hated, by his men. High in his expectations, he was short on praise—a soldier rendered meritorious service because that was what the government paid him to do. It was no more than Mackenzie expected of himself.[5]

Those who knew this complex man realized that he was "a man of very deep and intense feeling, of a high-strung and nervous temperament. . . . "[6] They admired his virtues and forgave his vices. General Henry Lawton and General James Parker both served under him. Ten years after Mackenzie's death, Lawton told Parker, "Whenever I am in a tight place, whenever I am uncertain what to do, I say to myself, 'What would Mackenzie do?'"[7] Parker's own assessment of Mackenzie was made in one simple sentence: "He was a *soldier*."[8]

CHAPTER 1

"Quiet, Modest to Shyness"

On May 18, 1873, regular soldiers of the Fourth United States Cavalry stormed through three Kickapoo and Lipan villages near the town of Remolino, deep in the Mexican state of Coahuila. The attack was a profound shock to the Indians. For more than a decade they had raided into Texas with impunity, retreating back into Mexico beyond the reach of U.S. troops. On the central plains of Texas the highly mobile Comanches and Kiowas had followed the same pattern, raiding at will and withdrawing into the impenetrable wastes of the Staked Plains, where no soldier dared venture.

The people of Texas clearly were on the defensive. Their line of settlement had been pushed back in the five years between 1860 and 1865, when their men and their soldiers were drawn away to fight in the Civil War. The return of United States military forces did little to alleviate the situation—the soldiers' primary mission was the enforcement of Reconstruction policies rather than protection of the settlers from Indians. During this period, hundreds of settlers were killed by the plains tribes, and a like number of women and children carried off into captivity.

During the decade after the Civil War, the situation changed entirely. The plains tribes were broken and the few scattered remnants were on the run. Large military forces regularly swept through the Staked Plains as if on a schedule, creating havoc among the Kiowas and Comanches. The raid on Remolino showed the Kickapoos and Lipans that Mexico was no longer safe—United States forces were poised on the Rio Grande, ready to strike. If the Mexicans failed to police their Indians, forces from the United States would do it for them.

All this was, in great measure, the work of one man. A new kind of officer, he feared no desert, respected no boundary, and had the support of the highest levels of government. Daring and imaginative, he hounded the hostile tribes to exhaustion. His name was Ranald Slidell Mackenzie.

Originally his family's name was Slidell and, even in an age noted for color, the Slidells were a remarkably colorful group. The first Slidell of importance seems to have been Ranald Mackenzie's paternal grandfather, John Slidell. Both wealthy and involved in politics, he represented the notorious Battery and Castle Garden areas on the New York City Council in the late eighteenth century and was president of the Mechanics' Bank and Tradesmen's Insurance Company. He may also have been a ship owner, or at least had substantial influence in the shipping industry. The family was Episcopalian, and Slidell was vestryman of Grace Episcopal Church in New York when it was incorporated in 1809.[1]

This Slidell had five children: Jane, Julia, John, Thomas and Alexander Mackenzie Slidell. Jane married Commodore Matthew C. Perry, who negotiated the first western powers treaty with Japan, while Julia married Rear Admiral Raymond Rogers. Thomas, a Yale graduate, eventually became chief justice of Louisiana.[2]

The most notable member of these offspring was John Slidell, an 1810 graduate of Columbia College. He became a social outcast after a duel over a New York actress, and moved to Louisiana where such affairs were better understood. After establishing a thriving law practice in New Orleans, like his father he entered politics and became the most powerful figure in the state's Democratic Party. In the 1844 presidential election, Louisiana was a swing state in the race between Henry Clay and James K. Polk, and Slidell's Plaquemines Parish became a swing district within Louisiana. Polk was Slidell's choice. To insure a victory he chartered two steamboats to haul loyal voters to poll after poll in the riverside precincts. Plaquemines Parish gave Louisiana to Polk, and Louisiana helped give him the presidency. Never a man to shirk on debts, Polk appointed Slidell minister to Mexico, with instructions to buy California and New Mexico. The purchase attempt failed, and it was not until after the Mexican War that the U.S. was able to acquire these territories.

In 1853 Louisiana elected Slidell to the U.S. Senate. He became President James Buchanan's senior advisor and, to some extent, was the power behind the Buchanan presidency. When Louisiana seceded and joined the Confederacy, Slidell detected new opportunities and made himself available to the southern government.[3]

If his uncle John Slidell was the most notable of the siblings, Ranald Mackenzie's father, Alexander Mackenzie Slidell, was perhaps the most talented. A naval officer, Alexander reversed the order of his name in 1837, becoming Alexander Slidell Mackenzie at the behest of a well-to-do maternal uncle, a bachelor and the last of his immediate line, who wanted the name Mackenzie preserved.[4]

Alexander Mackenzie was a romantic. As a junior officer he used his time at sea to read French and Spanish classics, particularly stories of Moorish Spain. His chosen profession was ideal for the romantic side of his personality, since in those

3

Alexander Slidell Mackenzie, Sr.
(National Archives)

John Slidell
(Author's Collection)

days officers with independent incomes took extended leaves after long cruises, and could frequently arrange their duty schedules to suit themselves. Accordingly, Mackenzie took time off and went to France to satisfy his romantic streak and to follow his literary inclinations. In 1826 he crossed the border into Spain, smuggling forbidden works by Voltaire in his baggage. He moved into rooms in the Puerta del Sol in Madrid and took lessons in the Castilian language from a gentleman of Cordoba.[5]

Mackenzie's interest in Spain's romantic period was shared by his acquaintance Washington Irving, who arrived in Spain to work on *The Voyages and Discoveries of the Companions of Columbus*. Mackenzie read the manuscript and provided some nautical information. When Irving left Madrid for Granada, Mackenzie toured the country. The result of his travels was the book *A Year in Spain*, which was published through Irving's assistance. It received critical acclaim and the twenty-nine year old Mackenzie found himself a celebrity.[6]

A Year in Spain was followed by *Spain Revisited, The American in England* and *Popular Essays on Naval Subjects*. He also wrote a two-volume life of John Paul Jones, biographies of Oliver Hazard Perry and Stephen Decatur, and *A Library of American Biography*. The books were successful and Mackenzie's prestige grew.[7] His navy career progressed as well, and he worked his way up to a command position.

Like many American literary works of the period, his biographies sometimes colored fact with nationalism. James Fenimore Cooper criticized the book on Perry as "absurd."[8] Ironically, Cooper's own romantic portrayals of the American Indian would influence Washington's government policy for much of the nineteenth century and would hamper the efforts of Alexander Mackenzie's son in the very real and savage world of plains warfare. On the other hand, some of Mackenzie's writings have withstood the test of time. As late as 1959, the eminent naval historian Samuel Eliot Morison called the two-volume biography of Paul Jones, "An excellent work by a professional naval officer. . . ."[9]

But author Mackenzie the romantic was totally different from Captain Mackenzie on the quarterdeck. He was a "sundowner,"[10] a navy term for a ruthless, hard-driving, sometimes psychotic officer who expected absolute obedience. In the earlier age of John Paul Jones and fighting sail, when a captain had to be tougher than the toughest forecastle sailor, such men had been the backbone of the navy. But as the nineteenth century progressed and the service underwent rapid modernization, a ship's officer became more of a technician than a quarterdeck autocrat. Men such as Mackenzie became obsolete. His "sundowner" personality cost the lives of three men and almost ruined Mackenzie's career when, in 1842 while commanding the brig *Somers* on a West African cruise, he panicked and ordered three men hanged for mutiny. Two of the men, Boatswain's Mate Samuel Cromwell and Seaman Elisha Small, were disreputable forecastle rats, but the third was Apprentice Midshipman Philip Spencer, ne'er-do-well son of Secretary of War John C. Spencer. When the *Somers* returned home, the elder Spencer pressured the navy and Mackenzie was court-martialed for murder. Although the "mutiny" existed largely in Mackenzie's mind, he was acquitted. Still, his career was permanently tarnished.[11]

Though he may have operated under a shadow, Mackenzie was far from finished. The summer of 1846 found him in Havana where, on a mission from President Polk, he met with exiled General Antonio López de Santa Anna, of Alamo infamy, to explore an end to the Mexican War. He then sailed to the Rio Grande, where he visited General Zachary Taylor's headquarters at Camargo.[12] He finished out his war service as commander of the USS *Mississippi*, after which he returned to his farm and family in New York.

His family had started when he married Catherine Robinson, daughter of Morris Robinson and Henrietta Elizabeth Duer, the latter a member of a prominent New York family. Catherine's grandfather was Colonel William Duer, who had once served on the staff of Clive of India and who had been assistant secretary of the treasury under Alexander Hamilton. Her grandmother was Lady Catherine Alexander, a daughter of Lord Stirling.[13]

Against this brilliant but often stormy background, Alexander Slidell Mackenzie and Catherine Robinson had a son, born in New York City on July 27, 1840. They spelled his name "Ranald" in the old Scots fashion and gave him the family name Slidell as a middle name.

Like so much of his private life, Ranald Slidell Mackenzie's boyhood remains an enigma. Most of what we do know is taken from an article by one of his officers, Lieutenant J.H. Dorst, which appeared in the *Twentieth Annual Reunion of the Association Graduates of the United States Military Academy* in the summer of 1889. Published only a few months after Mackenzie's death, the article was printed as an appendix hurriedly written in order to be included in the reunion book.

The article notes that, when Ranald was only a few weeks old, his parents moved to a farm on the Hudson River between Tarrytown and Sing Sing.[14] This is Irving country, and Washington Irving may have influenced the choice of moves. It is quite possible that Alexander Mackenzie wanted to be close to his friend in what little time either of them had at home (Irving was appointed minister to Spain in 1842).

More children followed: Alexander Slidell Mackenzie, Jr., called Sandy by the family, and another brother, Morris Robinson, and a sister, Harriet, called Hattie, both of whom also received the family name of Slidell as middle names. Sandy, following his father into the navy, entered as a midshipman in 1857, served with distinction in the Civil War, and rose to the rank of lieutenant commander before his early death. Morris also chose the navy and was graduated from Annapolis in 1866.[15]

It is unlikely Ranald saw much of his father. He was two years old when the *Somers* incident occurred, and thereafter Alexander was involved in the inquiries and various duty assignments which culminated in his Mexican War service.

Much of the boy's upbringing appears to have fallen on his mother, who "impressed it upon him that he must never hurt anyone smaller or weaker than himself," words which sank "deep into his generous nature." He was said to have been truthful and brave.[16]

When Ranald was three years old, he sustained a sunstroke from which he suffered for years before complete recovery. This early illness might have had some influence on his nervousness, irritability and ultimate breakdown. According to Dorst, "any long confinement to the house was certain to bring on headache and depression of spirits."[17]

A few months after his father returned from the Mexican War in the spring of 1848, his health gone, Ranald was playing by the gate of the yard when his father came riding out. The boy opened the gate and Captain Mackenzie stopped, chatted with him a few minutes, then leaned down, kissed him and rode off. A short way down the road he had a heart attack and was dead before anyone discovered him. He was forty-five.

Financial problems forced Catherine Mackenzie to sell the farm, and in the spring of 1849 she moved the family to Morristown, New Jersey. Henceforth, Ranald would regard Morristown as home. As he grew up, he developed a strong protectiveness for his mother. Shy and reserved, he had a speech impediment and a high, shrill voice which never completely changed. He allowed himself to be largely overshadowed by younger brother Sandy, who seems to have been at ease in school or at social events.[18]

Ranald showed no youthful interest in any real profession. When he reached his mid-teens, he finally agreed to his uncles' wishes that he study law. He prepped at Maurice's School in Sing Sing, New York, and in the fall of 1855 entered Williams College in Williamstown, Massachusetts.[19] Class-

Williams College, Williamstown, Mass. *(Williams College)*

mate Washington Gladden, later a noted hymnist, recalled that when he entered, Ranald wore "a kind of Eton jacket. Very quiet, modest to shyness, and with a little lisp, Ranald was a good fellow."[20] He gained self-confidence, was well-liked, made friends, and was initiated into Kappa Alpha fraternity. He was even fined two dollars for disturbing the rooms of freshmen.[21] His scholarship was indifferent. As Gladden said, "he had not at that time given any indications of the kind of character he was to develop."[22]

In Ranald Mackenzie's junior year his family faced further financial setbacks. He concluded that he needed a career which would earn immediate income, and the U.S. Military Academy at West Point offered both a salary and a chance to continue his education. Accordingly he wrote his mother for

9

permission and to ask her help in securing an appointment. An uncle agreed to get the appointment but doubted he would measure up, an opinion shared by friends and other relatives. Although most believed he would disappoint his mother with failure at the academy, the verdict wasn't quite unanimous. One of his teachers, a Mr. Morris, had decided three years earlier that, "With time he will always be equal to what is required of him."[23]

If Mackenzie knew of his family's concern, he did not show it. Perhaps in preparation for West Point, he wrote a paper entitled *Military Tactics* for presentation to the Junior Rhetorical Exhibition at Williams College. He failed to appear for the reading, apparently because a death in his mother's immediate family occurred about the same time.[24] A month later he left Williamstown; a presidential appointment to West Point had come through and he would enter at-large, representing no particular state. "We all loved him and were both sorry and proud when the appointment came to him," Gladden wrote.[25] Williams College did not forget him either. In 1863, as his army career began to soar, he received an A.B. and was restored to the Class Roll for 1859. Ten years later he was given an A.M.[26]

Ranald S. Mackenzie entered West Point July 1, 1858, and soon became a general favorite of the academy. A member of his class, Morris Schaff, wrote he "was easily the all-around ablest man in it . . . . He had a very immobile, inexpressive face as a boy, and a little impediment in his speech; there was very little of the spick and span ways of a soldier about him, but he had a very sweet smile, and earnest gray eyes." He made friends easily, ran with the crowd, and involved himself in pranks which, according to Dorst, brought "more than the average number of demerits."[27]

A few of his classmates, doubting his ability, held a discussion before their first encampment and generally agreed that Mackenzie's cadet career wouldn't survive the first examination. Instead he finished the year fifth in his class. When the second year was over and he stood second, the family clergyman told Catherine Mackenzie, "No, it is not possible. . . . Madam, you surprise me; I had ventured to hint to my wife—in strict confidence—my certainty of the disappointment in store for you."[28]

The young cadet went into an emotional slump during his junior year. The southern states were leaving the Union, and before the term was out the North and South would be at war. The Slidell-Mackenzie family found itself divided when Uncle John Slidell entered the Confederate diplomatic service. The national rift found its way into the barracks at West Point as well. Mackenzie lived in Company D, which housed many southern cadets, and many of his friends resigned and went south or, upon graduation, accepted their degrees but refused military commissions. When the school year ended, he had dropped to twelfth place in the class.

His final year went much better, so well that he was appointed assistant professor of mathematics. Years later one of his instructors, Lieutenant Colonel G.K. Warren, wrote "He is a master of the knowledge of mathematics which he comprehends so easily as to take no special pride in it."[29] In addition to his talent for math, he had inherited his father's literary interests. Though he himself never wrote much more than military reports and dispatches, he kept up with current literature throughout his life and his opinions were widely respected.[30] Aware that the war would be long and bloody and would involve him for several years after graduation, he also studied the problems of war and "chafed at his enforced

Mackenzie with friends at West Point. *(Civil War Library and Museum, MOLLUS, Philadelphia, Penn.)*

detention" at the academy, wishing the year would end so he could get into combat.[31]

While Ranald Slidell Mackenzie waited out his final year of training to become a Union officer, his uncle spent part of the time as a Union prisoner. John Slidell had passed the winter of 1860-61 feeling out the diplomatic community in Washington on the possibility of recognition for an independent South. He spoke French and was well-connected, and consequently Jefferson Davis asked him to be part of a three-man diplomatic mission to Europe. When Slidell refused this mission because he had a private quarrel with one of the other members, Davis asked him to be part of a second mission which included James M. Mason of Virginia. This time Slidell accepted, and he and Mason slipped through the blockade. On November 7, 1861, they sailed out of Havana on the British Steamer *Trent,* but were overhauled the following day by the USS *San Jacinto,* which had been waiting for the *Trent* in the Bahama Channel. Mason and Slidell were taken off, carried to Boston and imprisoned at Fort Warren. The British were furious at this violation of their neutrality, and the federal government was soon forced to release the two diplomats and allow them to continue.[32]

As the diplomatic storm raged about his uncle, Ranald Mackenzie prepared for graduation and entry into the United States Army. He finished first in a class of twenty-eight on July 1, 1862. In individual courses he was first in engineering, ordnance and gunnery, fourth in ethics, fifth in minerals, geology, and artillery tactics, sixth in infantry tactics, and ninth in chemistry. He placed only sixth in cavalry tactics, although he would eventually master the field.

His class picture shows a proud, somber young man. The absence of any trace of humor is not necessarily an accurate depiction, since the photography of the period required a person to sit absolutely still for several minutes, often with the head locked in an iron brace, and almost all studio portrait photographs of the period are grim. His record of conduct and "more than the average" number of demerits—122 for the year and fifty for the six-month period ending June 6—give a much clearer insight to his personality at the time. Scholastics aside, Ranald Mackenzie was a typical cadet.[33]

Mackenzie at West Point, 1862
(Special Collection, US Military Academy)

CHAPTER 2

"The Noble Bravery and Example of Colonel Mackenzie"

U pon graduation, Ranald Mackenzie accepted a commission to the permanent rank of second lieutenant in the Corps of Engineers and was appointed engineering officer on General Ambrose Burnside's staff. He was soon transferred to Major General J.L. Reno and was serving with him during the Second Battle of Manassas on August 29-30, when the North suffered a crushing defeat at the hands of General Robert E. Lee's Confederates.

On the afternoon of August 29, while carrying a message, he stopped to ask information from a wounded soldier and was fired upon from behind a fence. The bullet entered Mackenzie's right shoulder, passed under the skin across his right shoulder blade and spine, grazed the left shoulder blade and exited the left shoulder. Still conscious after he fell, he asked the southern marksman and his companion for water when they approached. The two Confederates replied they would "gladly give it but they had none themselves," then they helped themselves to his pistol and money but left his watch.[1]

All night Mackenzie lay where he fell. The following day he was found and taken to Centreville, where he was packed into an ambulance with other wounded and shipped to Washington. Learning that he was hurt, his brother Sandy searched

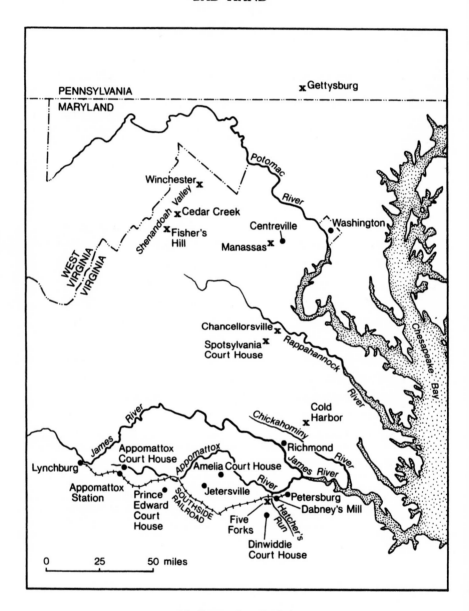

Civil War in Virginia

the hospitals until he found him quartered in a hotel which had been taken over for wounded officers. Their mother arrived the next morning. "I am wounded in the back," he told her, "but I was not running away."[2]

Although Dorst said the wound was "serious and painful but not dangerous," Mackenzie's medical certificate states he "could not rejoin his regiment at present without serious risk to life."[3]

The incident caught the attention of the association for the Williams College Class of '59. The group's yearbook reported he was "desperately wounded and left for dead on the field, was plundered by the rebels, but managed to crawl off the field, was taken home and is now in a fair way of recovery."[4]

He returned to duty October 19 and was breveted to first lieutenant "for gallant and meritorious service" retroactive to the date of his wound.[5] General Reno had been killed at South Mountain, so Mackenzie found himself back with Burnside until he was transferred to an engineer battalion under Lieutenant C.B. Comstock. Here he performed the mundane, but often dangerous, support duties which keep a combat soldier in action. On one occasion he was sent to select new positions for artillery batteries. On another, he had to inspect a dam across the Rappahannock, to see if the pond could be drained while the Confederates held the opposite bank. The construction of blockhouses, redoubts and other fortifications was continual. Mundane but nevertheless important, his work carried responsibility. In one set of instructions Comstock told him, "you should decide on a plan of operations, size of working party, &c., so as to be ready to begin at once when the order is given."[6] He was gaining the experience he would later need to lead troops in the field.

Mackenzie continued to see action as the Army of the Potomac moved against the Confederates to counter Southern advances. As the war progressed, he received increasing attention and additional honors in the form of brevet commissions.

The brevet rank was a temporary one which the government issued to build up a temporary officer corps in an emergency, while preventing the army from becoming top heavy with officers in peacetime. A soldier accepted the brevet commission knowing that he would take a reduction in rank if he stayed in the service when the crisis ended. Thus George Armstrong Custer, a brevet major general, held the permanent rank of lieutenant colonel at the time of his death. H.H. McConnell of the Sixth Cavalry called it "a cheap kind of honor with which the government rewarded multitudes of officers during the war . . . at the close of the war, and for years afterward, it was a conundrum as to who or where or what had become of the *privates* of the late war."[7]

In Mackenzie's case, the brevets piled up. He was commissioned to the rank of captain on May 3, 1863, for service at Chancellorsville, and to major on July 4 for Gettysburg, where he was temporarily attached to General George Meade's staff. A minor wound received at Gettysburg was not enough to incapacitate him, and it does not appear on his service record.[8] Despite his meritorious service, he detested the Corps of Engineers. In his letters, which have since disappeared, he called a pontoon a "bore," and referred to a pontoon train as his "pet aversion."[9] He wanted to lead troops in the field.

His chance came during the Richmond Campaign in June 1864, when the new General-in-Chief of the Armies, Lieutenant General U.S. Grant, committed what would be one of the very few tactical blunders of his career, a direct assault on a heavily fortified Confederate line at Cold Harbor. Amid the slaughter Colonel Elisha S. Kellogg, commander of the Second Connecticut Volunteer Artillery, was killed, and on June 6 Mackenzie was ordered to take over the regiment. On June 18 he was breveted to lieutenant colonel. He was not yet twenty-four years old.[10]

His new command, the Second Connecticut, was part of Brigadier General Emory Upton's First Division. Mackenzie had seen Upton in action at Spottsylvania Court House a month earlier, and his performance had left a lasting impression. Years later he recalled' Upton's "high, quiet courage *which subordinates all things personal to the procurement of a result* [italics added]." He praised Upton's willingness to risk his own safety where necessary along with his concern for the personal welfare of his troops. "In camp and on the march no officer was more careful of the comfort and the needs of his men, and none in attention to his duties or in correct and honorable bearing gave a higher example to his subordinates."[11] Upton's stamp began to appear on Mackenzie's own actions. Consciously or unconsciously, he seemed bent on following what he saw as Upton's example. If he didn't always succeed, it wasn't for lack of effort.

After Cold Harbor, when Grant swung around Petersburg in an effort to cut the Confederate line of supply, his forward command blundered and allowed General Pierre Beauregard to lead a Confederate defense born of desperation, giving General Robert E. Lee time to arrive in support. Rather than risk another Cold Harbor, Grant dug in around Petersburg and prepared to starve out Lee's Army of Northern Virginia.

During these preliminaries, the Second Connecticut and other units of the First Division, Sixth Corps, crossed the

Chickahominy River on June 13, and camped near the James River by 11:00 A.M. the following day. On June 17 the division crossed the James, a move which had been Lee's greatest nightmare. On the 18th the order to attack was given but then countermanded, a bluff which cost Lee valuable time as he moved to counter the feint. Over the next several days the Sixth Corps maneuvered into position. On June 22 the two armies met and there was fighting in some sectors, although a general battle was averted. In the Second Connecticut's zone, a shell fragment tore off the first two fingers of Mackenzie's right hand,[12] an injury which would later bring him two names on the Western Plains—"Three Finger Jack" from the troops and "Bad Hand" from the Indians. When he was nervous or irritated, he would snap the stumps against each other.[13]

For Mackenzie, on recuperative leave until July 9 when he returned to his regiment, the war had made its mark in other ways besides physical injury. No longer the prankster who had been fined at Williams College and who had piled up demerits with such aplomb at West Point, he had become cold and efficient. An officer who later served under him in the Fourth Cavalry said he was "irascible, irritable and difficult to deal with," yet "one of the few officers of that period who was always ready and willing to assume the gravest responsibilities, and he would never hesitate to take the initiative while awaiting definite orders."[14]

Mackenzie displayed both initiative and efficiency when he returned to the field, where he faced two enemies—the Confederate Army of Northern Virginia and the despair within his own Second Connecticut. Though nominally artillery, the regiment was functioning as infantry and, after Cold Harbor, was beaten and exhausted. The adjutant, Lieutenant

T.F. Vaill later wrote that the surviving troops were "so supined and stupid that they could hardly be called survivors."[15]

At first, Mackenzie did nothing. He waited, observing the men and identifying problems before initiating a rigid discipline to force the troops to act like soldiers. They were drilled, and they were punished, and they hated him. "By the time we had reached the Shenandoah Valley," Vaill wrote, "he had so far developed as to be a greater terror to both officers and men than Early's grape and canister."[16]

When General Jubal Early, sent by Lee up the Shenandoah to threaten Washington and thus relieve federal pressure on Richmond, smashed through the Army of the Shenandoah, he ruined the reputations of several prominent Union officers. Over President Lincoln's objections, Grant placed Major General Philip H. Sheridan in charge of the tattered Shenandoah defenses, confident that he would do better. Throughout the late summer and fall of 1864, Sheridan laid waste to the valley, driving Early before him. Within the Army of the Shenandoah, Lieutenant Colonel Ranald S. Mackenzie relentlessly pressured the Second Connecticut, until plots began to form within the ranks. Vaill wrote:

> There is a regimental tradition to the effect that a well defined purpose existed among the men, prior to the battle of Winchester, to dispose of this commanding scourge during the first fight that occurred. If he had known it, it would have only excited his contempt, for he cared not a copper for the good will of any except his military superiors, and certainly feared no man of woman born, on either side of the line.[17]

The men saw his iron nerve under fire when the Battle of Winchester opened in confusion on the morning of September 19. The various Union forces became intermixed, "making it extremely hazardous, if not impossible, to restore the proper order while under fire."[18] Taking advantage of the confusion, the Confederates threw back the Union's XIX Corps. The Second Connecticut, placed on the extreme right of the Second Brigade to check the Southern advance, took up a position in a hollow about three hundred yards to the left of the XIX Corps. When General George Crook moved up his forces to make a charge, Mackenzie shifted his across an open field to begin a heavy covering fire.

Pressed by Crook on one hand and Mackenzie on the other, the Confederates withdrew in confusion until they reached a stone fence where they dug in and held their line. Southern artillery opened up and pounded away at the Second Connecticut. The XIX Corps wavered again, and Mackenzie was ordered to move in at a right angle to the wall. "As soon as in position, he opened fire, enfilading the wall and driving the enemy quickly from his position."[19] Colonel Joseph Hamblin's 65th New York linked up with the Second Connecticut, and Mackenzie moved to flank the retreating Confederates and link up with Crook. The Southerners retreated to a crest, where they were exposed to a concentrated fire from Mackenzie and Hamblin which pinned them down and slowly forced them back. Then the Union forces charged the crest.[20]

Mackenzie "seemed to court destruction all day long," Vaill recalled. "With his hat aloft, on the point of his saber, he galloped over the forty-acre field, through a perfect hailstorm of Rebel lead and iron, with as much impunity as though he had been a ghost." When a shell cut his horse in half, skinning his leg as it went past, he tied a handkerchief around his wound and with some humor remarked that it was "dismounting without numbers."[21]

The Union forces gained the crest, giving them command of the final Confederate position, and the Third Brigade emerged from a wood in "beautiful order and giving great confidence to the troops engaged."[22] The Northerners surged forward and carried the day.

In his battle report, General Upton wrote, "Colonel Mackenzie is entitled to especial mention for the fearlessness with which he led his regiment and the ability he displayed in commanding it during the entire action. His regiment on the right initiated nearly every movement of the division and behaved with great steadiness and gallantry."[23]

The regiment's losses were heavy, as they would be throughout the Shenandoah Campaign. With one officer killed and seven wounded, including Mackenzie, sixteen enlisted men killed and 101 wounded, and two officers and fifty-one men missing, the Second Connecticut's losses were higher than any other regiment in the Second Brigade.[24] The missing included one entire company which was surrounded and taken prisoner while on picket that morning.[25]

The soldiers of the Second Connecticut had come a long way from the "supine and stupid" troops of two months earlier, and they knew it. When the Battle of Winchester ended, so did any plots they might have had against their colonel. As Vaill wrote, they "could not draw a bead on so brave a man as that."[26] They never loved him, none of his soldiers ever would, but they would follow him anywhere.

Sheridan continued his push through the Shenandoah, defeating the Confederates again at Fisher's Hill. But at dawn October 19, while Sheridan was returning from a conference in Washington, General Early caught the Union forces off-guard at Cedar Creek. Acting in Sheridan's absence Major General Horatio G. Wright deployed his troops, confident they would hold the line, but the surprise had shaken the soldiers. Men who previously had excellent combat records "broke before the enemy fairly came in sight, and under a slight scattering fire retreated in disorder down the pike."[27]

Wright redeployed and the Second Brigade, including the Second Connecticut, was placed in line facing the rear. During several subsequent maneuvers, the troops on the left were forced to withdraw, and the Second Brigade was attacked while holding one of the roads. It stood fast and the Confederates were forced to halt, but heavy fire continued for nearly half an hour. Mackenzie's leg, grazed earlier in the day, now received another more serious wound, but he stayed on. A short time later, a piece of shrapnel struck him in the chest, momentarily stunning him and temporarily paralyzing his arms. Recovering his senses, he ordered his men to place him on his horse and continued to direct the movements of his troops.

The line on the right was forced back, and the Second Brigade was ordered first to provide covering fire, then to take a position on a crest a few hundred yards to the rear. When the Confederates took advantage of a gap in the Union's left flank and swarmed through only two hundred yards away, the Union withdrawal speeded up and a new line was formed some fifteen hundred yards back. Joe Hamblin, who commanded the brigade in addition to his own New Yorkers, was wounded too badly to remain on the field, and Mackenzie assumed command.

For the next several hours the brigade continued to retreat as the Army of the Shenandoah fought to survive. The Second

Brigade finally joined with First Brigade, forming into two lines, where they held.[28] When Sheridan arrived after a hard ride from Winchester, he gathered reports, reviewed information on enemy strength from prisoners, and considered his position carefully before making his move. About 3:00 P.M. he ordered a general attack.[29]

Writing in the third person, Lieutenant Colonel Egbert Olcott, commanding the First Brigade, reported:

> The first line [under Mackenzie] moved gallantly to the edge of the wood, then meeting a galling fire, it hesitated, but, inspired by the noble bravery and example of Colonel Mackenzie, it pressed forward to a crest some 150 yards in front. It appearing unable to advance farther, and in some danger of being forced back, Lieutenant-Colonel Olcott, agreeable to instruction from General Wheaton, charged with the second line. The two lines joined in the charge, and drove the enemy from a commanding crest 400 or 500 yards in advance. In this charge, Colonel Mackenzie, while in front of his men, was again wounded and taken off the field. The command then fell to Lieutenant-Colonel Olcott. [30]

Sheridan added:

> My whole line as far as the eye could see was now driving everything before it, from behind trees, stone walls, and all such sheltering obstacles, so I rode toward the left to ascertain how matters were getting on there. As I passed along behind the advancing troops, first General Grover, and then

Colonel Mackenzie, rode up to welcome me. Both were severely wounded, and I told them to leave the field, but they implored permission to remain till success was certain.[31]

Success became certain. In his report to Grant the following day, Sheridan noted the victory had been recovered "from disaster by the gallantry of our officers and men." Listing officer casualties, he said, "Col. R.S. Mackenzie, commanding brigade, wounded severely; would not leave the field."[32]

Virtually every senior officer recommended or endorsed Mackenzie for a general's star. Two brevets came through, both retroactive to October 19. One was for a colonelcy of the Regular Army; the other named him brigadier general of the Volunteers.[33]

Mackenzie was out of action, recovering from his wounds, until November 13. When he returned, one of his concerns was pay. Throughout his life he worried about money, understandable in view of his financially troubled childhood and because he lived in an age when congress begrudged every nickel spent. The fact that his appointment was retroactive did not mean the government was automatically willing to pay him retroactively, or even beginning with the date of the order. The letter of appointment as brigadier general was written November 30 but did not reach him until December 28, delaying for twenty-nine days the administration of his oath making it official.[34] Making his case for an earlier increase in pay, Mackenzie wrote:

I have understood that when a long time elapsed between the date upon which an appointment was sent and its receipt, that pay was allowed from the date when [the] letter should have reached its

Mackenzie in 1864/1865 *(Brady photograph, National Archives)*

destination without extraordinary delay. I was during the time referred to cmdg. a Brigade.[35]

There was also a question of seniority, another point about which he was touchy throughout his life. Joe Hamblin and Colonel William H. Penrose were also breveted to brigadier general effective October 19, and Mackenzie was apparently dissatisfied with his own assignment in relation to theirs. In a letter to Colonel George Ruggles, assistant adjutant general of the Army of the Potomac, he complained:

> Brevet Brigadier Generals Penrose and Hamblin were appointed as such to date from the 19th day of October, 1864.
>
> I was appointed as a Brigadier General from the same date.
>
> As Colonels, Brevets Brig. Genls. Penrose and Hamblin were Senior to myself, and they have been assigned to duty by the President, according to their Brevet rank.
>
> Brevet Brig. Genl. Penrose is also Senior to myself as Captain in the U.S. Army.
>
> I request information as the relative rank of myself and the two officers named.
>
> It seems to me that the full Commission should rank the Brevet appointments of the same date.[36]

The issue of pay may have been resolved—the records are not clear—but the army was unimpressed with Mackenzie's seniority problems. The letter to Ruggles made its way up the chain of command, gathering unfavorable endorsements at each step until it reached the adjutant general's office in Washington, where it was pointed out that Penrose had served as colonel since April 18, 1863, and Hamblin since May 26, 1863. Since Mackenzie's appointment as colonel of Volunteers dated from July 10, 1864, Penrose and Hamblin therefore had seniority by Regular Army brevet and were assigned accordingly.[37]

We can only imagine what might have been going through Mackenzie's mind. Most young officers are concerned with pay, credit for achievement and seniority, but Mackenzie's concern became almost obsessive. As he grew older, he became increasingly convinced that he alone understood all the aspects of a particular problem. Professional jealousy became deeply seated, and even the most minor rebuffs, when added together, convinced him that the entire Washington establishment was against him. As the years went by, this obsession became paranoic.

Despite pay and seniority disputes, he soon received an assignment in keeping with his rank: command of the Cavalry Division of the Army of the James. The assignment, perhaps awarded as a means of mollifying a brilliant but troublesome young officer, to soothe his ego and give him something to do as the federal noose tightened around Petersburg, was nonetheless a stroke of genius—Ranald Mackenzie understood the role of the horse in war as few men in history have done.

Ulysses S. Grant *(National Archives)*

CHAPTER 3

" The Most Promising Young Officer in the Army"

On March 29, 1865, the three principal federal commanders, Lieutenant General Grant, Major General W.T. Sherman and Rear Admiral David D. Porter, conferred with Abraham Lincoln on the *River Queen*, the President's floating headquarters. The siege of Petersburg was ten months old, and it was obvious to both sides that the Confederacy was going to lose Richmond as well. Even so, the Army of Northern Virginia was far from beaten and, as his situation grew increasingly desperate, General Lee had become even more daring and imaginative. Grant's biggest fear was that Lee would break out, make for the Carolinas and unite with General Joseph Johnston, thus combining forces and prolonging the war. If he tried a breakout, Sherman was to move to contain him, before the link was made, until Grant could catch up and crush him. Grant preferred to make the first move himself, maneuvering around Lee's left, trapping him in Virginia and cutting him off from Johnston.

On the *River Queen*, Lincoln asked if the war could be ended without another battle, and was told by the generals that the decision rested with Lee. After discussing the political ramifications of a Confederate surrender, the group broke up and the officers returned to their respective headquarters.

Grant spent the rest of the day positioning his troops. The XXV Army Corps, under Major General Godfrey Weitzel, was placed in front of Richmond; Wright's VI Corps and Major General John G. Parke's IX Corps were positioned at Petersburg; Major General Edward O.C. Ord's available forces from the Army of the James extended south to where the Vaughan Road crossed Hatcher's Run; Major General Andrew Humphreys' II Corps was west of the crossing beyond Dabney's Mill; and Major General Gouverneur K. Warren's V Corps was situated on the extreme left to the junction of the Vaughan Road and Boydton Plank Road. South of Warren, Phil Sheridan's Army of the Shenandoah was placed at Dinwiddie Court House, also on the Boydton Plank Road.[1]

These were the obvious moves, but Grant had already made other preparations in total secrecy. Days before, he had directed Ord to withdraw several large units, including Mackenzie's cavalry division, and place them in camps far enough away from the Confederate lines that "they could not be seen or heard." Ord's remaining forces were "kept in motion, changing camps frequently." On the night of March 28, the main body of troops was sent to the left front of the Petersburg defenses. Their camps were left intact, fires lighted, tents standing and bands playing the usual calls. The bridges they would have to cross had already been covered with damp straw and compost to muffle the sounds of movement of a huge number of soldiers—Mackenzie alone started with fifty-four officers and 1,629 enlisted men—over a distance of thirty-six miles. "Although my lines were within rifle shot of the rebels and I had to cross two bridges overlooked by them, the movement was not, as I afterward learned from rebel officers, even suspected," Ord reported.[2]

Throughout March 30 and 31, troop movements continued. As Warren, the West Point professor, advanced to drive the Confederates from White Oak Road, he was met with a fierce counterattack and thrown back. Meanwhile Sheridan was advancing toward Five Forks, where all the roads came together, but the Confederate infantry which had thrown back Warren was now free to reinforce its cavalry and push Sheridan back toward Dinwiddie Court House.

Sheridan refused to be routed. Instead, he deployed his own cavalry on foot, forcing the Southerners to form a long offensive line and slowing their progress, and began an orderly withdrawal toward Dinwiddie Court House, notifying Grant of the situation.

Mackenzie, whose division was in camp as general guard over wagon trains, was asleep when an order came to join Sheridan. He gathered up a thousand men and moved toward Dinwiddie Court House, arriving about 9:00 A.M. on April 1. Warren with one division of his V Corps was also sent to assist. In the interim Sheridan had already stabilized his line, held fast, and counterattacked at daylight. Mackenzie was ordered to rest his men in an open field about half a mile north of the court house, but Warren was delayed so long that, by afternoon, Sheridan was faced with a possible Confederate thrust down White Oak Road which would expose his right and rear to attack. To offset this vulnerability, he ordered Mackenzie to "gain the White Oak road if possible, but to attack at all hazards any enemy found, and if successful to march down that road and join me."[3]

Mackenzie encountered Confederate breastworks and ordered two companies of the Eleventh Pennsylvania Cavalry to charge them. The breastworks were overrun and the defenders scattered. Years later, Mackenzie confided to Sheridan that the works were so strong he would not have attempted to take them "had it not been for the great urgency of your orders." After leaving a battalion of the Fifth Pennsylvania to picket, Mackenzie moved down the road toward Five Forks, where Sheridan appeared with infantry from the V Corps. Completely preoccupied with a situation which could still go either way, Sheridan's attitude nevertheless struck Mackenzie as "entirely kindly toward me [but] very positive and required vigorous action." Again it was the type of leadership the young general so greatly admired, and would strive—not always successfully—to provide his own men.

Sheridan ordered Mackenzie to move to the right flank of the infantry, a signal for Major General Wesley Merritt's cavalry to assault the Confederate works, which were taken at several points. Mackenzie had to change direction several times to avoid becoming tangled with infantry, but the defenses of Petersburg were broken and between five and six thousand prisoners taken. The remainder of the Southern forces fled westward, chased by Mackenzie and Merritt until long after dark. Merritt's cavalry division finally went into camp on the battlefield. Meanwhile, Sheridan had relieved Warren and placed Major General Charles Griffin in command of the V Corps.[4]

On April 2 Mackenzie was assigned to Merritt, who commanded the cavalry of the Army of the Shenandoah. Merritt, who had already secured the South Side Railroad earlier in the day, was ordered to march to Scott's Forks, five miles north of the line. Confederate General W.H.F. "Rooney" Lee's cavalry sporadically attempted to block the Union advance and, at one point, Merritt's First Division engaged in a "spirited fight" with Southern infantry and artillery. The Union line trailed out over too wide an area for a concentrated attack, but was nevertheless too strong for the Confederates to oppose. Although there were no decisive actions, when the day ended Merritt was just short of his goal and had linked up with infantry from the V Corps. That night, the Confederates abandoned Scott's Forks.

The next morning, the Northern steamroller pushed on. Pressed from all sides and cut off from Joe Johnston, the Army of Northern Virginia moved toward the Appomattox River, looking for places where its troops could mass. Merritt ordered the First and Third Divisions up the Namozine Road in pursuit, while Mackenzie was sent to follow the actual line of retreat "to pick up stragglers and others cut off by our movement."[5] Mackenzie's forces reached the Appomattox River at two points, capturing about three hundred prisoners and four guns. Then he turned toward Deep Creek to rejoin Merritt.[6]

It was becoming obvious that the Confederates planned to concentrate for a possible stand at Amelia Court House, and by nightfall their infantry had found a strong point along Deep Creek where they destroyed the bridges and obstructed the fords. Once again Merritt was forced to go into camp just short of his goal. That night the Confederates withdrew.

The Union march resumed at 6:00 P.M. on April 4. Mackenzie's training as an engineer proved useful as his troops set about "clearing obstructions from the best ford on Deep Creek, the energetic commander superintending the work," Merritt wrote. "It was intended to cross the entire command at this ford, but after General Mackenzie had crossed it was found that the ford, which was very deep and muddy, was impassable for wheels and impracticable for mounted men. The other two divisions, with all the wagons, were therefore marched to the south side. . . ."[7]

On the north side, Mackenzie had a "sharp skirmish" with the Confederates and pushed on to Five Forks, about a mile from Amelia Court House. After another scrap in the vicinity, his division went into camp, having fought "more or less during the entire day."[8]

About 10:00 P.M. Merritt was ordered to move his troops to Jetersville,[9] but Mackenzie's division remained behind. In explanation, Mackenzie wrote:

> I received information from many and different sources that the main body of General Lee's army was at this time at or in the immediate vicinity of Amelia Court-House, and during the night received orders from General Sheridan to remain where I was, to be watchful and demonstrate, but not push the enemy. This was done to the best of my ability. On the 5th and during the afternoon I made a demonstration with Colonel [A.W.] Evans's brigade, which caused the enemy to attack with a strong force of infantry, but without their inflicting any damage beyond the loss of a few men.
>
> I have reason to believe that the enemy were considerably delayed in their movements by our skirmishing at Amelia Court-House, and during our skirmishing they there destroyed a large amount of ammunition and other ordnance property, caissons, limbers, &c.[10]

Mackenzie's peculiar instructions, to stay in place and harass the enemy, were based on a more or less spontaneous decision by Sheridan, who found himself in a tight spot. The

Union forces had moved so rapidly over so wide an area that when Lee consolidated and entrenched at Amelia Court House, Sheridan had "but one corps of infantry with a little cavalry confronting Lee's entire army." General Meade was so sick he could hardly stand but, on receiving Grant's orders, he rushed up with reinforcements. Humphreys and Wright were ordered up before 4:00 A.M. on April 5, without time for rations. With more troops moving up, Lee was nearly trapped. Later in the morning Grant recalled, "I sent word to Sheridan of the progress Meade was now making, and suggested that he might now attack Lee. We now had no other objective than the Confederate armies, and I was anxious to close the thing up at once."[11]

Sheridan had learned that the Army of Northern Virginia was virtually without rations; if it could be kept from reaching its supplies, Grant felt it could be starved into submission.[12] General Henry Davies attacked and destroyed a supply train of 180 wagons which had been working its way toward Lee, and on April 6 Major General George Crook destroyed another four hundred wagons and captured artillery and prisoners, a move which also cut off three divisions of Confederate infantry from their line of retreat. Meanwhile Mackenzie was moving up through Jetersville, Burkeville and Prince Edward Court House, toward Appomattox Station, on the Lynchburg Railroad about five miles south of Appomattox Court House. Some thirty prisoners were taken during a skirmish at Prince Edward Court House.

On April 8 Mackenzie was assigned to Crook's Second Division. That night, Brigadier General Charles H. Smith's brigade was sent to hold the road from Appomattox Court House to Lynchburg. The lines were quiet and the troops settled in, while General Grant and General Lee exchanged notes discussing the possible surrender of the Army of Northern Virginia.

At 9:00 A.M. April 9 Crook's forces were attacked by General Bryan Grimes, as the Confederates in that sector made one last effort to break clear. The gray-clad ranks slammed into Mackenzie's front, while Confederate cavalry moved to his left and rear. He ordered three regiments dismounted and formed into a line across the Lynchburg Road, but Confederate pressure forced them back. Colonel Evans, whose Fifth Pennsylvania made up part of the line, was ordered to remount his men as soon as possible, but "some unauthorized person," Mackenzie later wrote, had moved their horses too far back, and time was lost in the remount. Meanwhile, "the same mentioned individual" sent Lieutenant Colonel Egbert Olcott with one gun around to the left, where it was overrun and captured.[13]

Although Union reports downplay the fight, the fact remains that Crook's line was broken. Mackenzie's troops were scattered in confusion and, for a brief moment, the cheering Southerners managed to clear the road to Lynchburg. The arrival of the XXIV Corps shored up federal forces and, as Mackenzie put it, "the command was extricated from a very dangerous position."[14] Crook was reorganizing his forces for a counterattack when word arrived that a truce between the two armies had been declared.[15]

Grant and Lee met the afternoon of April 9. Terms for the surrender of Lee's forces were offered and accepted. Sheridan was present and, when the formalities were over, reminded Lee that he had sent several notes protesting Grimes's attack, since it had been made after the truce was in effect. As Sheridan had not had time to make copies of his notes to Lee, he asked to borrow back the letters for that purpose. Lee took them out of his pocket and handed them over "with a few words expressive of regret that the circumstances should have occurred, and intimating that it must have been the result of some misunderstanding."[16]

The Army of Northern Virginia was formally surrendered to the United States forces on April 12, 1865. Two days later, Joe Johnston met Sherman and surrendered the Army of Tennessee. Although some fighting was still taking place in the Deep South and in Texas, for all practical purposes the great slaughter was over.

Even though the fighting was done, the army was still busy. The Confederate government was on the run but had not surrendered. Federal forces had to secure all government property and reestablish U.S. authority in a region which had lately been a separate nation.

As part of the task of reestablishing federal authority, on the night of April 10 Mackenzie had sent an officer and eight men from the Fifth Pennsylvania into Lynchburg. They returned the following day with a delegation of citizens to discuss the surrender of the city, and about 3,500 Confederate soldiers in Lynchburg formally surrendered on April 14. Mackenzie, who had moved his command into the city earlier in the day, captured fifty-six field pieces, six heavy guns, forty mortars, seventy-five caissons, fifteen thousand muskets, and a large quantity of ammunition, commissary and quartermaster supplies. A squadron of the Eleventh Pennsylvania was sent to Red Oak Church and returned with thirty prisoners, a battle flag, and thirty-six gun carriages and caissons. With the area secure, Mackenzie left Lynchburg on April 16, arriving in Richmond eight days later.[17]

For Ranald Mackenzie, the war was over. Already a brevet brigadier general of the Volunteers, he had been breveted to the same rank in the Regular Army on March 13, 1865. Now he would be breveted to major general of the Volunteers, retroactive to March 31, becoming the highest ranking officer of West Point's class of 1862.[18]

A final commendation on Mackenzie's Civil War service came twenty years later, as a dying Ulysses S. Grant struggled to complete his memoirs while still strong enough to hold a pen. Looking back on his officers, he wrote:

> Griffin, Humphreys, and Mackenzie were good corps commanders, but came into that position so near to the close of the war as not to attract public attention. All three served as such, in the last campaign of the armies of the Potomac and the James, which culminated at Appomattox Court House, on the 9th of April, 1865. The sudden collapse of the rebellion monopolized attention to the exclusion of almost everything else. I regarded Mackenzie as the most promising young officer in the army. Graduating at West Point, as he did, during the second year of the war, he had won his way up to the command of a corps before its close. This he did upon his own merit and without influence.[19]

It is unlikely Mackenzie read or appreciated the supreme commander's assessment, for Grant's memoirs were not published until 1886 and, by then, Ranald S. Mackenzie had slipped into the dark world of insanity.

CHAPTER 4

"Scouting Parties Have Been Kept Out Constantly"

At war's end Mackenzie retained command of the cavalry for the Department of Virginia until August 11, 1865, after which he was listed as "awaiting orders." Apparently he spent much of the time on leave in New York with his Duer relatives, since he notified the War Department in October and again in November that he could be reached in care of George W. Duer, Bank of the State of New York. On January 15, 1866, he was mustered out as brigadier general of the Volunteers. Like most soldiers who remained in the Regular Army, he had to take a reduction in rank. He was still entitled to be addressed as "General" on official occasions, and could wear the shoulder straps of a brigadier when sitting on courts-martial, but his rank was reduced to that of a captain of the Corps of Engineers. He remained on leave until February 23, when he was assigned to assist with construction of harbor defenses at Portsmouth, New Hampshire.[1]

While Mackenzie was going about his duties at Portsmouth, the army was undergoing a reorganization which raised Mackenzie's hopes that he might receive both a promotion to major and a field command. In the spring of 1867 friends told him the colonelcy of the Forty-First Infantry was available. Because it was a black regiment, several other officers had already turned down the command assignment. Mackenzie was advised that if the position were offered him,

he would do well to take it even though the idea of commanding black troops was not appealing. Like most Northerners of
the period, he was opposed to slavery but unwilling to view
blacks as equals. Nonetheless, the assignment was not only a
way out of the detested Engineers—it would also jump him
three grades, far beyond the rank he had hoped to receive. The
offer was made, and on March 11 he wrote the War Department, "I have the honor to acknowledge the receipt of appt.
of Colonel of the 41st Rgt. of Infantry US Army. I accept the
same and will report as directed." At twenty-six, he was now
the second youngest colonel in the army.[2] Two days later he
passed the examining board and medical examination in New
York. On April 26 he was handed Special Order No. 209 from
the Adjutant General's office, telling him to report to his
regiment at Baton Rouge, Louisiana. He returned the order
with a note across the bottom, saying he considered it as
notification and acceptance of the appointment and would
comply "as soon as I can make the necessary arrangements for
my change in station and rank."[3] He was back on the line.

His second-in-command was Lieutenant Colonel William
R. Shafter, who had managed the regiment until a colonel was
appointed.[4] No more perfect match could have been found;
in many ways Bill Shafter and Ranald Mackenzie were alike,
both men arrogant and egotistical with a stubborn determination. But there were differences as well. Mackenzie was me-
ticulous about detail and made certain there was paperwork
on everything. He filled every blank space in his regimental
and post returns unless there was absolutely nothing to record,
and even that was often noted. Shafter saw situations more in
overview, and often seemed indifferent to finer points so long
as the proper results were achieved. His record keeping, at this
time at least, was a bureaucrat's nightmare. His returns con-

William R. Shafter
(Fort Davis National Historic Park)

tain enormous gaps. He was also a family man and relatively gregarious, while Mackenzie remained alone and aloof. The two were dissimilar physically as well. Although Mackenzie fleshed out over the years, he could never have been considered overweight. He was neat, and his hair and moustache were always trimmed. Shafter grew to gargantuan proportions. With a fat, square face staring out from under a mop of white hair, and a lip hidden by an oversized brush of a moustache, he looked like an unkempt walrus in blue.

The similarities and differences blended in almost perfect harmony. Indeed, it might even be said that Shafter was the closest thing to a friend Mackenzie had during his years in the army. A trace of affection shows through the military formality of Mackenzie's official letters. For his part, Shafter sent notes containing both military and personal information, including some references to Mackenzie's private life which others would not have dared mention.

The situation the two officers faced in Baton Rouge was discouraging. The black troops were little more than uneducated field hands newly liberated from slavery. One of Mackenzie's first acts was to make Shafter superintendent of the Regimental Recruiting Service. Officers were sent to Detroit and Chicago and a concerted effort made to enlist Northern blacks, who were generally considered better educated.[5] Once again, Mackenzie needed to reverse a bad situation. If he could overhaul a bunch of stubborn, independent volunteers during a war, he could certainly do the same with ex-slaves during peacetime.

In late June 1867 the Forty-First set out for its first Western assignment at Fort Brown, Texas, and Ranald Mackenzie entered the frontier where he would serve for the rest of his career. Unknown to him his brother Sandy, who had risen to lieutenant commander and who was serving on the remote China Station, had died earlier the same month. On June 13 he had led a landing on Formosa to avenge the deaths of American seamen in attacks by local natives, and was killed in a charge.[6] Nothing has been found of Mackenzie's reaction to his brother's death, but there can be little doubt that he was deeply affected by the tragedy. The Mackenzie brothers and their sister were a tightly knit group, and Ranald and Sandy appear to have been especially close.

Despite his personal loss, Mackenzie continued to upgrade his regiment while reestablishing federal authority on the frontier. The army which served in Texas in 1867 was an army of occupation, sent to pacify citizens whom the federal government considered to have been in rebellion. In South Texas there was the additional problem of French intervention in Mexico. The United States was committed to the republican regime of Benito Juárez, but along the border the Texans' relations had been cordial with the Mexican imperialists and their French allies, and they viewed the fate of the former Emperor Maximilian with some concern.[7]

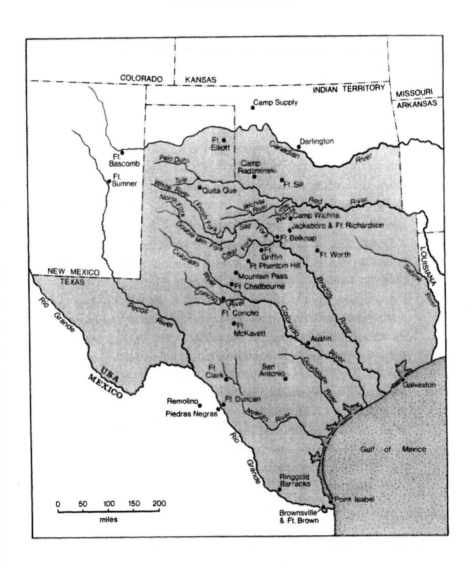

Military Department of Texas

Fort Brown was located at Brownsville in the southern-most part of Texas, one of the most urbane and cosmopolitan towns in the Southwest, having prospered both from the cotton trade during the war, and from the trade with the imperialists in Mexico. Northerners, Southerners and Europeans had flooded the city, taking advantage of the boom as Southern cotton was exported through Mexico, and luxuries and munitions imported. The fort had been established in April 1846 when no one was sure whether or not it was even on U.S. territory. In fact, its very existence was a point of contention with the Mexicans and one of the causes of the Mexican War. When that war ended in 1848, the fort's primary function was to guard the border from periodic raids by Mexican bandits and filibusters. Surrendered by the North in 1861, it was taken over by Confederates until November 3, 1863, when, as Union forces approached Brownsville, General Hamilton Bee panicked and abandoned the city. To prevent the post from falling into enemy hands, he ordered that it be set on fire. Flames reached the powder magazine, which exploded "with a concussion as if heaven and earth had come in collision. . . . Men and women on the side walks, in the streets, and those keeping vigil over their effects at the ferry were shocked, stunned and many were thrown to the ground." Flames spread into the city itself and several blocks were destroyed.[8]

Now, almost four years later, Mackenzie arrived to administer the city and rebuild the ruined post. Until new barracks could be finished, troops were quartered in town, which created incidents with local citizens.[9] Not everyone in town was unhappy, however. With tension along the border, the Brownsville *Daily Ranchero* was realistic in its view of the regiment's arrival:

The Saint Mary brought over from Galveston about a thousand colored troops who are now at Brazos Santiago. These troops are to be stationed at various points along the Rio Grande.

We wish it were fifty thousand, for obvious and diverse reasons. There is work for them in this latitude, and we should like, well, to see them on hand and getting at it; the sooner the better.[10]

Soon they were "getting at it." Because the area was under martial law, military commissions handled much of the business normally considered beyond their jurisdiction. A key duty was enforcement of registration laws under the Reconstruction Acts. Contemporary accounts report several trials for violations during that summer and fall.[11]

Fort Brown was also headquarters of the Sub-District of the Rio Grande and, in addition to commanding a regiment and superintending the long, tedious job of rebuilding the post, Mackenzie had duties as the sub-district commander. The men of the Forty-First were scattered between Brown, Brazos Santiago near Point Isabel, and Ringgold Barracks another hundred-plus miles upriver.[12] In August and September of 1867 Mackenzie stayed at Ringgold, a post in somewhat better condition than Fort Brown but also hopelessly dilapidated and obsolete and undergoing reconstruction. He returned to Brownsville in time for one of the worst hurricanes in the city's history. On October 7 and 8, according to the post surgeon, "A heavy North East wind sett [sic] in, accompanied by rain and hurricane which caused Brazos de Santiago to be overflowed, sweeping away most of the houses and other buildings, and causing the loss of sixteen (16) lives." Most of the newly constructed buildings at the post were destroyed, and work had to begin all over again.[13]

All the while, Mackenzie and Shafter maintained pressure on the regiment, with patrols along the Rio Grande and pickets along the most-used fords. As they settled into a routine of field service, construction and discipline, the men began acting more and more like soldiers. Command of black troops in 1867 carried a special burden which officers of white units did not experience. Most blacks of the time had been denied any sort of education, and what little education some of them might have was generally rudimentary. Consequently, officers of black units found themselves performing duties normally handled in white units by sergeants and clerks, ranging from paperwork to sanitary needs. On the positive side, the added responsibilities created officers generally much more efficient than their counterparts in white regiments.

The regiment also had to deal with racial prejudice which existed on the border. Mackenzie alleviated racial problems by constantly shuffling units between the various posts under his command, so there would not be enough time for major incidents to develop between individual soldiers and local citizens.[14] Thus he continued to gain experience in handling troops, experience which would stand him well within the next few years. In the process, the Forty-First became a superior regiment boasting the lowest desertion rate in the Army.[15]

By the beginning of 1868 the border was quiet. In February Mackenzie was ordered to Fort Clark, farther west, and the regiment followed a month later. Soon after it arrived, however, he went to San Antonio for courts-martial duty, where he remained until November despite having lost Bill Shafter, who was assigned to command Fort Duncan on March 24.

During his stay in San Antonio, Mackenzie lived in a

boarding house owned by Warrick Tunstall near the Fourth Street Bridge. Tunstall had an eighteen-year-old daughter, Florida, and by most accounts the twenty-seven-year-old colonel fell in love with her. His relationships with women were never one of his strong points. As a youngster he had always deferred to Sandy in social functions, and he had apparently gained little confidence as he grew older. On at least one occasion on the frontier, one of his officers recalled he was "a little slow, diffident or bashful," which perhaps prevented his forming a strong relationship with Florida Tunstall. Perhaps, also, he held back because she seems to have been already romantically involved with Dr. Redford Sharpe, an army physician nineteen years her senior, whom she married in 1869 when she was twenty.[16]

Mackenzie returned to his regiment at Fort Clark on December 14, where he remained until March 1869 when the Forty-First was transferred to Fort McKavett in Menard County. McKavett was another old post which had fallen into disrepair during the war. Although it was the headquarters post of the Forty-First, the fort was shared by units of the Ninth Cavalry, a mounted black regiment. As post commander, Mackenzie had charge of these units as well. At last he again had horse soldiers.

Fort McKavett was closer to the Indian frontier than Forts Brown or Clark. Mackenzie noted that large numbers of free-roaming cattle in the area were "driven off by the Indians, and by white thieves, whose organizations extend from Mexico, through the Indian Territory to Missouri and Kansas. Horses or blooded stock cannot be raised on account of such depredations."[17]

Given this opportunity to hunt down and engage a wily enemy, it must have been frustrating for him again to be

Fort Clark, Texas, 1903 *(National Archives)*

ordered to San Antonio for courts-martial duty. This time, however, he was finished in San Antonio by May 12, and seven days later rode out of McKavett with two lieutenants and forty-two enlisted men of the Ninth for a scout in the direction of the mouth of the Pecos River. He was gone until July 13. No contact with hostile Indians was reported.[18]

Other scouts fared better though, as shown by this report a few months later:

> The detachment of two officers Capt. Carroll and Heyl and 61 enlisted men of Companies F and M 9th Cavalry, Capt. Carroll commanding, that left this post Sept. 2nd returned on the 13th instant [October] having had one engagement on the 16th of Sept. with a party of about two hundred Indians (Kiowas and Comances *[sic]*) near the head waters of the Salt Fork of the Brazos River in which, during a running fight of eight miles[,] twenty five Indians were Killed and wounded. The casualties were Privates Pope Lane and Basil Fontery, Co. M, 9th Cavalry, wounded. The command was out

forty two days, and marched a distance of six hundred and thirty seven miles.[19]

The same return stated, "The Head Quarters of the 24[t]h Infantry, Bvt. Brig. General MacKenzie, Col[.] were established at this post and companies D and I 41st U.S. Infantry, consolidated forming Co. D 24[t]h Infantry. . . ."[20] The Forty-First had been consolidated with the Thirty-Eighth Infantry as part of the Army Reduction Act, an economic measure passed in 1869. The new Twenty-Fourth Infantry thus created became one of the four regiments of black troops which were to win high honors on the Western Plains as the "Buffalo Soldiers."

Amid scouting expeditions and unit consolidations, Mackenzie was also preoccupied with various administrative concerns involved in rebuilding the dilapidated post. Many of the post returns for 1869 contain the sentence, "The greater portion of the garrison present is engaged in repairing and building quarters, building stables, etc." He had trouble obtaining skilled laborers and materials such as finished lumber, shingles and cement.[21]

Another source of irritation was the post sutler, Samuel Wallick, a private citizen who dispensed liquor and other commodities to the troops on credit. Interest rates were exhorbitant and many soldiers were perpetually in debt. Although the men had grievances against Wallick, matters remained quiet until July 1869 when the firm of Reynolds and Kintz opened a competing store, which Mackenzie closed on the grounds that two stores created too much unrest. To begin with, he said, they would try to draw customers away from each other by allowing "loud boisterous and improper conduct in the vicinity of their shops, and make much trouble generally." He added a sentence which also summed up his feelings toward blacks. "The men run up bills with several [stores] and are unable to pay or do not and if allowed to go unpunished for their dishonesty the slave habit of stealing is made more difficult to break up."[22]

Regardless of what he thought about his black soldiers, he was merciless toward anyone who mistreated them. One old settler, John M. Jackson, offended by what he considered the excessive and unwanted attentions of a mulatto sergeant toward his daughter, took his rifle and went after the man. The several different accounts of what happened all agree that Jackson killed the wrong soldier.

Mackenzie was determined to arrest Jackson and spent months detailing search parties, but Jackson knew the country and had the support of the local population. The soldiers received no cooperation, in spite of their colonel's efforts to pressure the magistrates. At one point Jackson was captured but managed to escape with the help of family and friends. Several other times he barely avoided capture but was still at large when Mackenzie was transferred elsewhere.[23]

Besides Mackenzie's other problems, there was also a question concerning the actual ownership of the post. Like most Texas military installations of the period, Fort McKavett was built on leased land, in this case land owned by the estate of Joshua D. Robinson who had acquired the property and the government lease in 1858. The administrator of the estate, A.O. Cooley, submitted a request for rent money but, instead, Mackenzie recommended the Department of Texas exercise the government's option to buy the reservation. Overruled, he was ordered to pay the bill.[24]

This was not the only dispute with the Department, and particularly its commander, Colonel J.J. Reynolds. When a load of corn, purchased under a contract with the San Antonio firm of Adams and Wickes, contained fifteen percent dirt, Mackenzie convened a board of officers to inspect it and wrote to Reynolds requesting credit for the difference. Reynolds ordered the entire bill to be paid. Thinking the order was a mistake, Mackenzie asked for clarification but again was told to pay the bill. This was the first of several confrontations with Reynolds which would have repercussions over the next seven years, and which would do much to convince Mackenzie that the departmental commander was "a bad officer."[25]

To further complicate Mackenzie's life in general, Florida Tunstall's new husband, Dr. Sharpe, was the post surgeon at Fort McKavett. Fortunately for both men, Mackenzie was absent much of the time. Although his service record does not so state, he was also commander of the Sub-District of the Pecos at this time, and often visited the various other posts under his jurisdiction. Planning to inspect Fort Concho in September, he sent word ahead that he wanted preparations made for a large scouting party. Upon arrival, he toured the post hospital and told Dr. William Notson, the surgeon, that the police of the facility was not "as good as it might be." He didn't bother to explain what he meant, and the conscientious surgeon was left wondering what he was supposed to correct.

The scouting party, which left Fort Concho on September 6 with one hundred men of the Ninth Cavalry, fought a large band of Indians for two days on the Salt Fork of the Brazos. When the party returned, it had been out exactly one month. A second scouting party, this time with 150 men, left for the Upper Brazos country on October 10 and was joined by another twenty-five troops and an equal number of Tonkawa Indian Scouts at Fort Griffin. This larger party clashed with several hundred warriors, swept through an Indian camp, and returned with eight women and children as prisoners.[26]

Mackenzie returned to Fort McKavett on January 11, 1870. During his absence, his own Twenty-Fourth Infantry had several fights with Indians. These actions kept pressure on the Indians, and few encounters were reported during the remainder of his service at the post. In March 1870 the post returns stated, "Scouting parties have been kept out constantly during the past month, but nothing important has been accomplished against Indians." Mackenzie spent the next several months on detached service and on an extended leave. He returned to Fort McKavett on October 1, but remained only a short while. On October 17 he was relieved of command of both the regiment and post, and was ordered to Washington as a member of a special board.[27]

While Mackenzie was in the capital, the following notice appeared in the December 29 issue of the Austin *Daily State Journal*:

> General Order No. 126, issued by the War Department December 15, by direction of the President, transfers and assigns a number of commissioned officers to fill vacancies to the present date, prominent among whom are Col. Joseph J. Reynolds, transferred from the Twenty-fifth Infantry to the Third Cavalry. . .Col. Ranald S. McKenzie, Twenty-fourth Infantry to Fourth Cavalry vice Graham, retired. . . .[28]

This order, giving him command of a cavalry regiment, was to change Mackenzie's life and the history of the Plains.

CHAPTER 5

"A Blessing to this Whole State and Frontier"

M ackenzie prepared to assume his new command at the worst possible time. On the surface his assignment was clear enough—protect the settlers and bring the tribes under control—but policy was made in Washington, far from the plains and under the influence of an Eastern establishment whose policies often differed from those advocated by the western settlers. It was often hard to tell whose side the government was on, and official policy often hindered the performance of a soldier's duties.

Peace with the Indians on the Texas frontier was the responsibility of the Department of Texas, until 1871 an administrative area of the Military Division of the South assigned the primary duty of enforcement of the state's reconstruction. After November 1871 the department was attached to the Military Division of the Missouri. Headquartered in Chicago, this division with its four departments occupied the middle two-thirds of the United States, extending to the western boundaries of Montana, Wyoming, Utah and New Mexico. For the next two decades, this vast theater of operations was the center of the United States' military efforts.

The majority of the officers in the division detested the Indian service. To them, "war" meant the late conflict between North and South, where two organized armies met each

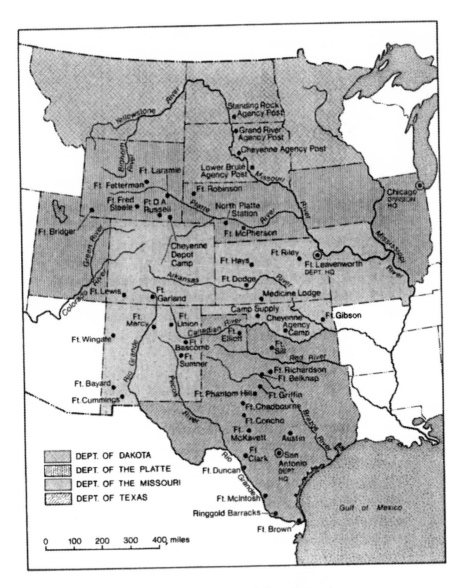

Military Division of the Missouri

other in the field according to a mutually understood code of conduct. There was no glory in fighting a primitive people. As General John Pope told the Social Science Association in 1878:

> To the Army officer a state of peace with Indians is, of all things, the most desirable, and no man in all the country east or west would do more to avert an Indian war. To him war with Indians means far more than to anyone else except the actual victim. He sees its beginning in injustice and wrong to the Indian, which he has not the power to prevent; he sees the Indian gradually reach a condition of starvation impossible of longer endurance and thus forced to take what he can get to save himself from dying of hunger, and cannot help sympathizing with him for doing so; but because he does so the officer is ordered to use force against him. . . .If successful, it is a massacre of Indians; if unsuccessful, it is worthlessness or imbecility, and these judgments confront the Army in every newspaper and in public speeches in Congress and elsewhere— judgments passed by men who are absolutely ignorant of the subject at all, or by those who, knowing better, misrepresent for a purpose.[1]

With this sense of frustration, the army went to war on the frontier.

Many government leaders shared the attitude of the officers, and in the late 1860s they attempted reconciliation with the warriors of the plains. Federal officials met in October 1867 with representatives of the leading tribes at Medicine Lodge, Kansas, where the government demanded the Indians move to reservations, end their raids and allow railroads through the plains. In turn, they would receive non-exclusive hunting rights in their traditional buffalo ranges south of the Arkansas River, they would be issued annuities and be given schools, churches, farming implements and other essentials of white civilization.[2] Such a one-sided negotiation was cause enough for a breakdown in relations, since the tribes saw nothing of value in these essentials of white civilization. Additionally, the traditional ranges south of the Arkansas extended into Texas, where the federal government had no jurisdiction over public or private property.[3]

The Indians were not blind to the situation and were quick to reply. Most of their answers were delivered by the Kiowas, generally acknowledged as the best orators, led by Satanta, whose posturing arrogance belied his very real ability as a warrior.

> All the land south of the Arkansas belongs to the Kiowas and Comanches, and I don't want to give away any of it, I love the land and the buffalo, and will not part with it. . . .I hear a good deal of talk from the gentlemen whom the Great Father sends us, but they never do what they say. I don't want any of the Medicine lodges (schools) within the country. I want the children raised as I was.

Referring to one Comanche band which had accepted government largess, he fumed:

> Look at the Penatekas! Formerly they were powerful, but now they are weak and poor. I want all my land, even from the Arkansas south to the Red River. My country is small enough already. If you

build us houses the land will be smaller. Why do
you insist on this? What good will come of it?[4]

Satanta's speeches were unsettling to the government
agents. He spoke long and often, earning the sarcastic title
"Orator of the Plains" from those whites present who were
less-than-impressed with his personality. Through it all, the
old chief Satank sat quietly. He was a *Koiet-senko*, a member
of an elite society of the ten bravest warriors of the Kiowa
nation. On October 24 after the Kiowas had signed their part
of the treaty and were preparing to leave, Satank went straight
to the point. He told the group that whites had originally
come as friends and had gained the confidence of the tribes.
Now they were invaders who told the Indians "to be gone, as
the offended master speaks to his dog." By accepting peace
with the whites, "I have been made poor. Before, I was rich
in horses and lodges. Today I am the poorest of all." Nevertheless, Satank voiced confidence in the treaty, and pledged
his trust.[5] The Kiowas and Comanches agreed to a reservation
near Fort Sill in the western Indian Territory.

The grievances of the Indian were many, but so were those
of the whites. Plains Indian society was a warrior society,
where proof of manhood was based on proficiency and courage in battle. As early as 1837 a traveler noted that the people
of Texas "must expect to be harassed; their homes reduced to
ashes; their wives and children will be butchered, and what is
worse than all, the whole country kept in perpetual fear and
anxiety as long as government has not the means or the power
to impress [the tribes] with terror."[6] Now, more than thirty
years later, the Indians had nothing to gain by accepting the
reservation, whereas raiding the settlements brought them
plunder and prestige. Many of the Kiowas, treaty or no treaty,

Kiowa Chief Satank *(National Archives)*

intended to continue their depredations in Texas.

This was the situation Mackenzie faced in 1871 when he arrived at Fort Concho to assume command of the Fourth Cavalry. Before many months passed Satanta and Satank would become his greatest concern, but first, as usual, he was primarily interested in whipping his regiment into line. The

Fourth had a short but honorable history. It had been organized in 1855 as the First Cavalry, and had served against Indians and guerrillas in Kansas before the Civil War. Its ranks included J.E.B. Stuart and Joseph E. Johnston, both of whom later gained fame as Confederate generals. When Robert E. Lee submitted his resignation from the U.S. Army, he had signed his name as the regiment's colonel. Renumbered as the Fourth in 1861, when the army's mounted units were reorganized, it had distinguished itself throughout the war.

The regiment had arrived at Fort Concho in July 1870, a shadow of its former self with discipline slack and the officers indifferent. With abundant game and well-stocked rivers in the vicinity of the post, the officers spent much of their time hunting and fishing when they should have been seeing to their men.

There was also a number of incapacitated officers on the rolls even though they did not serve. In the nineteenth century, the army retirement list was severely restricted. Many disabled officers were unable to retire because they had no means of support, so they stayed on regimental rosters for years. Humane as this might have been, it blocked promotion and restricted the commanding officer's flexibility.

There was the additional problem of Fort Concho itself, which had experienced eleven commanders in the three years prior to Mackenzie's arrival. Dr. Notson, the post surgeon, felt this continual change of command had been generally detrimental, with the problems of one administration carrying over into the next and the efforts to solve them never consistent.[7] The regiment was a mixture of various nationalities, with Irishmen composing their usual high percentage. Some troopers were former officers with drinking problems, and others were former Confederate officers who were barred

Fort Concho, Texas *(National Archives)*

from holding commissions in the federal armed forces. As did all the other military units, the Fourth had its quota of troopers fleeing from the law or from social obligations. Normally, at least ten percent of any western command landed in the guardhouse on payday, and there was no reason to believe the Fourth was any different.[8]

The arrival of Mackenzie meant change. Writing home about his new regiment he said, "I intend that it shall not be on account of any laziness of mine if it falls below any other."[9] Once again, the screws began to tighten. On February 25, 1871, the day after he arrived, he ordered all sporting rifles and shotguns packed and stored, although he himself was fond of hunting. He successfully lobbied for retirement of his incapacitated officers, opening the door for advancement. Inept officers were transferred out and new ones brought in. Under Mackenzie, the Fourth became known for rapid promotions;

a lieutenant might make captain in twelve years, whereas in other outfits it might take more than twenty.

One of the replacement officers was Lieutenant Robert Carter, who was to serve Mackenzie faithfully for the next four years and who would do more than any other man to perpetuate his memory. Carter arrived at Fort Concho just in time to pack his own hunting gear but, as he noted, the regiment would soon be hunting "larger and more troublesome game."[10] After a month of drilling and discipline, the Fourth was ordered to garrison Fort Richardson in Jack County near the Indian Territory some seventy miles west of Fort Worth, on the outer reaches of the frontier and the center of some of the worst raiding.

Lieutenant Robert G. Carter
(National Archives)

On Monday, March 27, Headquarters, Companies A and E and the band prepared to march out of Fort Concho. As with any major move, things invariably went wrong. Mules kicked packs loose, and coffee, flour and bacon were scattered all over the parade ground and had to be repacked. A vicious horse had to be whipped into line. Some soldiers had spent the previous night in the cantinas of nearby St. Angela and were too hungover to be of any use. Several officers were taking their wives to the new garrison, a situation which the bachelor Mackenzie viewed with both amusement and irritation. Finally, at 11:00 A.M., everything was ready and the march command given. The rest of the garrison assembled and gave three cheers as the column rode out of the fort, splashed across the Concho River and headed north. It made fifteen miles before halting to camp at 4:00 P.M., resuming at 7:00 A.M. the following day. The soldiers began to see buffalo, part of the vast southern herd which often blanketed the Texas plains for miles at a stretch. A light drizzle, which had begun early in the morning, continued into the night and a chill set in. Mess kettles were piled full of mesquite wood to serve as stoves for the women.

The third day's march was warm, the weather clear, and the column made seventeen miles before stopping to camp at old Fort Chadbourne at 1:00 P.M. This post had been founded in 1852 and was now abandoned except for a corporal and three privates guarding the mail station. Hundreds of buffalo grazed around the area, even on the old parade ground.

A cold, wet norther blew in about noon on the day the column left Fort Chadbourne, and it rained heavily that night. The following day the weather remained "wild and boisterous" as the column came to Mountain Pass, about nine miles south of what is now Merkel. The pass through the escarpment was a favorite ambush spot, and a thorough reconnaissance was made before the column descended it.

The plains below were dotted with herds of buffalo which became alarmed as the wind carried the scent of the column down to them. The scattered herds began consolidating into one vast herd which moved toward the column, coming so close that it crowded the lead company. When several of the horses took fright and became unmanageable, Mackenzie grabbed a carbine from one of the troopers, dismounted, and began firing at the herd in an attempt to head it off. The nearest buffalo swerved but those behind kept coming, completely surrounding the column and frightening the men, who started firing into the gigantic animals. The pack of mongrel dogs, which the soldiers kept for pets, charged in and began snapping and tearing at the buffalo. Between the dogs and the gunfire, the herd finally veered off and the command was given to cease fire. King, a seventy-five-pound English bulldog who belonged to the regimental band, attacked an immense bull which had been wounded in the shooting, grabbing the bull by the nose just as he had been trained to bring down cattle in the slaughter pen at Fort Concho. The buffalo went to his knees, stood up again and began to shake his head, but the dog held on tight as he had been trained to do. Blood and foam spattered both the buffalo and the dog, and the bull began to weaken.

"Kill the animal, and put him out of his misery!" Mackenzie shouted impatiently, and two soldiers went over, pointed their carbines behind the buffalo's shoulder and fired. He quivered for a moment, then collapsed. With the animal dead, the bulldog let go. Months later, when one of the periodic orders went out to kill the dogs which had accumulated at Fort Richardson, King was spared by a special paragraph citing "gallant conduct."[11]

The next several days of march were relatively routine, and the column camped among the ruins of old Fort Phantom Hill. Here, in one of the loneliest spots on the frontier, Mackenzie uncharacteristically waxed poetic. "Quarters for 5 or 6 Companies must at one time, have been completed," he wrote, "but there is nothing now left save the Chimneys which seem to have been well built, and are standing alone in silent desolation, commemorative of time's decay."[12]

After Fort Phantom Hill came the heavily garrisoned post of Fort Griffin, a "jumping off place" for the empty expanses of Northwest Texas. The remnant of the Tonkawa tribe camped nearby under the fort's protection. The Tonkawas hated the plains tribes and were proving to be one of the army's most valuable assets as scouts. Beyond Griffin was the abandoned post of Fort Belknap, about a day's march from Fort Richardson across an open plain known as the Salt Creek Prairie, perhaps the most dangerous place in Texas at the time.

"Passed a mound on which two wooden crosses are erected with the remark 'Three Negroes killed by Indians January 3rd. 1871' cut on the wood," Mackenzie wrote,[13] and Carter added:

> There were other rude head boards marking the last resting place of some "freighter," or cow boy, or rancher, who, in passing along this dangerous stretch of stage road, had sacrificed their lives in encounters with the Indian raiders and murderers. . . . We had occasion to pass the markers for the dead, of which there were 21, many times. . . .[14]

The Fourth entered Fort Richardson at noon on April 8, after a march of 220 miles from Fort Concho. Headquarters and six companies of the Sixth Cavalry had already left for Fort Harker, Kansas, and the remaining companies were busy packing and turning in the regiment's surplus stores and unserviceable arms and equipment. The Sixth had held up well enough in combat, but had never actively pursued Indian raiders. Comparing the two regiments, H.H. McConnell of the Sixth admitted that Mackenzie "believed it was more important for the troops to scout the frontier and perform

Fort Griffin Officers' Quarters and Cannon, 1872 *(Lawrence T. Jones III Collection)*

military duty than it was to build chicken-coops for officers and interfere with the citizens of the country." To McConnell, the change of command "was to prove a blessing to this whole State and frontier, and to reflect credit on the National government and on his own command."[15]

Fort Richardson was a motley collection of picket barracks and pecan log huts. A few of the principal buildings such as the hospital, guardhouse and magazine, were made of stone. There was a stone commissary building which had originally been intended to enclose the sally-port of a quadrangle that was never built. Some of the officers lived in quarters of sawed cottonwood facing the parade ground. With the companies of one battalion of the Sixth still at Fort Richardson, space was at a premium and most of the Fourth went into camp outside the post. Bachelor officers of the Sixth offered their quarters to the ladies of the incoming regiment, small comfort since the rough huts were infested with fleas.[16] As the Fourth settled in and waited a few weeks for the remainder of the Sixth to leave for Kansas, the officers and men became better acquainted with their new commander.

Mackenzie was quick to criticize, but not very free with praise. "Sometimes when I most hoped for a word of commendation from General M— I received nothing or if anything a few caustic remarks," Trooper John Charlton said. "The greater the trust reposed in me the more I felt I had accomplished in gaining his favor, but I felt hurt and rebellious many times, because of his manner."[17]

But there was another side to the man, which Charlton discovered in their first encounter. He had never before met Mackenzie, since his own company had been transferred from Fort Griffin rather than from Fort Concho and had arrived at Richardson ahead of the others. Subsequently detailed as a

Picket Building

Guard House
Fort Richardson, Texas, 1872
(Lawrence T. Jones III Collection)

teamster to help move the Sixth as far as Fort Sill, on the night of his return to Richardson, Charlton was grooming a mule at stable call when the animal stepped on his foot. He instinctively hit it with a curry comb. When he looked up, he saw a man in a gray suit standing nearby. After stables, Sergeant Faber, the corral boss, told Charlton that Mackenzie had ordered him to report to the first sergeant.

"Huh," Charlton said. "What does General M— know about me? I never saw him in my life."

"That was he standing behind you when you struck that mule," Faber replied.

Charlton knew he was in trouble. He had committed the unpardonable sin of the cavalry. He had mistreated an animal. He hurried over to the first sergeant's office to get it over with.

"The Gineral is goin' to make you a Corporal, Charlton," the sergeant said.

"Phew!" Charlton breathed with relief. "If I had known that *I'd have killed that darn mule and maybe he'd have gotten me a commission.*"[18] If Charlton had broken a key rule in hitting the mule, he had also reacted quickly and instinctively. Mackenzie wanted that in a soldier. Less than a month later, Mackenzie's judgment was proved right when Charlton was again quick to react, this time in a far deadlier situation.

CHAPTER 6

"You Will Not Hesitate to Attack"

Eighteen seventy-one was a year of terror for the settlers on the Texas frontier. "The entire border was ablaze, and the stories that these wretched settlers brought in from time to time of murder, rapine, burning, pillaging and plundering was almost heartrending," Carter wrote.[1]

By March, it appeared that some major movement was afoot among the tribes of the Indian Territory. Lieutenant Colonel J.W. Davidson, Tenth Cavalry, commanding Camp Supply in the northwestern part of the Territory, speculated that the Kiowas were buying all the water kegs they could find so they could send their families to a secure spot on the Staked Plains, while they consolidated with the Comanches and part of the Cheyennes west of the Wichita Mountains. He ordered large military escorts out of Camp Supply, since small ones "only invite attack." Davidson was a tough, level-headed officer who only reported the information he considered most reliable: "Did I send out every rumor that reaches my ears I would have my hands full," he wrote to departmental head-quarters.[2]

South of the Territory, depredations were almost routine around Fort Richardson, some occurring within sight of the post itself. Twelve persons had been murdered in Jack County during the first four months of 1871. The Sixth Cavalry had taken a lackadaisical approach to the problem, partly through

71

indifference and partly through the government's failure to provide enough horses and equipment to keep a mobile unit in the field.[3]

The Fourth likewise suffered problems of enough mounts, but its colonel was undeterred, sending a detail with Lieutenant Peter Martin Boehm to the city of Sherman to acquire new horses. One, an iron gray, particularly impressed Boehm. When the detail returned to Fort Richardson, Boehm, undoubtedly aware that Mackenzie's war wounds caused him considerable pain and made him a poor rider, took him to the road behind his quarters and rode the horse up and down to show off its gaits. Mackenzie liked it and designated the gray as his own mount.[4]

As more of the regiment arrived, scouts were sent out—Lieutenant George Thurston with Company E on April 20, and Captain Wirt Davis with Company F the following day. Although both returned without meeting any hostile Indians, they had covered 131 miles and 113 miles respectively. Mackenzie's arrival at Fort Richardson signified an end to the lackadaisical approach to the Indian problem.[5]

Except for a few scattered bands, the Indian raiders in Northwest Texas were almost exclusively from the Kiowa-Comanche Agency near Fort Sill. Like other agencies in the Indian Territory, it was under the administration of the Society of Friends—the Quakers—who sought to pacify the Indians by example rather than by military force. Fortunately, the Quaker agent in charge at Fort Sill, Lawrie Tatum, realistically recognized his charges to be undisciplined marauders.[6] In his own peace-loving way, he could be as iron-fisted as the Indians under his care and sometimes subdued them by sheer force of personality. Tatum might have succeeded had his ideals and determination been balanced by a

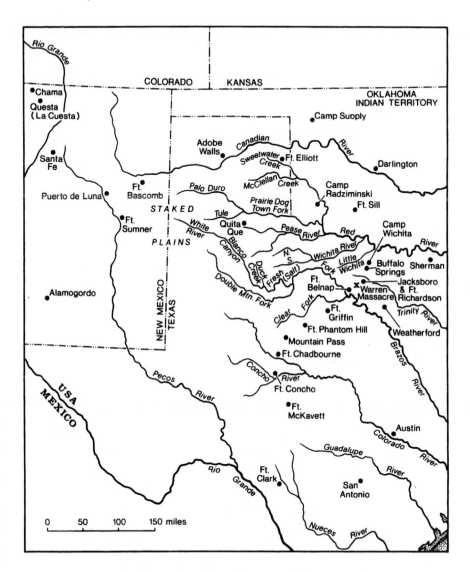

Central and Northern Texas

strong show of force at Fort Sill, but the post commander, Colonel Benjamin Grierson, was totally sympathetic to the government's Quaker policy. Even though he established patrols along the Red River in a futile attempt to turn back raiders en route to Texas, and occasionally made personal inspection tours of the reservations with a military escort, his belief in the pacification policy of the Quakers often colored his judgment. To some extent, in fact, he appears to have depended on his contacts among the Indian commissioners to protect him from being relieved from his position because of what William and Shirley Leckie call "his too Quaker-like opinions regarding Indian policy."[7] Even had he desired to use force, Grierson was hampered both by the dispersion of his Tenth Cavalry throughout the Indian Territory and Kansas, and by a government policy which greatly restricted the army's options on a reservation. Consequently both agent and soldier were powerless to prevent raiders from coming and going as they pleased.

Although Mackenzie's troops were in the field more or less continually, two movements deserve particular attention. On May 10 a scouting party consisting of Lieutenant Boehm and twenty-five enlisted men were sent out to patrol the area between Fort Richardson and Fort Griffin. Meanwhile Company B was arriving by detachments from Fort Concho, some on May 6 and others on May 18, six weeks after the rest of the regiment. While the reason for the delay in their arrival is not stated, Boehm's scout and the fragmented arrival of Company B may have been designed for security during the visit of General W.T. Sherman, General-in-Chief of the Army.[8]

Sherman was conducting a first-hand inspection of the frontier in response to the continuing outcries which poured into his headquarters. He left San Antonio on May 2 for a

Lawrie Tatum
(Oklahoma Historical Society)

Benjamin Grierson
(National Archives)

wide swing west, through Fort McKavett and Fort Concho, and then to the northeast. Like most military men in the East, he considered the stories of Indian depredations exaggerated, and possibly even fabricated, in an effort to draw troops away from reconstruction duties. His inspection trip was extremely important to the people living on the frontier, since it would determine whether they received additional protection. There were even those who hoped that some of the inevitable depredations would occur during the general's visit. By the time he arrived at Fort Griffin on May 15, Sherman had still not seen any sign of Indians. He did, however, order a picket at old Fort Belknap, to protect the few families who lived around the abandoned post.

Sherman remained skeptical as he covered the last few

William Tecumseh Sherman
(National Archives)

miles between Fort Belknap and Fort Richardson on May 17. He declined an additional escort at Fort Griffin and continued to travel in an ambulance, a semi-enclosed coach, with only seventeen infantrymen from San Antonio as outriders. The local commanders were better informed and, in addition to Mackenzie's units, sent out two scouting expeditions from Fort Griffin. The large number of troops scouting the area probably prevented the general-in-chief from seeing any hostile Indians.[9]

If Sherman doubted the Indian stories, his travelling companion, Inspector-General Randolph B. Marcy, who had served in Texas following the Mexican War, accepted them wholeheartedly. Marcy noted the destruction in the area around Jacksboro and was blunt about who he thought should take the blame. In his journal, he described:

> remains of several ranches. . .the occupants of which have been either killed or driven off to the more dense settlements by the Indians. Indeed this rich and beautiful section does not contain today so many white people as it did when I visited it eighteen years ago, and if the Indian marauders are

not punished, the whole country seems to be in a
fair way of becoming totally depopulated.[10]

As Sherman's group rode through the Salt Creek Prairie,
a powerful Kiowa war party watched from a nearby height.
Some warriors wanted to attack but their leader, the medicine
man Maman-ti, held them back. He had seen this group in a
vision, and said it should be allowed to pass unmolested. A
second band of whites would come through later and could
be attacked with better results. Perhaps Maman-ti had noticed
the military outriders and decided these whites might cause
more trouble than they were worth.[11]

Mackenzie had detailed Lieutenant Carter to ride out and
meet the party on the road with fifteen "carefully selected
men" and a change of mules for the ambulance. He was also
told to offer Sherman the use of Mackenzie's quarters. Carter's
detail had reached Rock Station at the western edge of the
prairie and was resting the mounts when Sherman's party
arrived. He mounted his men and saluted as Sherman drew
up.

General Sherman was in a good mood. He greeted Carter
like a "long lost brother" and presented him to his staff. He
declined the offer of the mules, saying his were still fresh. As
for accommodations he said:

> That is kind in Mackenzie to tender the use of his
> quarters, but I have got plenty of canvas and we
> will pitch our tents right behind and close to him.
> Your horses look warm. It would be too hard on
> them to try and keep up with us. If you will put us
> on the right road, you had better come in at your
> leisure. I appreciate it just as much—and I will
> thank Mackenzie personally for his kindness in

sending you and such a fine looking detachment
out to insure my safety.

With that, he continued on his way, leaving Carter to catch
up later.[12]

Sherman arrived at Fort Richardson without incident.
After receiving courtesies from the officers, he met with a
delegation of citizens who presented him with a petition for
action against the plains tribes, listing 129 deaths in Jack
County from August 1859 through April 1871, including the
twelve from the preceding four months. He listened politely,
but "was inclined to be very incredulous and shook his head
in such a manner as to cast doubt upon the pleadings of these
poor harassed settlers who had been expecting so much from
him." Once the citizens had been ushered out, Mackenzie
took Sherman around the post, calling on the sergeants and
visiting the messes. Finally, the general turned and said,
"Now, Mackenzie, let's go see the ladies." They talked with
the wives and children of the officers, and Sherman assured
them of his interest and support.[13]

It began raining hard the next day. Sometime after midnight, two men appeared at the stables, where Captain
Clarence Mauck's company was tending the horses. One of
the two men, Thomas Brazeale, had a bad limp and appeared
to be severely wounded. "We are teamsters from Warren's
wagon train which was attacked yesterday about 3 P.M. by
about one hundred Indians on Salt Creek Prairie," he told
Mauck. "Seven of our men were killed—four men and myself
escaped—all are wounded but my wounds are the most serious."[14]

Presumably this was the second band of whites foretold
by the vision of Maman-ti. The wagon train, belonging to

Henry Warren of Weatherford, had been hauling corn to Fort Griffin under a government contract. It had been overwhelmed and plundered, and more than forty mules had been taken. ·

Brazeale was taken to the hospital. Sherman was summoned to his bedside and heard the story first hand. Realizing that he had passed over the same spot one day earlier and could very easily have become a victim himself, Sherman's doubts vanished and he reacted immediately, sending Henry Strong, a civilian scout, to Weatherford to fetch Warren. Mackenzie was ordered personally to take a detachment to the scene of the raid and pick up the trail. If it led to the Fort Sill Reservation, Sherman told him,

> I hereby authorize you to enter said Reservation, and if the trail be fresh, and you should overtake the party anywhere within thirty or forty miles of Red River, you will not hesitate to attack the party, secure the property stolen, and any other property or stock in their possession, and bring them to me at Fort Sill.[15]

To Colonel William H. Wood, Eleventh Infantry, commanding Fort Griffin, he wrote:

> A pretty strong party of Indians have attacked and captured a train of twelve (12) wagons this side of Salt Creek, ten (10) miles this side of Fort Belknap. . . .

> It is all important that this case be followed up with extreme vigor, and principally that we find out, whether or no, the impression be well founded that

the numerous robberies and murders on this Frontier have been done by the Fort Sill Reservation Indians.[16]

In Sherman's mind, however, the question was already settled; when the delegation of citizens from Jacksboro called again, later in the day, he listened.

Meanwhile, Mackenzie and four companies of cavalry made their strenuous way through the rain and mud toward the massacre site. The streams were swollen and the mud so heavy that they often had to dismount and lead their horses.[17] On reaching the scene about nightfall, Mackenzie sent a brief note to Sherman saying, "statements concerning the wagon train are not exaggerated. Five mules lay dead around the wagon. The sergeant in charge of the detail, who was sent out in advance, found five men about the wagons with heads split open and badly mutilated." Dr. Julius Patzki, the post surgeon who accompanied the expedition, went into more detail.

All the bodies were riddled with bullets, covered with gashes, and the skulls crushed, evidently with an axe found bloody on the place; some of the bodies exhibited also signs of having been stabbed with arrows. One of the bodies [Samuel Elliott] was even more mutilated than the others, it having been found fastened with a chain to the pole of a wagon lying over a fire with the face to the ground, the tongue being cut out. Owing to the charred condition of the soft parts it was impossible to determine whether the man was burned before or after his death. The scalps of all but one were taken.

A search turned up two more bodies, a good distance away

where they had been cut down as they fled. A burial detail under Sergeant Miles Varily made a single large grave, the rain so heavy that the men often had to stop and bail as they dug. The bodies were placed in a wagon bed which was lowered into the pit, covered, and two stones set up with seven marks cut into them. Then Mackenzie set out after the Indians.[18]

The war party had a twenty-four hour head start and the rain had obliterated the trail, so Mackenzie turned north toward Fort Sill. Lieutenant Boehm's scouting expedition was more successful; headed back to Fort Richardson it came across four hostile Indians who had remained behind to hunt buffalo. A brief fight ensued in which one of the Indians (actually a Mexican prisoner adopted into the tribe) and his horse were killed, and one soldier and two army horses slightly wounded. The remainder of the raiding party returned to the reservation where Maman-ti, a shadowy figure little known to the whites, temporarily vanished into self-imposed obscurity, leaving the others to take credit for the raid.[19]

Mackenzie, delayed by flooding on the Wichita and Red Rivers, arrived at Fort Sill on June 4. Sherman had already come and gone. Three Indian leaders, the aging war chief Satank, the tough, arrogant Satanta, and the young sub-chief Big Tree, were in irons under close confinement. Mackenzie learned that Satanta had strutted into Agent Tatum's office on May 27, boasting of the raid, naming himself as leader and implicating several others, including Satank, Big Tree and Eagle Heart. Tatum had gone immediately to Colonel Grierson and Sherman at the military post and asked for their arrest. The Kiowas were summoned to Grierson's house, where Sherman arrested Satanta and Satank. Eagle Heart, warned of the arrests, escaped, but troops arrested Big Tree near the post trader's store.

Sherman's orders were clear. The three prisoners were to be returned to Texas for trial in the state district court. He was especially emphatic about Satanta, who had a long and bloody reputation. "I think it is time to end his career," he wrote to Sheridan, who was now divisional commander. As for Satank, Sherman said he "ought to have been shot long ago."[20]

On June 8 the prisoners were led out from confinement. Old Satank moved toward Grierson as if to shake hands, but Big Tree jerked him back. It was later learned Satank had a concealed knife and had intended to stab the colonel. The Indians were loaded on two wagons with Satank in the first and Satanta and Big Tree following. Two soldiers were placed in each wagon as guards, and Mackenzie went into Grierson's office while the rest of the train started down the road toward Jacksboro. When shots suddenly rang out, Mackenzie sent a trumpeter to find out what had happened but, without waiting for an answer, went to see for himself.

Satank was dead. The old warrior had slipped his handcuffs and stabbed one of the soldiers guarding him. Both guards jumped out of the wagon in such a hurry that one left his carbine behind. Satank grabbed the seven-shot Spencer and tried to lever a shell into the chamber, but it jammed. Reacting immediately, Corporal Charlton stood up in the second wagon, leveled his own carbine and fired. Satank went spinning backwards, sat up and again tried to work the lever, but was killed by several more shots from Charlton. The guard was only slightly wounded in the stabbing, but one of Charlton's shots went completely through Satank and injured a teamster.[21]

Mackenzie, taking no chances, ordered Satanta and Big Tree searched, but no other weapons were found. Charlton was placed in charge of the guard, with orders to stretch the two Indians lengthwise each night, with their arms and legs extended and tied to stakes driven into the ground. Charlton thought this was too harsh but, as a soldier, had to obey. One night, however, he went to check on them and watched Satanta's muscles swell and strain against the ropes as hundreds of mosquitoes bit him. "Old fellow," he said, "War is H— and you're a *blood thirsty savage, but by criminy, I'm not, and I'll be d—d if those mosquitoes shall bite you while you are helpless.*" Each night until they reached Jacksboro, he posted a sentry over each of the Indians with orders to fan them with leafy branches to keep off the mosquitoes.[22]

When the detachment arrived back at Fort Richardson, the chiefs were placed in the post guardhouse under heavy security, and preparations got underway for the trial. Reporting to Sherman, Mackenzie wrote, "Satanta now says that he never came to Texas at all being so great friend to the whites and that it was all Satank who was a fool and very bad." He also sent a note to Tatum, asking that agency interpreter Matthew Leeper be sent to Jacksboro as a witness. "The attendance of Mr. Leeper if present on any occasion when these Indians admitted their guilt, is of course of the first importance to the ends of justice."[23]

On July 1 the grand jury of the Thirteenth District Court convened in Jacksboro and ruled that Satanta and Big Tree "with force and malice not having the fear of God before their eyes, but being moved and seduced by the instigation of the devil" murdered S. Long, James Elliott, N.J. Baxter, James Williams, Samuel Elliott, John Mullins and James Bowman by gunfire in Young County* on May 18, 1871.

Big Tree's trial began on July 5, held before Judge Charles A. Soward of Weatherford, with Samuel W.T. Lanham as prosecutor, and Thomas Ball and J.A. Woolfork appointed to defend the Indians. Lanham went through a parade of witnesses who established that the victims had been massacred by Kiowas, since Kiowa arrows had been found in the bodies, and that Satanta had boasted of the raid and implicated Big Tree. Mackenzie was one of the witnesses.

When testimony was completed, Lanham made his closing arguments. First he described the two Indians in the idealistic terms by which they were seen in the East, "where distance lends enchantment." Then he said, "We who see them to-day, disrobed of all their fancied graces, exposed in the light of reality, behold them through far different lenses!" He called Satanta an "arch fiend of treachery and blood" and said Big Tree was a "tiger-demon, who has tasted blood and loves it as his food."

He attacked the government's policy of purchasing peace with the Indians, saying it led only to more bloodshed in Texas. "If the entire management of the Indian question were submitted to that gallant and distinguished army officer (General Mackenzie) who graces this occasion with his dignified presence, our frontier would soon enjoy immunity from these marauders," Lanham commented.[24] It took the jury only a few minutes to convict Big Tree and recommend the death sentence.

---

* Although Jacksboro is in Jack County, Young County had been disestablished after the Civil War and attached to Jack County for judicial purposes in 1871.

Kiowa Chiefs Big Tree and Satanta *(Texas State Archives)*

"Big-tree was tried and sentenced to death to day," Mackenzie noted. "Satanta, if a jury can be impanelled will be tried to morrow, and as the evidence is much stronger in his case than in Big-tree's, the result is not doubtful." He was correct in his prediction. The same jury tried Satanta and likewise recommended the death sentence. The two Kiowas were sentenced to hang on September 1.[25] A month later, Governor Edmund J. Davis commuted the death sentences of the two Kiowas to life imprisonments in the state penitentiary in Huntsville, on the recommendation of Judge Soward and Tatum. The people of Texas were outraged and Sherman was furious.

By then, however, Mackenzie was out on the plains, hunting other hostile Indians. As he had written Sherman:

> The Indians who depredate in Texas west of the Guadalupe river all come from one of two points[:] the Head of the Brazos, or the Reserve. They are generally Comanches and Kiowas, and those from the Reserve are mixed up with the bands on the edge of the Staked plains in their depredations.
>
> To obtain a permanent peace and to give Mr. Tatum whom I regard as an Excellent man an opportunity to elevate these people, the Kiowas and Comanches should be dismounted, and disarmed, and made to raise corn &c.[26]

The Staked Plains, flat, waterless and devoid of any features or landmarks, had always been a forbidden zone for the army. Somehow the Indians managed to survive in its wastes, and Mackenzie felt soldiers could, too. At any rate, he did not intend merely to scout for chance encounters with wandering marauders. He would seek out the hostiles wherever they went.

CHAPTER 7

"One Soldier Wounded"

Mackenzie prepared thoroughly for his expedition into the plains. Ten companies of the Fourth Cavalry poured into Fort Richardson from throughout Texas, the greatest concentration of the regiment since 1865. Many of the units, coming from places like Brownsville, Laredo, Fort McKavett and San Antonio, had never seen their commanding officer.[1] Despite his personal animosity toward Mackenzie after their dispute over the corn shipment at Fort McKavett, Colonel Reynolds, the departmental commander, gave him a free hand to operate as he saw fit, placing Forts Concho and Griffin under his command for the duration of the expedition.[2]

To support this vast operation, Mackenzie brought Lieutenant Henry W. Lawton, from the Twenty-Fourth Infantry, to serve as his commissary officer. The choice reflected Mackenzie's instinctive judgment of men. Lawton was a superb organizer with a talent for getting things done and no patience for red tape. As Carter would later write, "Lawton made his own rules and fitted them to the problems and situations as they came up to be solved, and he wasted no time in discussions."[3] Much of Mackenzie's success over the next twelve years would be due to Lawton's ability to keep him supplied in the field.

The expedition was a joint action between Mackenzie and Grierson, commander at Fort Sill. Mackenzie was to suppress any hostile Indians in Texas and force any reservation Indians back towards the Territory, where Grierson would round up

Lieutenant Henry W. Lawton
(National Archives)

the reservation tribes, return them to the agency, and collect an indemnity for the mules stolen during the Warren raid. Sherman's orders were very clear in dividing responsibility between the two commanders. The Indian Territory was in a different department and under a different military division. Mackenzie was not to cross into the Territory unless Grierson asked him to. "The latter has ample force to deal with the Kioways, and can force them to surrender an equivalent for the mules taken from Warren's train." At the time, the sentences of Satanta and Big Tree had not yet been commuted, and Sherman felt their hanging would be a good example to the Indians. "If the Kioways propose to resent this we are now as well prepared as we are ever likely to be," he said. He was already considering another expedition for that autumn which would cover the western headwaters of the Brazos.[4]

For his part, Mackenzie was absorbed with preparations for the expedition and, at the same time, appeared to be using these preparations in a way calculated to infuriate Reynolds. On July 1 he bypassed regulations by directly invoicing forty-six pack mules to the officers of four of his companies, instead of going through the post quartermaster. Then he directly requisitioned $50,000 worth of ordnance equipment from the departmental depot in San Antonio without first submitting the request to Reynolds. Angry over these breaches of protocol and regulations, the departmental commander demanded Mackenzie rectify the error, which he did. Although Reynolds furnished a portion of the equipment requested, Mackenzie sent several letters to the assistant adjutant general of the Division of the South, bringing up his old complaints about corn contracts.[5]

Since Reynolds and Mackenzie openly detested each other, one can only conclude Mackenzie was taking advantage of the upcoming campaign to force a showdown. Perhaps he was beginning to consider himself indispensable. If so, then the timing was right to engineer the removal of Reynolds and rid himself of a nuisance. Ambitious subordinates try this from time to time but rarely, if ever, do they get away with it. As events would show, however, Mackenzie was one of those rare subordinates who was—for the moment, at least—as indispensable as the thought he was.

Reynolds aside, the summer of 1871 was a busy one for Mackenzie. On July 9 he left for Fort Concho to serve as a witness at a general court-martial. Ten days later he was on the road to Fort Sill "on business connected with the Indian expedition under this command," returning on July 26.[6]

Two days later, several companies under Captain N.B. McLaughlen set out from Fort Richardson for the Little Wichita with orders to prepare for the arrival of the train and to bridge the stream if necessary. Over the next several days, other units were sent to the Red River. Despite orders establishing separate jurisdictions, Mackenzie, Grierson and Agent Tatum apparently worked out a plan for joint operations along the boundary area between Texas and the Indian Territory. Mackenzie was particularly concerned that someone—his men or Grierson's—occupy the abandoned post of Camp Radziminski to cover his northern flank and, perhaps, induce the Indians to return to the reservation.[7]

Among the units on the expedition was a band of Tonkawa Indian Scouts from Fort Griffin under the command of Lieutenant Peter M. Boehm. His position gave Boehm some leeway in dress, and he wore a white, broad-brimmed cowboy hat which was cooler and provided better protection from the sun than the black campaign hat the other officers were required to wear. The other officers also began to think of their own comfort. With no idea of how long they would be in the field, they were concerned not only about protecting themselves from the heat, but from the bitter cold of the plains as well.

As expedition adjutant, Carter inherited the task of bringing the officers' comfort to Mackenzie's attention. The colonel, however, was as indifferent to the comfort of his officers as he was to his own. When Carter asked if they could wear cowboy headgear he replied, "No! Boehm is in command of the Indians. As such he is outside the marching column, a sort of 'free lance'. . . ." Officers in the column would wear regulation hats.

"Could we pack any buffalo robes on the mules to use in event of cold weather?" Carter asked, but Mackenzie indicated he did not intend to pack one for himself and saw no reason why the other officers should. As for tents, he said he intended to share a wall tent with Carter and Matthew Leeper, the interpreter, and then only in bad weather. Two or more officers could make do with wall tents and the men could use pup tents, all to be painted a dull, lead color. End of discussion.[8]

On the morning of August 2, Companies C and L under Captain John A. Wilcox left Fort Richardson to join troops from Forts Concho and Griffin. Mackenzie himself left about 8:45 P.M. the same day, taking the headquarters unit and Boehm and the Tonkawa scouts. They arrived in camp at the West Fork of the Trinity later that night.[9]

After their arrival on the West Fork, the summer campaign became a series of gross misunderstandings which hindered the entire operation. After the Kiowa chiefs had been arrested, their people fled the reservation, going into the hills and out onto the plains. Kicking Bird, who headed the tribe's peace faction, had followed them. Despite Sherman's explicit orders to force hostile Indians in Texas back into the Territory, Mackenzie apparently assumed that Kicking Bird had bolted as well, and that his mission was to hunt him down. Kicking Bird was, in fact, trying to round up the others and bring them back. Encountering some Comanches on the road, Kicking Bird told them he didn't really care what happened to Satanta and Satank, after all the trouble they had caused. He fully intended to raise a number of mules equal to those lost in the Warren massacre, as an indemnity for the raid.[10]

Unaware of these developments, Mackenzie made a tedious march in hot, dry weather. At Buffalo Springs the soldiers found the water holes undrinkable, littered with dead cattle in various stages of decomposition. Pushing on to old Camp Wichita, they discovered the water was drinkable but unpleasantly saturated with sulphur and other minerals. The command followed the trail left by McLaughlen's advance column, and met it at the Big Wichita where the troopers were constructing a bridge across the stream. The bridge was finished the following morning and the march continued. Deer and wild turkey were plentiful, and the Tonkawas kept Mackenzie well supplied with fresh game. The column finally arrived at Otter Creek on the old Radziminski Trail, where Grierson awaited with his Tenth Cavalry.[11]

As the regiments stripped down for scouting, the two commanders made a personal reconnaissance of the country and conferred on the campaign. Although Grierson knew that Kicking Bird was not on the run, he apparently failed to tell Mackenzie, for the latter continued under the assumption that Kicking Bird's band was the object of the expedition. Why Grierson apparently kept this information to himself is beyond understanding.

Mackenzie's column resumed its march on August 17. On the trail he was overtaken by a courier with an official letter. According to Carter, Mackenzie "seemed much agitated" after reading it and spent the rest of the day riding in silence. Although Mackenzie never revealed the contents of the letter, Carter later learned that it placed Grierson in overall command of both his and Mackenzie's columns as long as they operated in Indian Territory. Mackenzie was to ascertain Kicking Bird's whereabouts, but was not to attack.

The officers of the Fourth believed that pressure to draw the reins on Mackenzie had been brought to bear on the War Department by the Indian Ring, the corrupt eastern businessmen and politicians who profited from Indian troubles. Aware of Grierson's personal sympathy with the Indians, the Fourth Cavalrymen also concluded that the Ring found him willing to collude with its aims and conspired with him to guarantee the campaign would fail. There is, however, no evidence the Ring was involved. The orders came from Sherman himself, who had simply reiterated his, previous stand that Mackenzie was to operate separately and stay out of the Indian Territory unless in pursuit. In such a situation Grierson, with military seniority, would naturally have overall command. As early as June 19, before his conferences with Mackenzie, Grierson informed his own departmental headquarters that Kicking Bird had already collected the indemnity and was enroute back to the reservation with the mules. This information he forwarded on to Sherman but, again inexplicably, did not pass down to Mackenzie, a lapse for which Mackenzie never forgave Grierson. This incident destroyed Grierson's credibility among the officers serving in the Northwest Frontier, and Sherman ultimately had to transfer him elsewhere. Almost before it started, the summer campaign was a failure.[12]

While Mackenzie sulked in his saddle, the column entered the wild country leading into the gypsum belt. At Marcy Creek, Carter found "The water so perfectly vile and nauseating that one was made sick as soon as it was drank [sic]. After a bath in the stream, the body, before one could dress, was at once crusted with gypsum which was removed with difficulty." The rugged terrain was almost impassable for the wagons. The second day led through vast buffalo herds, and when the column camped for the night the soldiers found the water contaminated not only with gypsum but with buffalo urine and excrement. Men and animals became sick. Dr. Julius Patzki, the surgeon, developed such a bad case of diarrhea he could hardly sit on his horse. Several of the men had to be carried on horse litters.

One night around the camp fire, Mackenzie said, "Gentlemen, we shall all have a new stomach when it gets thoroughly coated with a crust of gypsum . . . I think my coating is now about that thick!" he indicated with his fingers. Taking a swallow of gypsum-laced coffee, his stomach revolted and he disappeared into some bushes. When he returned, an officer asked him what was the matter. Mackenzie managed a weak smile and replied, "Oh, *heap* sick! *heap* Sick!" The polluted water had made Captain Clint Powers, already dying of tuberculosis, terribly weak. Mackenzie motioned Carter to one side and quietly said, "You have got the only brandy in the command, you brought it out for me; let's give it to poor Powers; we will not need it." Powers was given the brandy with Carter's compliments.[13]

As the days passed, Mackenzie became more irritable. He slept badly, and at night the sound of a mule clanking his chains or a horse snorting would cause him to spring up from his cot. Carter and Matthew Leeper, the agency interpreter from Fort Sill, shared his tent and took the full burden of his nervous outbursts. One night they decided they'd had enough and, no matter what happened, would pretend to be asleep for as long as possible. A thunderstorm struck and sheets of rain came down, filling the roof of the tent. When the ridgepole broke and the roof collapsed, dumping a torrent of water on the sleeping colonel, Mackenzie "plunged around" and shouted out for his orderly and then for Carter and Leeper. Both appeared to be asleep.

"How in the name of Jehovah," he demanded, could they sleep through that?

"General," Leeper replied, "I am always a very heavy sleeper in the field. It takes more than a storm like that to wake me."[14]

By now, the sick and exhausted animals were giving out. On August 31 Mackenzie had to abandon ten horses and two mules.[15] The following day the command returned to the base camp at Otter Creek, only to find Grierson had already gone back to Fort Sill and that Kicking Bird was back on the reservation. Mackenzie was bitterly disappointed, and Carter noticed it "seemed to possess his soul and disturb his peace of mind." He found some relief in the base camp where Captain Lewis Carpenter, Tenth Cavalry, was an excellent host. He invited Mackenzie to a dinner consisting of wild game and fish, served on a table covered with a red cloth and set with dishes. The officers sat in comfortable camp chairs, and a soldier of the Tenth served as waiter. To the officers of the Fourth, used to sitting on cracker boxes while they ate food spread on a poncho on the ground, this was a real luxury.

Then came dessert. Looking at it, Mackenzie began snapping the stumps of his missing fingers excitedly and exclaimed, "prune pie! Well, I'll be d—d! *and in the field*; what do you think of that?" Even on the ride back to his own camp, he repeated several times, "prune pie! prune pie! Well, I'll be ——! What do you know about *that?*"[16]

There was now no point in continuing the expedition. On September 7 Mackenzie dispatched Captains Clarence Mauck and Wirt Davis with part of the command to Fort Griffin. They were to go into camp there and rest the men and animals in preparation for a second expedition in the fall. He sent a note to Colonel Wood, post commander at Griffin, asking him to assist. "Many of the animals need shoeing and some of the wagons need repairing," he wrote. Mackenzie himself returned to Fort Richardson and remained there until leaving for Griffin to rejoin his command on September 25.[17]

In camp on the Clear Fork of the Brazos, near Fort Griffin, Mackenzie began planning his new expedition. Fort Richardson was stripped bare, leaving only a few troops on the post to construct winter shelters. He had to employ a civilian blacksmith to shoe horses for the supply train, since

Clear Fork of the Brazos from Mackenzie's Ford
(Lawrence T. Jones III Collection)

he had discharged his own smith "on account of worthlessness," and the company blacksmiths were ordered to shoe their horses and mules as soon as possible. Colonel Wood was asked to supply a company of infantry, equipped for an expedition of six weeks, and to issue each soldier two hundred rounds of ammunition.[18]

This time Mackenzie planned to go after the Quahadi Comanches, who had been raiding along the frontier and who had attacked a ranch on the Clear Fork of the Brazos even as the soldiers camped nearby. The Quahadis were not a party to the Medicine Lodge Treaty and therefore not restricted to a reservation. Roaming through the Staked Plains at will, they operated out of more-or-less permanent refuges in the canyons which cut into the edges of the caprock. Their principal chief was the wily and gifted young warrior Quanah Parker, whose mother had been a white captive raised in the tribe. Mow-way and Para-a-coom were powerful subchiefs. On October 3 Mackenzie marched out at the head of six hundred soldiers. Boehm and his Tonkawas were already well ahead, fanning out over the countryside looking for trails. An advance guard covered the column against a surprise attack. At the various creeks and washes, officers with Union Army experience were sent to help with the wagons, since they knew how to bridge and move supply trains in a hurry. The troopers were rested and cheerful and occasionally would break out in the old regimental song, "Come home, John, don't stay long; Come home soon to your own Chick-a-biddy!"

The column saw vast herds of buffalo throughout the second day. That night it camped at some springs which had foul water but excellent grazing, in the midst of buffalo which moved off from the camp a mile or two but otherwise surrounded it. A hunting party was sent to kill enough of the animals to provide fresh meat for the entire command. The night grew cold as the soldiers settled in, and the noise of the wind drowned out all other sounds. Just before midnight, the sentries heard a different sound, barely audible above the wind, of hooves and snorting and bellowing. Something had sent the buffalo stampeding straight toward the camp. Unable to shoot since the noise might stampede the horses, and with no time to call out to the others, the guards grabbed blankets and started waving them at the lead animals. The buffalo veered to the left, stampeded by the horse herd and ran off into the night. Many of the men, now well awake, thought the horses had stampeded. Had the buffalo not veered, the horses would have certainly been lost.

The next day the command marched toward Duck Creek. En route they found several abandoned stations used by Comancheros, Mexicans and renegade Americans from New Mexico who traded guns, ammunition and other supplies to the Comanches and who occasionally trafficked in white prisoners. With a base camp established at Duck Creek, Mackenzie decided to send out the Tonkawas that night to hunt for signs of hostile villages. If they found any, he hoped to make a night march to surprise the Indians. The scouts didn't like the idea of a night reconnaissance in a new country, but they went.

The next day the Tonkawas had not returned. Mackenzie sent Carter with a detail to look for them and to watch for signs of a Comanche trail, but it returned the same day having found nothing. Mackenzie then decided to make a night march without waiting for the return of the scouts. The wagons were corralled and fires left burning, to give the impression the entire command was in camp. After a hard night ride through rough country, they reached the Fresh Fork of the Brazos about 9:30 A.M. October 9 and the men unsaddled, built fires and fixed breakfast. A reconnaissance squad found the remains of a hostile camp nearby.

That afternoon, as the command rested, Captain E.M.

Heyl was sent out on a second reconnaissance and was spotted by the Tonkawas, who headed toward him. As the Tonkawas rode along the edge of a ravine they ran into four Comanches, who had been watching Heyl, and gave chase. But they had been without food or sleep for two days, and the Comanches soon outran them. When they caught up with the soldiers, they reported they had discovered a trail leading to a Quahadi village. At 3:00 P.M. Mackenzie ordered the command to move out.[19]

Many of the animals bogged down in quicksand while crossing the Fresh Fork, and by the time the tail of the column reached the other side, the vanguard was far ahead. Strung out as it was, the column was vulnerable. When a shot rang out, Mackenzie galloped to the rear, demanding to know the cause, then without waiting to find out sent orders for the lead companies to fall back and consolidate. By the time he learned an enlisted man's carbine had accidentally discharged, time had already been lost.

About sunset, the command went into camp in a depression, with a line of small hills to one side and the Fresh Fork on the other, near the mouth of Blanco Canyon at the foot of the Staked Plains. A series of rises, gullies and ravines led to the canyon itself and on into the caprock where the plains began. Horses were securely picketed and the men allowed to light fires. The camp was quiet, except for the noise of the horses pulling at their lariats as they tried to find more grass. As the fires died down, their embers continued to glow, lighting up the area.

About 1:00 A.M. pandemonium broke loose, with yelling and shooting near the horses. The men jumped up, and those camped on the outer perimeter went into action. By the flashes of the muzzles, the soldiers could see Comanches riding past, waving buffalo blankets, screaming and ringing bells. There were more yells as the Tonkawas joined the fray.

"Get to your horses!" someone shouted, but by then it was too late. The Comanches were already in the middle of the horse line and the animals were beginning to stampede. "Every man to his lariat! Stand by your horses!" came the commands above the noise.

In the light of the muzzle blasts, the horses could be seen rearing, pulling at their picket pins and running off. Men ducked the sharp iron picket pins swinging wildly in the air. Some grabbed lariats and were dragged along the ground, others suffered rope burns as the lariats tore through their hands. As the Comanches, with their newly captured horses, thundered off into the distance, the soldiers secured the animals which had been unable to escape and began to sort through the tangle of lariats, pins and lines. Firing parties were sent to the tops of the ridges to cover the camp as it tried to reorganize. Among the losses was Mackenzie's own gray which Boehm had secured for him. (Five years later, after the Quahadis had surrendered and Mackenzie commanded Fort Sill, Quanah Parker went to see him and offered to return it. Mackenzie declined.)

Mackenzie was now faced with a partially dismounted cavalry unit in the middle of a hostile wilderness. The survival of the command could easily depend on having a sufficient number of horses and, at first light, several detachments were sent out to try and recover them.

The Comanches, slowed by the captured horses, divided into smaller groups and scattered. Heyl's detachment soon overtook one group of about twelve Comanches, who abandoned the horses and scattered among the ravines. Heyl, detaching some of his men to take the horses back to the camp,

Comanche Chief Quanah Parker
(National Archives)

chased after the Indians until, suddenly, the Comanches turned. Augmented by others who had returned to the scene, the Indians began riding down on the soldiers. Heyl was caught in a trap with raw recruits who began to panic, but the detachments commanded by Carter and Boehm rode up to reinforce him. Boehm took most of the troopers back to a nearby ravine in more or less good order, but Heyl completely lost control of his men, who milled about aimlessly until they finally made the ravine. Carter and a squad of five troopers were isolated some distance to the rear, and one of the men, a Private Gregg, yelled that his horse was giving out. The others, unable to ride back to help if they hoped to make the ravine themselves, could only urge him on, but one of the Indians (Carter maintained it was Quanah) rode up and dispatched Gregg with a pistol shot to the head.

Back in the camp, Mackenzie heard the firing in the distance and sent Wirt Davis to help. By the time Davis arrived, the Indians had been beaten back and had scattered up the Fresh Fork toward the Staked Plains. Carter led a group in pursuit, but suffered a bad leg injury when his horse stumbled and fell on him.

The Blanco Canyon fight was over. Private Gregg was buried with a soldier's funeral, a simple salute and a few words, and stones were piled over the grave to protect it from wolves. Pickets were thrown out and the horses, still saddled, were allowed to graze under strong guard. Saddles of the lost horses were cached, in hope of recovering them later. Mackenzie had sent out the Tonkawas, and about 2:30 P.M. they returned to report a fresh trail leading up the canyon to what they surmised was Quanah's village. Orders were given to move out, but the pace was slowed by the large group of dismounted soldiers.[20]

Morale was low. "A dismounted cavalry trooper is a much more demoralized man than a tired-out, straggling infantry soldier," Carter explained, "since, from force of habit, he has learned to rely almost wholly upon the strength and brute courage of his faithful horse, rather than in his own powers of endurance. . . ."[21] The men had to be pushed and threatened. Not used to walking, they chafed and their feet blistered. The officers decided the soldiers would be useless for further action, and reported their opinions to Mackenzie that night in camp.

The next morning, Mackenzie summoned Carter and said he was sending back the dismounted men, since they would impede the march. He noted Carter's injured leg was now in splints and asked if he wanted to lead them back, but Carter said he would prefer to remain with the command. "Another thing," Mackenzie said, changing the subject, "I have been told that Captain Heyl did not behave well in that action yesterday morning. I had him transferred to this regiment because of his ability, efficiency, and reported gallantry in action. What do you care to say about it? You were a close witness of his conduct."

"I will merely say that under all of the circumstances of that affair, in my opinion he committed a very grave error of judgment, and you can draw your own conclusions," Carter replied.[22]

Mackenzie let the matter drop. Perhaps he assumed that Heyl was already miserable enough over the mistake. If so, he was correct, for Heyl later confided to Lawton that it was "the bluest moment of my military life."[23]

The following morning, October 12, the mounted column rode away from the dismounted soldiers, ascended the caprock and came out on the broad emptiness of the Staked Plains. A norther started blowing in, the temperature plunged, and the wind bit into the soldiers in their summer uniforms. The Tonkawas dismounted so they could follow the trail more closely through the dry grass stubble. At the brink of a canyon the rest of the column dismounted to follow a trail down to the bottom. There they found the Comanches had fled, leaving the canyon by many different trails. The scouts found what appeared to be the main trail leading up the opposite side, and the soldiers ascended again. At the top, they found a broad trail marked with lodge poles from the travois and hoofprints of a large herd of stock.

The day grew colder but the trail grew fresher, marked now and then by wagon ruts of the Comancheros, leading up from the Pecos River area. From the top of a low ridge they saw horsemen, off in the distance, who the Tonkawas said were Comanches. Mackenzie moved the command forward at a fast pace and soon they found themselves with a large body of horsemen on either side, swarming around "like angry bees" in an attempt to lead the soldiers away from their women and children. It was tempting to break off and chase them, but Mackenzie was determined to stay on the main trail. When the Indians saw their ruse had failed, they started moving in. The soldiers closed up in columns of fours and filled their blouse pockets with ammunition. One squad was sent to form a square around the pack mules, and mounted skirmishers were dispatched to the front while flankers moved out to the sides. The Tonkawas slipped off their riding horses, ran over to the horse herd to catch their war ponies, and began painting themselves and putting on their war bonnets.

It was growing late, but the soldiers could see the Indians' families in the distance, rushing to get away. They had been camped around a shallow depression, filled with rainwater, where the column paused briefly to give their horses one last chance to drink. Scattered all around were lodge poles, skins used to cover tepis, tools and abandoned cooking fires.

The soldiers pushed on. Rain, mixed with snow and sleet, blew in their faces as they drew closer to the fugitives. When night fell they were less than a mile from the Comanches and, to Carter, "It seemed as though a great black curtain or pall had suddenly dropped in front of our eyes, shutting off every object." The men were ready to push on, but the horses were exhausted. After the fiasco at Blanco Canyon there were no remounts, so Mackenzie gave the order to dismount.

The storm now broke in full fury. A large defensive ring was formed around the pack mules, and each man held his horse. Their clothing, soaked by the rain and sleet, became frozen by the cold wind. The Comanches, thrashing through the darkness trying to make their way back to their people, suddenly stumbled onto the line of soldiers. Shots were ex-

changed and the Indians fled off into the night. Davis took a
detachment to give chase, and soon the others could see
muzzle flashes in the distance. When it grew quiet, the Tonkawas in camp started yelling and were answered by those with
Davis. Davis' detachment, which had become lost in the storm
less than five hundred yards from camp, managed to find its
way back.

The mules were unpacked and tarpaulins, robes and blankets were pulled out as the men tried to protect themselves
from the storm. Mackenzie sat shivering until someone produced a buffalo robe and wrapped it around him.

The storm blew out during the night and the next day
dawned beautifully. The trail was still fresh and the column
followed it for some time, but the men had taken all they
could. Mackenzie was far from base and his supplies were
running low, so he decided to turn back. Several days' march
brought them back to Blanco Canyon, after which Mackenzie
adopted a more leisurely pace to rest the men and horses. Most
of the men were half asleep in their saddles and the horses
moving out of habit when suddenly the advance scouts and
the leading company came dashing back. The troopers sat up
immediately and closed ranks. The Tonkawa scouts had discovered two Comanches, dismounted and leading their
horses, following the soldiers' original trail up the canyon.
When they spotted the scouts, the two abandoned their horses
and fled into the ravines, from which they opened fire. The
Tonkawas went up on one of the bluffs to cut off their escape
in that direction, and to try and drive them out toward the
soldiers.

Mackenzie deployed his men to seal off the openings
where the Comanches might escape, then ordered Boehm to
take fifteen men and drive them out of the ravine. Becoming

impatient, he dismounted and joined Boehm. An arrow struck Mackenzie's thigh, and he was carried to the rear where the surgeon cut it out. After the two Comanches were killed, the Tonkawas scalped and mutilated them (the surgeon, Dr. Rufus Choate, later went out and cut off their heads for study.) The engagement over, the command bivouacked on the spot. One of the farriers had been shot through the intestines, but survived.

Because infection did not set in, Mackenzie's wound would leave no long-term physical effects, but it was painful enough to incapacitate him for awhile. His injury, combined with the exhaustion of the campaign, put him in a foul mood. He was so irritable that, by the time the command reached the base camp at Duck Creek, no one wanted to be around him. Dr. J.R. Gregory, a civilian physician attached to the expedition, decided to liven things up by telling Mackenzie the leg had to be amputated, just to see the reaction, but got more than he bargained for. As soon as the word "amputate" was mentioned, the colonel grabbed a crutch and headed toward the doctor, who beat a hasty retreat "to save his own head from amputation."[24]

Mackenzie's official report of the entire fall campaign was less than one page long, mentioning only the loss of the horses, the death of Private Gregg, and the effort to trail the Comanches. "On the return," he wrote, "two Indians were killed, and one soldier wounded." He made no mention of his own wound.[25]

The events of 1871 brought profound changes to warfare on the Southern Plains, and in Washington caused the military to realign itself completely. Sherman was aware that the designation of Texas as a Southern rather than a Western state had created some of the jurisdictional problems which had hindered the summer campaign. To him, it was obvious that the federal government's biggest problem in Texas was Indians, not ex-Confederates. "This case convinces me that Genl. Sheridan's command ought to be extended to the Texas frontier," he wrote.

On November 1 Texas was placed under the Military Division of the Missouri, the center of the War Department's efforts against the plains tribes, and the Indian Territory was added to the Department of Texas. Reynolds was transferred to Fort McPherson, Nebraska, and Brigadier General C.C. Augur was named departmental commander.[26] Henceforth Indians, and not Reconstruction, would be the army's top priority.

Aside from policy considerations, the reorganization of the department and Reynolds' transfer removed a potentially explosive situation between Reynolds and Mackenzie. To get one last shot, Reynolds initiated court-martial proceedings on the bases of the high-handed way Mackenzie had made his requisitions and reports, as he organized the summer expedition, and on his resurrection of the corn contract dispute. The charges were disobedience, contempt and disrespect toward his commanding officer, conduct unbecoming an officer, and conduct prejudicial to the good order and discipline of the service. The charges made their way up the official ladder until they reached Secretary of War W.W. Belknap, who referred them to the judge advocate general, who suggested the matter be dropped. Belknap agreed,[27] for reasons which are a matter of speculation. Perhaps the officials in Washington felt Mackenzie was too good an officer to face trial on what was obviously a personal dispute. In addition, Belknap himself was implicated in the allegations of corruption in army contracting, and he may have feared that if Mackenzie went to trial, some of Reynolds' nefarious dealings might be traced all the way to the top.

His expeditions on the plains had a profound effect on Mackenzie. Many former Union officers on the frontier never made the mental adjustment from the Civil War to the Indian Service, and attempted to counter the Indians' hit-and-run tactics with the same procedures they had used against Confederates in the East. This failure to adapt at all levels ultimately led to the Custer disaster at the Little Bighorn.[28] Mackenzie avoided this mistake. The 1871 campaigns taught him to "think Indian." Henceforth, he would turn their own methods against them and hit them where they were most vulnerable—their families and their possessions. Because of his ability to adapt, he became one of the most successful officers in the West.

CHAPTER 8

"It is a Regular Business"

A fter the fall campaign of 1871 the Indian raids subsided, as they always did with the onset of winter. The relative peace on the frontier allowed Mackenzie to disburse the regiment to various posts for winter quarters, and gave him some rare leisure time to go hunting with Henry Strong, the scout. In the northern part of Jack County they bagged turkeys, several cats, and two bears.[1]

While Mackenzie may have done well on the hunt, he was not so successful at social functions where he seemed to lose what self-confidence he had acquired in school. Any contacts with women, however slight, continued to give him trouble. When Henry Lawton's clerk married a Jacksboro girl, Mackenzie was assigned a lady as a partner for dinner, which followed the tradition of calling guests to the tables by couples. He and his partner were called, but he hesitated until one young officer "gave him a vigorous slap on the back and asked him why he didn't 'move out' instead of 'blocking the traffic.'"[2]

Overall, however, life was routine and Mackenzie could settle into the job of regimental and post commander. Among other things, he found time to recommend clemency for a trooper in confinement awaiting court-martial. "The offense committed by him was of a serious nature," he wrote, "but at the time he was very much intoxicated. He has many of the excellent qualities of a soldier."[3]

As regimental commander, Mackenzie was also responsible for the assessment and grooming of young officers. One of these was Second Lieutenant John A. McKinney of Tennessee, fresh from West Point where he had been cadet adjutant of his class. He was assigned to the Fourth in August 1871 and arrived at Fort Richardson with a recruit detachment from Corsicana. Mackenzie was impressed with him and told Carter, "He looks like a very promising officer." Soon, however, he discovered McKinney owed money and sent for him.

"Mr. McKinney," he began, "I understand you are in debt. I don't like to have young officers when first joining my regiment to be in debt. What is the amount?"

"Five hundred dollars," McKinney replied.

"Here is my personal check for the amount. I do not want any note from you. Pay it whenever you can conveniently, and keep out of debt."

Not long after that, Mackenzie noticed the young lieutenant was starting to become a heavy drinker. He called Carter in and told him to take him under his wing and guide him. "Just look after him a little," he said, and as usual Mackenzie's initial judgment was right. McKinney developed into a brave, competent officer. His death in the Dull Knife Fight four years later put a severe strain on the colonel's sanity.[4]

In February 1872 Mackenzie received orders to report to Fort Sill as president of a general court-martial. Carter, placed in command of the escort with orders to run it as he saw fit, selected Sergeant Thomas Brown, whom he considered "one of the best duty sergeants in the regiment," as senior noncommissioned officer. Besides Carter and Mackenzie, there were four other officers, two of whom brought their wives. The colonel intended to relax and play host, leaving Carter to work out the military details.

The first day out they came upon the nude, scalped body

of an Indian, lying in the middle of the trail, who had been killed the day before by a party of settlers. There had been an Indian scare earlier and everyone was nervous. The ladies were so upset by the sight that it was necessary to camp early. Mackenzie, edgy from having been jolted about all day in the military ambulance, recalled the previous October when Quanah Parker had stampeded his horse herd, so Carter assigned a herd guard with orders to graze the horses in full view of the camp. One third of the entire escort was ordered to remain saddled until dark or until the herd was brought into camp.

Mackenzie, on a tour of inspection, found only two herders on guard. Snapping the stumps of his missing fingers irritably, he stormed over to Carter. "How many men are out on herd guard?" he demanded. Carter told him three, with a corporal in charge.

"You must not neglect your duty!" Mackenzie raged. "I told you that you were to Command the detachment, and in your own way, and I should not interfere with their control. I want no care nor bother, leaving it all to you, but I see only two out there, where is the other man?"

"Well, General," Carter replied, "I am responsible for those men, but shall hold them to a strict performance of their duty. I personally posted the men myself, and left them in charge of a good Corporal. If one is absent, it is probably on account of sickness or for some good excuse. I will attend to it at once, Sir, but I don't care to be accused of neglect, or even have it hinted at. I know how to perform such duty, but if I am supposed to stand here and see that these men are herding the animals properly, I prefer to mount my horse, relieve them, and herd them myself, then you may feel perfectly assured that they are being well guarded, and are safe."

Mackenzie went into a fury and rightfully so. "Carter, I like you very much. You have never failed me, but. . . . Sometimes you get a little insubordinate and you must not talk to me in that way."

"I shall not, Sir," Carter snapped, "unless you choose to reflect upon my performance of duty." Carter checked with Sergeant Brown and learned one of the guards had indeed become sick and a replacement already detailed. The matter was allowed to drop.[5]

When the group arrived at Fort Sill, Grierson and his officers proved to be excellent hosts, organizing breakfasts, luncheons, dinner parties and even dances. Grierson even gave a picnic party at the signal station on Mount Scott, overlooking the reservation.[6]

While Mackenzie enjoyed the brief interval from command responsibilities, the Indians were growing restless. In his annual report General C. C. Augur, the new departmental commander, pointed out that the northernmost settlements bordered directly on the Staked Plains and the Indian Territory. The plains tribes were openly hostile, while those in the Territory were only "quasi friendly," and there was open communication between the two groups. The reservation Kiowas were particularly notorious for their raids. "The Staked Plains and Indian Reservations afford by short lines, refuge and security to these outlaws and their plunder," Augur wrote.

To the south and west, he continued, the frontier was exposed to raids by Indians who either lived permanently in Mexico, or who retreated across the border to escape pursuit and sell their plunder. "In addition to these indian *[sic]* outrages the frontier Texan settlements are exposed to another enemy almost as fatal to their prosperity as the indians—the Cattle

Thieves from New Mexico on the northern line and the cattle thieves from Mexico on the western line."[7]

The first contact with these cattle thieves came on March 28, 1872, when a detachment of Fourth Cavalry from Fort Concho ran down what had been thought to be Indian marauders. There was a fight in which two of the raiders were killed, three wounded, and one captured who turned out to be Polonio Ortiz, a Comanchero from Chama, New Mexico. Under interrogation, he said two traders named Hughes and Church at Puerta de Luna, New Mexico, were furnishing Comancheros with goods to trade to hostile Indians. The Indians would raid into Texas, steal cattle and trade them to the Comancheros, who in turn would return to New Mexico and sell the cattle to Hughes and Church.

Ortiz said his raiding party had left Chama on February 10 and crossed the Staked Plains to Mucha Que, where they found a large village of Quahadi Comanches and Mescalero Apaches. The Indians, accompanied by some of the Comacheros, had left Mucha Que on a cattle raid on March 19. "As soon as the cattle are brought to the village the Mexicans buy them and return to New Mexico, but more will follow as it is a regular business," Ortiz said. But even more interesting, from a military point of view, was his assessment of the route.

> There is plenty of water on the Staked plain, it is permanent, the road is a good one. There is another road further north, that leads to a place called Quita-que; both are good roads with plenty of water. . . . Can ride on a good horse from Alamo Gordo to Mucha-que in five days, it would not be hard riding (supposed 200-240 miles).[8]

This was the break the army had been looking for. As Mackenzie had suspected, there was a way through the Staked Plains and, from Ortiz's description, it was an easy one. When General Augur offered a presidential pardon if Ortiz cooperated, Ortiz immediately became even more informative. He said his group was actually from La Cuesta, and they traded with a representative of a mercantile establishment in Santa Fe itself. He offered more detail about terrain and water holes in the Staked Plains, and gave an itinerary from Alamogordo to Fort Concho via Mucha Que. Major John P. Hatch, commanding at Fort Concho, forwarded the information to General Gordon Granger, commanding officer of the District of New Mexico, saying, "It may be of use in breaking up the trade, as the depredations would cease if no purchasers were found for the stolen stock."[9]

In April Ortiz accompanied a detachment of about one hundred men under Captain N.B. McLaughlen, Fourth Cavalry, which returned May 11 having verified the information. At the site of the large Indian village, recently abandoned, there was evidence of large cattle and horse herds.[10] In Chicago, Sheridan went over all the reports, then wrote to Augur:

> I fully authorize you to break up the illicit traffic with Indians on the Staked plains and if any of the parties engaged in it are caught they should be turned over to the United States Civil authorities of the State of Texas. We have had similar cases in the Department of the Missouri and the persons and property captured were turned over to the United States Marshal in the territory of New Mexico. [New Mexico was a district within the

Department of the Missouri][11]

Augur called a council of war in San Antonio. Mackenzie was ordered to establish a camp either on the headwaters of the Colorado or on the Fresh Fork of the Brazos, whichever he deemed best. The infantry was to guard and supply the camp while the cavalry scouted for the Indians. Three companies of the Fourth Cavalry and one company of the Eleventh Infantry were assigned from Fort Richardson, one company of the Fourth and one of the Eleventh from Fort Griffin, and two companies of the Fourth and one of the Eleventh from Fort Concho. Shafter would come up from Fort McKavett with three companies of the Twenty-Fourth Infantry. The expedition was to be supplied from Fort Concho.[12]

From Fort Richardson, Mackenzie wrote departmental headquarters that "the outrages committed by Indians have been more frequent than I have ever known them here or at any other period that I have served at in the Department." He included his scouting reports, which were forwarded on to Chicago. Reading them, Sheridan remarked:

> It is useless to disguise the fact that the depredations referred to by Colonel Mackenzie are committed by the Indians on the reservation at Fort Sill. . . . All the tribes on that reservation are engaged with them, as well as Indians from the upper reservation at Camp Supply. I do not know of any way of stopping this bad work except by action of the military at Fort Sill and Camp Supply; and the moment the Government will authorize me to stop this bad work I am ready to do it.

Meanwhile, Lawrie Tatum sent word from the Fort Sill Agency that he was losing control of the situation. Many of the Kiowas, as well as Comanches and Cheyennes, had already begun raiding into Texas. On June 9 Indians attacked the Abel Lee home near Fort Griffin, killing Lee, his wife and eight-year-old daughter. Three other Lee children were carried off into captivity. In a reversal of Quaker policy, Tatum authorized the military to attack and capture Kiowas, Quahadis and any members of Mow-way's band of Comanches "wherever they may be joined."[13]

While the generals fumed in frustration at their inability to control events, Mackenzie prepared for the expedition. He had tentatively decided to camp on the Fresh Fork of the Brazos, and told Shafter to leave Fort Concho no later than June 25 and meet him in the canyon at the headwaters. He felt Shafter could arrive there within six days if he pushed hard enough. "If at any time you hear firing ahead of you going up the Fresh Fork, make the very quickest time you can," he wrote.

He was particularly concerned that Shafter stay on the Fresh Fork and not be led away from it by Indians. Experience had taught him that if the Indians tried to lead Shafter away from the stream, he would "surely find a camp higher up [the stream bed]."[14]

While Mackenzie prepared for his expedition, rumors began circulating in the East that he and his command had been massacred by Indians. The newspapers picked up on the rumors and the War Department telegraphed Augur for a report "as soon as possible." Augur replied that there was "Not one word of truth in it. . . ."[15] It was the first of several reports of Mackenzie's death which would circulate during his career in Texas.

On July 6, after a march of twelve days, Shafter finally reached Mackenzie's supply camp on the Freshwater Fork of the Brazos. Due to the time and distances involved, Mackenzie decided to draw rations from Fort Griffin instead of Fort Concho.[16] The depredations were growing worse, with raids as far as the Pecos. Several cattle herds were attacked and some herders killed because Mackenzie's expedition had so reduced the garrison at Concho that Major Hatch could not provide sufficient escort. Consequently, he asked for one of the companies of cavalry which remained at Fort McKavett.[17]

Mackenzie left his supply camp with four companies of cavalry on July 9. McLaughlen had already been out scouting for a week with two companies of cavalry, and soon Shafter and Captain John Clous, Twenty-Fourth Infantry, went out as well. When everyone returned, Mackenzie compared the reports. His own scout had yielded nothing but, based on Shafter's and McLaughlen's report, he surmised there was a camp "on some of the head tributaries of the main Red River, either at Quitta Que or on the head of the Palo Duro. . . . The Mexican captured near Concho says that there are *always* Indians at the places mentioned."

Based on these reports, he intended to head for the streams emptying into the Red River, double back to his camp, then head on to the McClellan and Sweetwater Creeks. The only problem would be provisions. He would need to draw nine thousand rations and sixty to eighty thousand pounds of forage from Camp Supply, miles away in Indian Territory.

Concluding his report, Mackenzie shattered the notion that the Staked Plains were unable to support a large group of Indians for any length of time:

there is no country, in winter better adapted to all
the wants of the Indians than the head streams of
the Brazos, Pease and Wichita Rivers, while the
heads of the North Fork and Washita will answer
at any time: the only objection to the Brazos country at any time being the absence of buffalo in the
summer.[18]

He was convinced that he would find the main Indian
camps on the Staked Plains at any time of the year. More
importantly, if the area could support a large body of Indians,
it could also support a large body of soldiers. The U.S.
military forces on the frontier were about to confront their
dread of the plains, previously considered completely inhospitable.

Over the next several weeks, Mackenzie ranged back and
forth across the plains, crossing over into New Mexico where
he hoped to slip into Puerta de Luna and arrest the traders
who Polonio Ortiz had said were dealing with the Indians.
They could not be found, however, and he surmised they had
already fled to escape a local vigilance committee which was
"arresting cattle thieves and taking possession of stolen cattle."[19] Again short on supplies, he sent some wagons to Fort
Bascom where the soldiers escorting the wagons drew both
supplies and whiskey. According to Henry Strong, "you
never saw a more dilapidated set of men than they, the next
morning after the wagon train returned, for it rained that
night and the valley was as red as red paint and many of them
wallowed around in the mud, like hogs in a mudhole."[20]

While Mackenzie was in New Mexico, Colonel J.I. Gregg
of the Eighth Cavalry at Fort Bascom was combing the Staked
Plains. The Tonkawas sent with him found a large trail which

Gregg followed along the Palo Duro. Several Indians were sighted at a distance, but the scouts decided they were probably a small party "a long way from home."[21] Once again Mackenzie returned to his supply camp without finding the hostile Indian camps, but he planned one last try for September 21. If unsuccessful, he intended to break camp and return the men to their stations. Although no Indian contact had yet been made, the expedition could not be considered a failure thus far. Valuable information had been gained, Captain Clous was already working on maps of two routes across the plains, and Shafter was sending a scouting detail to map more of the area.[22]

In San Antonio, Augur was pleased. "This is the first instance, within my knowledge, where troops have been successfully taken across the Staked Plains," he wrote in his annual report. "This fact, that troops can be so moved, and the general knowledge of the country, and the specific knowledge of the routes and *modus operandi* of the cattle thieves, obtained by Colonel Mackenzie I regard as very important, and well worth the summer's labor."[23]

But Mackenzie wanted Indians. He fretted in camp almost three weeks while he rested his horses and men. Then, following the timetable he had set for himself, he left on September 21 with five companies of cavalry and one of the Twenty-Fourth Infantry. Eight days later the command reached McClellan Creek, where the Tonkawas found two fresh trails, one made by two horses and the other by a mule. Hoping the mule trail would lead toward the camp, they followed it into a vineyard of wild grapes, where they lost it. Captain Wirt Davis, noticing that grapes had been scattered under and beyond the vines, guessed the Indians had been harvesting grapes and packing them on the mule. He was right.

A trail of grapes was found where they had fallen out of the pack, and soon the mule trail was again located. After another twelve miles of rapid march, the hostile village was spotted about five miles away in a valley along the creek. The soldiers halted for a quick rest and to adjust their saddles.[24]

The command moved out at a gallop and struck the village about 4:00 P.M. Company F was engaged almost continuously from the time it hit, but Company D did not get into the fight until it went for the Indians' horse herd. The Indians were driven into a ravine, where they dug in and fought back. Company I was sent to head off an escape at the head of the ravine, but arrived too late. Company L chased the fleeing Indians and had a running fight until after dark.

One trooper was killed, one mortally wounded, and two others seriously wounded. The soldiers recovered a Mexican, Francisco Nieto, who had been held captive for two years, and seven Mexican women who had been with the Comanches so long that "they have become Indians." Indian losses in the fight are not known. Mackenzie counted twenty-three warriors killed and one mortally wounded, but he also speculated that more bodies had been thrown into a deep pool by the camp to prevent their falling into the hands of the soldiers. A Mexican woman told Strong she counted sixty-two bodies thrown into the water.[25]

When the Tonkawas began scalping and mutilating the Comanche corpses, Mackenzie put a stop to it and raised the ire of one scout named Henry. "What fur you no lette me scalp heme Commanche?" he demanded indignantly.[26]

The village of 262 lodges belonged to Mow-way, and there was no question that these Indians had been among the raiders responsible for depredations in Texas that year. Polonio Ortiz recognized most of the prisoners taken, and Francisco Nieto said he had been captured by the same band on the road between San Antonio and Fort Duncan. Most damning of all was a statement by José Carrión, survivor of a wagon train which had been massacred the previous spring "under circumstances of peculiar atrocity" at Howard's Wells in West Texas. He counted a total of forty-three mules found in the camp which had belonged to the train.[27]

About 130 prisoners were taken, mostly women and children. Some were seriously wounded, having been mixed up with the men while the fighting was underway. Mackenzie ordered the village burned, and left after dark with 124 prisoners. Those prisoners too old or too badly wounded to be moved were left behind. The surgeon tried to treat the wounded prisoners who were taken on the march, but could not make them follow instructions and eight died before reaching the supply camp.[28]

After leaving the ruined village, the troops first established camp about two miles away. Strong recommended the captured horse herd be placed in the center of the camp, but Mackenzie pointed out the herd guards were inexperienced and might not be able to control them. If Indian ponies got out of hand, they might stampede the cavalry horses; he had already lost army horses in one stampede and did not intend for it to happen again. Instead, the captured ponies were herded into a depression and staked out for the night.

That was a mistake. Before midnight the Comanches attacked, riding in wide circles around the campsite, whooping and occasionally firing shots into the camp. When they were sure of utter confusion, they cut into the herd and recovered many of the captured ponies along with those belonging to the Tonkawas. The next day Carter noted one of the scouts "leading a small, forlorn looking burro, packed with their saddles, every one afoot, looking sheepish and woefully dejected. . . ."

The command moved eighteen miles that day. Undeterred by distance, the Comanches hit the pony herd again that night and made off with most of the remainder of the captured horses. Of only fifty ponies and mules left of the "large number" originally captured, Mackenzie gave most to the Tonkawas as compensation for their losses.[28]

Mackenzie had destroyed a village and captured prisoners, but the Comanches were still mounted and capable of surviving and prospering. Never again would Mackenzie make this mistake; henceforth, captured ponies would be destroyed.

The encounter with the Comanches proved to be more successful than Mackenzie had first thought. Despite the recovery of their horses, the Indians were now on the defensive. One hundred and sixteen of their friends and relatives were prisoners, interned at Fort Concho too far away to be recovered in a fast raid. For the first time, the Indian leaders would be forced to negotiate with the whites for captives. As Major G.W. Schofield at Fort Sill reported in a letter to San Antonio, "The fact that these prisoners are in our hands has clearly been the principal incentive to cause their prompt compliance with the demands made on them."

The Kiowas, who had lost none of their people to the whites, were less inclined to end their raids,[30] but even with the Kiowas new developments were unfolding. Kicking Bird's peace faction was gaining control over the majority of the tribe. The indications that Satanta and Big Tree might be paroled from prison in Texas provided further incentive for the Kiowas to curtail their raids. The plains were beginning to grow quieter.

Back in Texas, nine Medals of Honor were awarded to enlisted men and non-commissioned officers of the Fourth Cavalry for gallantry at McClellan Creek on September 29, 1872.[31]

Southern Texas

124

CHAPTER 9

"You Must Assume the Risk"

Headquarters
Army of the United States
Washington, D.C.
Feb. 5, 1873

General C.C. Augur
Comdg. Dept. of Texas

General:

The President wishes you to give great attention to affairs on the Rio Grande Frontier, especially to prevent the raids of Indians and Mexicans upon the people and property of Southern and Western Texas.

To this end he wishes the 4th Cavalry to be moved to that Frontier, and it will be replaced by the 7th Cavalry to be drawn from the Department of the South. The 7th Cavalry is now scattered but it is believed the whole can reach Louisville or Memphis by or before the 10th of March. And if the Red River is up as it ought to be at that period of the year, the Regiment will be at or near Fort Richardson [by the end of] March. Its strength is now reported 1020 enlisted men, and the horses are believed to be in splendid order. This Regiment can replace the 4th in North West Texas. The 4th, as soon as it is safe to move should march to the Rio Grande, and the ninth [Cavalry] can be broken into detachments

125

to cover the Western Frontier and the road toward New Mexico.

In naming the 4th to the Rio Grande the President is doubtless influenced by the fact that Col. MacKenzie is young and enterprising, and that he will impart to his Regiment his own active character.

I have the honor to be,
Your obedient servant,
W.T. Sherman,
General.[1]

The Kickapoos were responsible for most of the raids on the Rio Grande frontier of Southwestern Texas. A woodlands tribe speaking an Algonquian language, they had moved from the area of southwestern Wisconsin to Illinois in the eighteenth century, then in the early 1800s again fled ahead of white expansion, passing through the Southwest in the middle decades of the century. Some Kickapoos had been in Mexico since the early 1850s, and they and the Lipans were responsible for a series of killings in Uvalde County in 1859.[2] Allowed to settle below the Rio Grande on condition that they protect the Mexican towns from attacks by Lipans and Mescaleros, they then worked a deal with local merchants who would buy any plunder they could bring back from Texas. With this source of income established, they negotiated yet a third arrangement with the Lipans. Secure on all sides, the Kickapoos and Lipans crossed the border at will, raiding between the Rio Grande and the Nueces. In Medina County alone during 1865 and 1866, the county judge reported, "The number of stock stolen by the Lipan and Kickapoo can not be ascertained, but will certainly number about one thousand head."[3]

The two tribes also trafficked in white prisoners. On January 27, 1865, Lipans encountered three boys who were out hunting steers northwest of Castroville. One of the boys, Augustus Rothe, was heavily armed and managed to fend off his attackers, but seventeen-year-old George Jacob Miller was tortured to death and thirteen-year-old Herbert Weinand was carried into captivity near Monclova Viejo, some thirty miles south of Eagle Pass. Two years later, Herbert and several other white children from western Texas were still being held in a Kickapoo camp near the Santa Rosa mountains in the State of Coahuila, although a wealthy Mexican from Monclova was trying to negotiate the boy's ransom.

Discussing the case in a letter to Governor Elisha M. Pease, Medina County Judge H.J. Richards wrote:

> All necessary information they receive from the border Mexicans in regard to the strength and movements of the U.S. Troops, chances of stealing etc. and are allowed to cross the Rio Grande at any time on their plundering raids to this part of Texas. W[h]y should Mexico not be made responsible, for the loss of property and outrages sustained by our citizens [?][4]

The Monclova businessman's efforts to ransom Herbert Weinand apparently failed, since he was still a prisoner in 1870. On April 27 of that year, Mackenzie wrote the Department of the Interior urging federal intervention. In a classic bureaucratic blunder, Interior presumed the Kiowas and Comanches were involved, and instructed Lawrie Tatum "to use every means at his command to find, and obtain the release of all captives held by those Indians."[5]

Eventually, the federal government turned its efforts in

the right direction. In 1871 the Mexican government yielded to U.S. pressure to try to clean up the border, but the Coahuila business community was thriving from the trade in stolen goods and blocked any attempt to stop it. When negotiations between the two governments broke down completely in 1872, it became obvious that special measures would be needed.[6]

In January 1873 Secretary of State Hamilton Fish decided to make one last effort to resolve the situation, but the United States government no longer believed Mexico would—or even could—put a halt to the depredations. Consequently, as Fish prepared to send commissioners to negotiate with the Mexicans, he was already discussing the possibility of military intervention with President Grant. The same month, in an announcement of a redistribution of military forces along the border, Grant also noted that Mexico would be held accountable for continued Indian raids originating in its territory.[7]

The government's skepticism proved well-founded. On May 8, even as U.S. commissioners were taking depositions from ranchers who had been raided, Kickapoos and Lipans drove off a hundred head of horses and cattle eighty miles northwest of San Antonio, and two days later raids were reported within sixteen miles of the city. William Schuhardt, United States consul in Piedras Negras, was unable to negotiate the ransom of a captive white boy because his Kickapoo captor was off raiding in Texas and could not be contacted.[8] The rumors in San Antonio, that a government wagon train bound from Austin to Fort Concho had been attacked near Fort McKavett and several teamsters killed, fed the local hysteria about the Mexican situation. By now, it was claimed that Indian raiders from Mexico had inflicted almost fifty million dollars in property damage to Texas, not including deaths and kidnappings.[9]

Fort Clark, founded at Las Moras spring, was at the center of the area most heavily raided. As headquarters of the Ninth Cavalry under Lieutenant Colonel Wesley Merritt, it should have been able to provide some defense against the attacks, but Merritt was burned out by service on the border and showed "more or less indifference or indecision" in dealing with the situation.[10] New blood was needed and the government was taking steps to provide it.

Wesley Merritt
(National Archives)

Under Grant's redistribution, units of the Fourth were drawn from throughout the frontier and concentrated at Fort Clark. On March 4 Companies A, B, C, E and K left Fort Richardson and Companies G and I and Headquarters were sent from Fort Concho. Company M was shifted from Fort Brown to Fort Duncan, opposite Piedras Negras, to cover the approaches to the Texas interior.

Like Brown and McKavett, Fort Clark was a pre-war post, old by frontier standards. Located on a hill overlooking the surrounding plains, it was dilapidated and short of quarters in 1873. With the Ninth still on post, the men of the Fourth bivouacked in an oak grove at the base of the hill, and a detail was set to work making the camp habitable. The grounds were cleaned and the dirt sprinkled down with water from an improvised cart to settle the dust.[11]

While his men were sprucing up their camp, Mackenzie was in San Antonio conferring with Sheridan and Secretary of War Belknap, both of whom he escorted to Fort Clark. Their arrival on April 11 was an event "which created no little stir in camp," and a mounted field inspection was ordered for the guests.

> They both expressed great satisfaction, and Mackenzie seemed much pleased, for the regiment was then, after several strenuous Indian Campaigns for some years past, at the full maximum of its field efficiency in horses, arms, equipment and rigid discipline. Its personnel in enlisted men, especially in its non-com officers, some of whom had been officers in fighting volunteer regiments during the Civil War, could not have been excelled in any army in the world.

That night, Merritt's regiment hosted a dance for their visitors and for the new command.[12]

The discussions at Fort Clark between Belknap, Sheridan and Mackenzie have never been officially recorded. Carter's account, in light of what later happened, is fascinating, but suspect as a possibly fabricated defense of Mackenzie's actions. According to Carter, Mackenzie described the discussions as beginning with directives from Sheridan.

> Mackenzie, you have been ordered down here to relieve General Merritt and the Ninth Cavalry because I want something done to stop these

conditions of banditry, killing, etc.,etc., by these people across the river. I want you to control and hold down the situation, and to do it in your own way. . . . I want you to be bold, enterprising, and at all times *full of energy,* when you begin, let it be a campaign of *annihilation, obliteration* and *complete destruction,* as you have always in your dealings done to all the Indians you have dealt with, etc. I think you understand what I want done, and the way you should employ your force. . . .

Carter says Mackenzie thus understood he was ordered to seek out and destroy the enemy wherever found, an order which raised the likelihood of invading Mexico and risking a war. But he had to be certain. "General Sheridan, under whose orders and upon what authority am I to act?" he asked. "Have you any plans to suggest, or will you issue me the necessary orders for my action?"

Sheridan exploded. "Damn the *orders!*" he shouted, pounding his fist on the table.

Damn the *authority.* You are to go ahead on your plan of action, and your authority and backing shall be Gen. Grant and myself. With us behind you in whatever you do to clean up this situation, you can rest assured of the fullest support. You must assume the risk. We will assume the final responsibility should any result.[13]

Sheridan's table-pounding explosion appears in Carter's *On the Border,* but in an account written by him forty-seven years earlier—an account in many places duplicated in *On the Border*—the scene does not appear.[14] Although his account

131

Philip Henry Sheridan
(U.S. Military Academy Library)

of the discussion may be a fabrication of Carter's old age, it is generally understood----as it was at the time—that the decision to raid into Mexico had been made in the highest circles. Otherwise, Mackenzie could not have requisitioned all the equipment he received. In 1885 Major E.B. Beaumont, a veteran of the raid, commented on it in light of the visit by Sheridan and Belknap, saying:

It is thought that the policy to be pursued in regard to border raids was determined during the presence of these distinguished officers, and the emphatic endorsement of the War Department of General Mackenzie's invasion seems to confirm this opinion.[15]

A strong case has been made by Richard Thompson that Mackenzie was probably given his instructions in a meeting with Sheridan, Belknap and General Augur in Augur's office in San Antonio, before the meeting at Fort Clark. There is no question that Augur was involved, particularly since he did not hesitate to approve the various supply requisitions to the Fourth at Fort Clark.[16]

Soon after Belknap and Sheridan's visit, Carter was summoned to Mackenzie's quarters, where he found the colonel "nervous and uneasy." After wandering around the quarters to make certain there were no listeners, Mackenzie told Carter in strict confidence that he had ascertained the location and numbers of the Indians who had been raiding into Texas from Mexico, and planned to lead an expedition against them.

> At his dictation I wrote a detailed letter to the department commander—the nature of which it would be improper for me, even at this late day [1888], to divulge . . . . [Later] I was shown a reply from department headquarters authorizing the necessary supplies on requisitions, for an expedition, the destination of which was only known to General Mackenzie and myself.[17]

That same night, only eight miles from Fort Clark, raiders from Mexico hit Dolores Ranch, making off with thirty-six horses. Merritt, who had not yet been formally relieved, dispatched a tracker with fifteen Seminole-Negro scouts and ranch owner Jerome Strickland. They followed the raiders' trail to the Rio Grande, then returned to Fort Clark where Strickland gave a deposition. In his own cover letter to Strickland's statement, Mackenzie wrote:

> On the trail scouts picked up a small water keg painted and a rawhide Lariat such as is used by the Kickapoos and two horses broken down from hard riding. The party taking the horses is supposed to have consisted of about six Mexicans and Kickapoos from the Mexican side of the river. None of the horses taken from the Dolorus Ranche [sic] have been returned and it is supposed they were crossed into Mexico.[18]

Time was spent in preparation, horses shod, pack animals tended, saddles overhauled and sabres ground. Companies went out in the field to "grazing camps," supposedly to condition their horses, where the men were drilled in rapid fighting on foot. In a time when a parsimonious War Department did not require target practice in an effort to save ammunition, the importance which the government gave the expedition may be seen in the large quantities of ammunition issued so that daily target practice could be held.[19]

Mackenzie's nervousness and irritability grew. At one point he thought Lawton had found out about the project and raged at Carter for violating a confidence. Although Mackenzie probably preferred Lawton to any other officer in his immediate command, he did not trust him with secrets. Lawton drank, and when he did he talked, but in this case he knew nothing and had only been speculating.[20]

At 11:00 P.M. May 16, Ike Cox, post scout, who had been prowling in Mexico with Green Van and Art McLain, "half breed" ranchers from along the river, rode into Fort Clark with a report of a Kickapoo camp on the headwaters of the San Rodrigo River near the village of Remolino. Orders were sent to round up the companies scattered at various camps around Fort Clark. Assembly was played, rousing sleeping soldiers from their blankets. Officers were told to leave company property and tents, which would be taken to Fort Clark in the morning. Five days' rations were packed on mules amid curses of sleepy soldiers. Soldiers saddled their horses and went into formation, while cooks prepared a quick breakfast.[21]

By morning the scattered companies were assembling on Las Moras Creek. There was a delay while the assembled regiment waited for Company M, which had become lost on the trip up from Fort Duncan and which did not reach the rendezvous on Las Moras Creek until 1:00 P.M. May 17. An hour later the command moved out under the blistering South Texas sun. It included civilian guides, six companies of the Fourth and twenty Seminole-Negro scouts under Lieutenant John Bullis—approximately four hundred men in all.

The column moved at a leisurely pace down Las Moras Creek toward the Rio Grande, since Mackenzie wanted to delay crossing the river until after nightfall. Despite several rest stops, the men suffered badly from the heat and lined their hats with wet sponges to prevent sunstroke. Finally he drew up the column near the mouth of the Las Moras and explained his plans and the risks involved. As Carter recalled, "If wounded, capture might mean hanging, the death of a felon, or, with back against a wall, his body riddled by Mexican or Indian bullets." The officers assumed Mackenzie was acting on specific instructions from the War Department. Only Carter knew the truth—there were no orders, only verbal generalities from Sheridan and supply authorizations from Augur.[22]

Shortly after 8:00 P.M. the Fourth began fording the Rio Grande into Mexico, a few miles from the present-day Texas town of Quemado. The opposite bank was too steep to climb

John Lapham Bullis
(The Institute of Texan Cultures)

135

and had to be cut down while the troopers waited in midstream, water up to their saddle-girths. Finally ordered forward, they made it to the top and emerged from the dense canebreaks that lined the riverbanks. They were in Mexico. Here the column halted briefly, and men ate, smoked their pipes and speculated on the outcome of their expedition.[23]

A path through a rocky ravine led out onto the open prairie. The order to trot was given, and the air was filled with the dull thud of hooves and the metallic clank of straining traces. Lamps were extinguished in the lonely ranch houses as the people inside cringed at the sound of the dark, mysterious horsemen filing past "at the dread hour of midnight."[24] The moon rose but was hidden by haze, giving an eerie cast to the riders. "The gait increased," Carter recalled. "We rode rapidly, going where—we knew not—led by half-breed guides on their fox-gaited beasts. They knew the importance of reaching the villages by daybreak, as planned, in order to surprise the enemy; also had measured the distance, and spared not their horses."[25]

The gait varied according to the pace set by the guides, sometimes a fast walk, sometimes a trot or a slow gallop or a "fox-gait" speed between a walk and trot. Dust obscured the column, making it hard for the rear companies to keep track of the rest. At every ravine they had to move slowly by files, requiring a gallop to close ranks once flat land had been reached.

A crisis occurred when the pack mules, loaded down with provisions, could no longer keep pace and disappeared from sight several miles to the rear, slowing the advance and increasing the column's vulnerability. If the Mexicans or Indians were to discover the column, they would be able to separate and attack the mule train and make off with animals and provisions.

Mackenzie was still unaware of his vulnerability, but other officers were beginning to realize what could happen. Several of them rode up to Carter, urging him to say something but, knowing Mackenzie's mood for the past month, he hesitated. Finally, he geared himself, spurred his horse and rode up to the colonel at the head of the column.[26]

Mackenzie went into a rage, using every word of profanity at his disposal. When he finally exhausted his vocabulary, Carter calmly reiterated the problem. "Yes!" Mackenzie snarled, the stumps of his missing fingers snapping furiously. "Tell the troop commanders I'll halt, and give just *five minutes* to 'cut the packs loose.' Tell the men to fill their pockets with hard bread."[27]

Carter rode back along the line to the rear, spreading the order, then rode on to urge the mule train forward. Once it caught up, knives flashed and the packs tumbled to the ground. Men stuffed their pockets with hardtack, little realizing they would have nothing else to eat for the next two days. Relieved of their burdens, the mules trotted along with the rest of the column, but the delay had cost time and, Carter estimated, hurt the outcome, since many of the Lipan warriors left early to hunt and were not in the target villages when the attack finally came, leaving the elderly, the women and the children.[28]

The men had been in the saddle for sixteen hours, some even longer, and had been awake almost thirty hours. In a daze, no one spoke. There was nothing but the steady drumming of hooves as dawn broke and they still had not reached the hostile villages. It was obvious the guides had not only failed to make allowances for the exhausted mules, but had miscalculated the distances as well. Still they pushed on. All the animals were beginning to show signs of fatigue, and the guides whipped and spurred their ponies, pushing them to keep pace. Someone suggested to Mackenzie that the column break into a gallop for the last few miles, but he refused to consider it. The horses would need all their strength for the charge into the villages.

Mackenzie and his staff rode with the guides, followed by Bullis' Seminole-Negroes, their dark features powdered white by the dust. Then came the troopers of the Fourth in columns of four, all coated with dust, their faces drawn from the long ride.

From the Burro Mountains, now clearly visible, the cool morning breeze swept down and eased the suffering of both man and beast. A halt was ordered at the water holes of Remolino, where men and horses drank deeply and the soldiers washed the dust out of their throats. At 6:00 A.M.,[29] in the bed of a stream concealed from the Indian camps, the troopers began shifting their saddles for combat, tightening their girths, and inspecting their weapons. There was not a cloud in the sky.

The soldiers rode out of the stream bed and began rounding the hill which separated them from the villages. The guides had advised a three-pronged attack which Mackenzie rejected in favor of a full frontal assault. The command was not to be divided. Orders were passed along the column, every man now wide awake and making a last minute check on his weapons. The mules were herded aside as the combat soldiers formed into rows of four, the sergeants riding up and down, tightening the formation. Up ahead the men could hear gunfire as the scouts engaged. The order was given to form platoons and prepare to charge.

Horses in hand. Don't scatter.[30]

Mackenzie turned to the commander of Company A. "Mr. McLaughlen, you have the honor of opening the ball," and Company A headed down the slope. Then word went to the rest of the column. "Left front into line! Gallop! March! Charge!"[31]

Cheering and whooping at the tops of their voices, the men of the Fourth stormed across the last mile separating them from their goal. McLaughlen hit first, pursuing the fleeing Indians out onto the open ground beyond the lodges. Then came each succeeding company, the lead platoon firing a single volley, wheeling to the right, then doubling back for another pass. Each platoon followed suit, reloading, firing again, then back through, sweeping the length of the three Indian villages.[32]

Recalling an earlier battle during the Civil War, Carter wrote, "I saw many charges of fifteen miles of country during that day, but I never saw such a magnificent charge as that made by those six troops of the Fourth U.S. Cavalry on the morning of May 18, 1873, at Rey Molina, Mexico."[33]

Despite the delays and general bad luck of the march, the Fourth had achieved surprise. The remaining warriors ran in every direction in a panic. Officers and sergeants had to restrain the men to keep them in their assigned ranks and not chasing individual Indians, but a few terrified government horses bolted and ran off with their riders. When the rear companies rode up, they dismounted and began a furious, methodical carbine fire. Out on the cornfields surrounding the villages, Company A continued its barrages of fire. The Indians' pony herds and cattle stampeded and soldiers were sent to round them up.

Carter reported it was short work. While Company I

pursued the escaping warriors, a search through the lodges uncovered contracts between the Indians and "prominent Mexicans. . . for the regular delivery of so many horses and head of cattle at so much per head." The soldiers had little doubt that the Mexican government was aware of the transactions as well.[34]

"Fire the villages!" Mackenzie shouted, and the dismounted troopers made torches out of grass and brush and went through the tepis and lodges, burning everything they could find. While Carter's company was rounding up the livestock and heading back, someone shouted that Indians were hidden under a bank. Carter turned, saw a warrior pointing a rifle, swung up his own carbine and killed him. Investigating, the soldiers found the dead Indian guarded by a little dog which snapped and growled as they approached, so they shot it. Behind the warrior's body they found two small children, one dead and the other dying of gunshot wounds, and a woman with a badly wounded twelve-year-old girl.[35]

Mackenzie reported finding nineteen bodies, although Carter estimated the death toll was probably much higher. Forty women and children were captured. Among the prisoners was the Lipan Chief Costilietos, who had been lassoed by one of Bullis' scouts. Another scout brought in an Indian, but "through some neglect" had failed to disarm him. When the Indian raised his rifle to shoot at Captain Mauck, Carter and a Corporal Linden fired simultaneously, spinning the Indian completely around before he hit the ground.

In his report, Mackenzie stated that "three Villages averaging from fifty to sixty Lodges were destroyed. They appeared to be well supplied with stores, including ammunition." Sixty-five ponies were recovered, some of which had

Ike Cox's brand. Government casualties included Private Peter Carrigan, mortally wounded; Private William Pair, "a splendid old soldier who has served in the Regiment since its organization," right arm amputated at the shoulder; and Private Leonard Kemppenberger, slightly wounded in the face but fit for duty.[36]

Although the majority of the Indians were away from the villages or escaped into the Santa Rosa Mountains, the raid was a success. Their base had been destroyed. Henry Strong recalled, "We just about exterminated what we did not bring back. The village looked like a cyclone had struck it."[37]

The sun was now high and the heat almost unbearable, but the soldiers had to withdraw to their side of the border as fast as they could. The return trip took the column directly through the village of Remolino where people, long since up and about, stood and watched as the soldiers rode through with the prisoners. Everyone recognized the U.S. Army uniforms and could guess what had happened. There were "black, malignant scowls" accompanied by low mutterings. The soldiers could feel the hatred.

With the excitement of the raid behind them, the two nights without sleep were beginning to tell on the soldiers. From time to time, the column passed lagoons where there were brief stops for rest and water. As night fell men drifted off to sleep, swaying in their saddles. Officers rode up and down the line, shaking them awake and pushing them on. Only Bullis' scouts were still alert, prowling the flanks and watching for any signs of ambush. During rest stops soldiers would lie down with their arms through their reins, then could hardly be aroused. Constant headcounts were necessary to make sure no one was left behind. Some began hallucinating, while others became depressed or quarrelsome.

The fears of ambush were well-founded. From time to time, Bullis' scouts rode in with reports of shadowy groups following the column in the brush. During a rest stop, one trooper wandered off a short distance to catch some sleep and awakened to find a Mexican standing over him. He jumped up, fired his weapon, then ran back to the trail and followed it to the river, finally rejoining the command the next morning. Meanwhile, officers continued to shake the men upright in their saddles with curses and threats. The prisoners also began to doze and fall off their ponies, and were finally lashed into place with lariats. Had the hostile Indians attacked along the trail they might have achieved a massacre. At dawn the column came into sight of the trees lining the Rio Grande.

The way to the ford was blocked by a farm surrounded by a fence. Pushing the gate open, they rode through and soon were plunging into the river. "Men and horses seemed to draw new strength from the refreshing waters," Carter wrote. Then they climbed the Texas bank on Green Van's ranch, where the order was given to go into camp. Saddles were removed from the exhausted horses for the first time in forty-nine hours. Men flocked to the river to bathe.[38]

Couriers were dispatched to Fort Clark, and soon Lawton was heading toward the camp with six wagonloads of rations. The men ate all day. In an effort to be hospitable, Van went to his ranch headquarters and came back with several buckets of potent mescal. The officers were about to issue it when Mackenzie ordered it poured out. If the troopers were to drink it while exhausted and with empty stomachs, he felt the results might be serious.[39]

A few hours later, a large group of Indians and Mexicans gathered on the opposite bank and shouted threats. Mackenzie sent the horses back into the canebreaks away from the river, then ordered the regiment's best sharpshooters to form a skirmish line covering the ford. The balance of the command was placed in a second line. Sleeping in shifts, the men settled down for the night. The following morning the troops marched a few miles to a more secure spot, then bivouacked for a longer rest.

That night several worried officers gathered around Mackenzie's campfire to discuss the raid, and Beaumont asked if Mackenzie had orders to cross into Mexico. Mackenzie had no written orders from Sheridan, and when he replied that he did not, Beaumont said, "Then it was illegal to expose not only the lives of your officers and men, in action, but, in event of their being wounded and compelled upon our withdrawal, through force of circumstances, to be left over there, probably to be hung or shot by a merciless horde of savage Indians and Mexicans."

"I considered all that," Mackenzie said.

"Your officers and men would have been justified in refusing to obey your orders, which you now admit as being illegal, and exposing themselves to such peril."

"Beaumont is right!" McLaughlen added, "and had I known that you had no orders to take us over the river, I would not have gone!!"

Mackenzie stood up and stared at them. "Any officer or man who had refused to follow me across the river I would have shot!"

"*That would depend, Sir,* upon who *shot first!*" snapped McLaughlen, himself one of the best shots of the regiment. There was a long, uncomfortable silence. Finally one officer and then another eased away, until the group broke up.[40]

Lessing Nohl has hinted that Mackenzie was ready to handle these officers as his father had done with the rebellious sailors on the *Somers*.[41] But Ranald Mackenzie was not his father, and McLaughlen and Beaumont were highly trained professional soldiers. Mackenzie was not threatening his officers, merely stating what he would have done had the situation required it. Now that the crisis had passed, Mackenzie could afford to tolerate some insubordination. He probably considered the argument the result of fatigue and nerves on the part of the other two officers. In his report, he said Beaumont and McLaughlen "acted handsomely and deserve consideration."[42]

About noon May 21 the command rode into Fort Clark, the raid over. It had been an attack on villages comprised mostly of women, children and old men, but in retrospect it had achieved results. When the warriors returned, they found their homes and supplies destroyed and their families held prisoner. The effect was overwhelming. As late as 1958 the Mexican Kickapoos at Nacimiento used the name "Mackenzie" to frighten stubborn children into obedience.[43]

The raid was over, but the furor had just begun.

CHAPTER 10

"The Grateful Thanks of the People of the State"

Mexico was in an uproar. On May 19, even as the soldiers were on their exhausting rush back toward the Rio Grande, the drums sounded assembly in Piedras Negras. Couriers were sent to various towns and villages and to the state capital at Saltillo, advising that some "600 gringos" had violated Mexican sovereignty. The mood was ugly until word arrived that these "gringos" were neither Texas Rangers nor Militia but United States regular troops, which dampened much of Mexico's enthusiasm for immediate retaliation. U.S. Consul Schuhardt told a crowd in Piedras Negras that the soldiers meant no affront to Mexico but had simply crossed over to punish Indians who had been raiding into Texas. The additional information that the soldiers had already crossed back into the United States allayed fears of an outright invasion. Several "more sober minds" also pointed out that if Mackenzie's soldiers were attacked, a much larger American military force would invade Mexico in revenge. For his part, Schuhardt immediately wrote a congratulatory letter to Mackenzie.[1]

In Chicago, General Sheridan was preparing to travel east for the funeral of General Edward Canby, who had been murdered by a Modoc Chief, Captain Jack, during a peace parlay in California. When word came of the raid, he dashed off a telegram to Secretary Belknap.

> It is more than probable that Mackenzie crossed
> into Mexico, and had his fight on that side of the
> Rio Grande. We must back him.[2]

Sheridan, privately delighted with the raid, admitted to Augur that a short time earlier he had told an unspecified higher authority that Mackenzie would cross into Mexico, and this higher authority had approved the action. Augur, who did not feel Mexico was in a position to make an issue of it, advised Mackenzie that he should correspond with that country's officials only on routine matters, indicating it was not necessary to justify the raid to the Mexicans. Despite support from the army command, other U.S. officers were not so enthusiastic about the raid. In Arizona, Colonel George Crook worried that Mexico might attack his jurisdiction in retaliation for Mackenzie's action. Colonel Edward Hatch, and others, believed the raid was part of a plan at the War Department to enhance Mackenzie's reputation and hasten his promotion to brigadier general.[3]

Meanwhile Mackenzie was involved with the more practical problems of the raid. There was the inevitable paperwork of a formal report, details had to be given, a count of the prisoners reported, government casualties listed and individual officers cited. Company reports had to be gathered, with a list of individual enlisted men deserving special notice.[4] Arrangements had to made to transfer the prisoners to the proper reservations.

But his most important concern was the possibility of Mexican reaction. As commander at Fort Clark, Mackenzie was responsible for his sector of the border, and it was imperative that he be ready to face any threat from the south. The leading citizens of the Mexican towns were worried that the breach between the two countries had grown too wide to be settled peacefully, and Coahuila went so far as to levy "such an extraordinary tax as is only done in cases of great revolutions or threatening war." Americans living in that part of Mexico were cautioned to look after their lives and property.[5]

On May 24 Mackenzie received word that Mexicans and Indians were preparing to gather on the opposite side of the river. He took two companies and scouted the area, returning two days later without making contact, but the scouts reported that Fort Clark could expect an attack anytime. The guard was doubled on the night of May 26 and picket lines established all around the post. Despite an electrical storm, families gathered in nervous little groups on the porches of the quarters. Amid the thunder and flashes of lightning a carbine went off, followed by more gunfire. Drums and bugles sounded assembly and troopers poured from the barracks, but investigation revealed that one nervous guard, firing at a hog, had started the whole line shooting. Officers were called to headquarters and the incident reviewed. There seems to have been no criticism; the false alarm was used as a means of evaluating preparedness for an attack and changes in procedure were made.[6]

Shafter at Fort Duncan was just as cautious but less jumpy than Mackenzie at Fort Clark. Located within shouting distance of Piedras Negras, Shafter was well aware of the chaos in Mexico; he knew that Mexico did not possess enough organization or unity to pose a major threat. Such danger as existed would come from Indians or local irregulars. In a note to Mackenzie, Shafter cited Schuhardt in saying that "the respectable people in Piedras Negras sustain you or rather are not offended." He also repeated a rumor that some three hundred Indians, gathered at Remolino to await Kickapoos from Santa Rosa, had refused an order from the Mexican commandant to disperse.[7] The Indians' defiance exemplified the weakness of Mexico, but the order also revealed that Mexico's government and military were getting tired of having Indians come and go as they pleased.

Mackenzie was at the forefront of the local diplomatic effort. He sent one letter to Schuhardt, intending that it be shown to the governor of Coahuila, stating his position on war with the Indians as opposed to war with Mexico. Another letter to Thomas G. Williams, U.S. commissioner to the Mexican Kickapoos, stated he wanted peace with the tribes but was ready to fight if need be. Meanwhile, he dispatched his prisoners to San Antonio with instructions for their care. He arranged for the Tonkawa Chief Castille and Lipan-Tonkawa Scout Johnson to visit old Chief Costilietos.[8]

Mackenzie's report, making its way up the chain of command, verified what Sheridan had known all along—that the raid had occurred in Mexico. In a follow-up telegram to Belknap, Sheridan said:

> If the government will stand firm we are near the end of all difficulties on the Mexican frontier. For twenty years there has been no safety for life or property on the Rio Grande, and at last when we are driven by a necessity which is the foundation of all law, namely that of protection of our lives and property, to cross a very crooked river to exterminate the murderers and robbers, we must

in all reason be sustained. There can not be any valid boundary line when we pursue Indians who murder our people and carry away our property. If the government will say that there shall be no boundary line when we are driven to the necessity of protecting our lives and property, there will never be another raid on the Rio Grande.[9]

On the border itself, however, the issue was far from settled. Mackenzie was keeping in close touch with events in Mexico and was doing his best to make sure the Indians remained isolated with no support from the Mexican population. He learned that the *alcalde* of San Fernando and the governor of Coahuila had refused permission for the Indians to attack the U.S. side of the border. "As I have never heard of their asking permission before I think they are taking at least one step in the right direction," he reported.[10] He sent a wagonmaster he had known at Fort Richardson to spread the word among the Mexicans that the Fourth was friendly toward them but hostile to raiding Indians. The wagonmaster was told to recite the Fourth's war record against the Comanches, "whom the Mexicans both hate and fear."

Concerning the rumors floating about that a large band of Indians and Mexicans were assembling at an undetermined point to make a major raid into Texas, "I am not a particle stampeded," Mackenzie told General Augur, "but think that now is the time to show pretty strongly and if needed to act. Should this big raid come off the Governor of Coahuila can hardly be free from the greater share of the blame." To Schuhardt he wrote, "The Indians can be well assured that they have not got nor can they get enough men to hurt me, and for every man of mine I will *hurt* many more Indians."[11]

Neither Carter nor Charlton commented on Mackenzie's physical or emotional state at this point, but the strain must have been considerable. Besides the border crisis he was responsible for the routine administrative duties of a regimental and post commander, such as deciding whether charges should be filed against an unduly harsh company commander. He apologized to Augur for the brevity of one letter, saying, "I am tired and very busy or I would write more at length."[12] There was an emotional complication as well. Florida Tunstall Sharpe, two months a widow, was at Fort Duncan. Mackenzie knew it and perhaps had seen her. At least Shafter thought enough of the situation to mention her in his letters, one mentioning that she had been sick and another that she sent Mackenzie her regards.[13]

Mackenzie continued, however, to display his capability for well-reasoned logic. He felt the Indian problem on the border was due to Mexico's internal struggles, rather than any deliberate acts of the Mexican people. Since incipient civil war in Mexico precluded any concerted effort by the country to police the border, he told Schuhardt it was wrong to hold the nation responsible, "just as it would have hardly been right when eight years ago our own country was distracted by a great war, to hold us responsible for the misdeeds of Indians or rebels." Instead he suggested some sort of agreement by which regular troops of either nation could cross into the other "for the purpose of punishing marauding Indians."[14]

He even worried about the Indians, and wrote Commissioner Williams that "I much regret that the Kickapoos suffered more than the Lipans: that I was more particularly in search of the Mescalero and Lipans than of the Kickapoos, but if their people will steal and associate with the Lipans and

Mescaleros they must take the Consequences." As for the Lipans, he suggested that if they wanted to return home, they could live with the Tonkawas at Fort Griffin "and they could steal horses from the wild Commanches [sic]."[15]

His most realistic suggestion was for a border open to the military. But Mexico, recently freed from French occupation and still touchy about its sovereignty, rejected the idea outright. To some extent Mexican anger was justified. Although tribes were also raiding across the northern borders of the United States, then taking refuge in Canada, the federal government was loathe to incur British wrath by a punitive expedition across the Canadian border. It was one thing to risk a war with Mexico, a war which the United States must surely win, but Great Britain with its world-wide empire and large standing army was another matter. The certainty of the outcome of any war with Mexico was recognized on both sides of the Rio Grande. Indian applications for permission to retaliate were met with polite indifference or outright rejection by the various Mexican government offices.

Sheridan, continuing to rant, made sure the federal government did not waver in its support of the colonel on the border. In his formal endorsement of Mackenzie's action report, Sheridan restated his earlier contention.

> There should be no boundary line when we are driven to the necessity of defending our lives and property against murderers and robbers. If the Government will stand by this action of Col. Mackenzie the troubles on the Rio Grande frontier will soon cease.[16]

The report went on to Washington, where Sherman gave

151

it a more detached endorsement. Forwarding it to Belknap, he wrote:

> The invasion of the Territory of a neighboring Friendly power in *hot pursuit* of an aggressive or robber force would be warranted by the Laws of nations. But in this instance Col. McKenzie did not clearly state the facts that convinced him of what is doubtless true, that these identical Kickapoos and Lipans were then engaged or had only recently been engaged in a marauder on the Border into Texas. Until the Mexican Government complains formally of the invasion of their Territory, I suppose there is no need of our making further enquiries on this point.[17]

Belknap agreed. He sent copies of the report to the Secretary of the Interior with the comment, "I have informed Colonel Mackenzie that his action is commended by this Department."[18]

The official reaction from the Mexican government was slow in coming for several reasons. Although Mexico officially opposed any armed incursion into its territory, its foreign minister, Ignacio Mariscal, had assured the U.S. minister that there would be no serious complaint at such a crossing. When Mackenzie did enter Mexico, the slowness of communications between Saltillo and Mexico City and thence to Washington impeded an immediate response. Finally, Mexico was apparently unwilling to lose further face by commenting immediately one way or the other. By June 2, two weeks after the raid, the Mexican minister in Washington still had no official report from his government and so was not ready to present its views to the Department of State.[19] The longer

Mexico delayed, the more time Sheridan, Grant and Belknap had to build their case and the less likely the Indians were to get support south of the border. By June 13 Sheridan was able to write, "I do not anticipate any raid from the Indians—in fact I consider the Mexican border troubles as drawing to a close. (Mariscal finally delivered the Mexican government's protest in January 1874; however, it was tempered with the assurance that while Mexico could not authorize armed intervention by a foreign power, the Mexican government would help stop border depredations.)[20]

There was one group that had no doubts about the validity of the raid into Mexico. As the warlords in San Antonio, Chicago and Washington pondered the raid with its implications, the Texas Legislature convened in Austin to approve the following resolution:

> Whereas reliable information has been received that General Ranald McKenzie of the U.S. Army with troops under his command, did on the 19th day of May 1873, cross the Rio Grande [border] with the Republic of Mexico, and inflict summary punishment upon the band of Kickapoo Indians who harbored and fostered by the Mexican authorities have for years past been waging predatory warfare upon the frontier of Texas, murdering our Citizens, carrying their children into captivity and plundering their property:
>
> Therefore, Resolved—by the Senate of the State of Texas. The House concurring. That the grateful thanks of the people of the State and particularly the Citizens of our Frontier are due to General McKenzie and the officers and troops under his

command for their prompt action and gallant conduct in inflicting well merited punishment upon
these scourges of our frontier.

Resolved. That his Excellency, the Governor, be
and is hereby requested to forward a copy of these
Resolutions to General McKenzie and the Officers
and troops under his command.

The resolution, adopted by the Senate on May 25 and by the
House of Representatives the following day, was signed on
May 30 by Governor Edmund J. Davis.[21]

On June 22 Green Van and a scout of forty troopers
picked up the trail of cattle thieves heading for the river about
forty-five miles below Eagle Pass. They caught the thieves
trying to cross the herd, and captured one Mexican on the U.S.
bank. The others were told that if they did not return, the
soldiers would cross the river and kill every man. Troops were
sent over to bring the cattle back, and they arrested a second
Mexican on the far bank. Eighty head were recovered. The
prisoners were taken to Fort Duncan, where they were inter-
rogated and jailed in the guardhouse. In a change of attitude,
the Mexican commander in Piedras Negras fully endorsed the
action and promised assistance whenever necessary.[22]

Relations on the border were changing, but one of the few
men who failed to recognize the change fully was Mackenzie.
Once set into motion he was hard to stop, and thus he
presented a new set of problems for the generals. He required
an active say in everything, including the decision as to which
of their commanders Mexico should send to the border for
joint action (his own choice was Pedro Advícula Valdez, who
the Americans called Colonel Winker). He appears to have
been looking forward to another confrontation with the

Indians.[23]

His zealousness prompted Sheridan to write, "Mackenzie has done very well; hope he will not spoil it by corresponding too much with Tom, Dick and Harry, on the subject." Still later, he told Sherman, "I have directed General Augur to draw the brakes a little tight on Mackenzie until there is additional provocation. I do not myself fear for some time to come any further outrages from Indians living in Mexico."[24] Augur himself wrote, "Colonel Mackenzie has been ordered not to cross again into Mexico, without further provocation."[25]

As Mackenzie sat at Fort Clark under the watchful eyes of his bosses, rumors once again reached the East that he had been killed in an obscure action in West Texas. The New York *Times* reported:

IMPROBABLE STORY OF A BATTLE—
GEN. MACKENZIE REPORTED KILLED.

The following is an extract from the Waco (Texas) *Examiner* of July 9: "Mr. Wm. Johnson, of the stage-coach line, arrived from a visit to Granbury, Wood *[sic]* County, evening before last. He informs us that news of a serious engagement between Mexican and Kickapoos on one side, and the American forces, under Gen. Mackenzie, on the other, had been received at that place. The battle occurred, according to this report, on the head waters of the Concho, the 3d or 4th of this month. The fight was made by Indians, it is supposed, to avenge the insult and injuries of the famous Mackenzie raid. The assailants were largely in excess to numbers, and the contest was bloody and severe, resulting in a victory to the Americans, though at the expense of many brave soldiers, including the commander, Gen. Mackenzie, himself. The Mexican loss is estimated at nearly 200 killed and wounded. The news was brought, says Mr. Johnson, by a man just from the vicinity of the conflict, and the people of Granbury seemed to think it all true."[26]

Four days later, the *Times* corrected itself, pointing out that Governor Davis had received a letter from Mackenzie written at Fort Clark several days after his supposed "death."[27]

Amid the rumors, personality conflicts and diplomatic maneuverings, the wheels of officialdom ground onward. The prisoners taken at Remolino were transported to Fort Gibson, Indian Territory, except for Costilietos who escaped. The federal government tried to negotiate the return to the U.S. of all Kickapoos, using the Fort Gibson prisoners as bait, but ended up having to offer cash inducements as well. About half of the Kickapoos agreed to return, arriving at Fort Sill on December 20;[28] the remainder were unwilling to relocate. In Mexico they moved about at will and were not confined to any reservation. The Mexican government balked at forcing their return—there was a limit to how far the Mexicans were willing to go without compromising their sovereignty. Furthermore, the Kickapoos did have some uses against more hostile tribes. Some of the Indians agreed to leave the Texans alone, while others withdrew further south into the mountains.

Meanwhile, Mackenzie's health was beginning to fail. On July 20 he suffered an attack of acute rheumatism, first in his right shoulder, then in his left forearm and legs, particularly in the joints and tissues around his right knee. A letter from Shafter expressed concern and advised against visiting Fort Duncan if he weren't up to it. He continued to deteriorate as the summer wore on. By mid-August his correspondence was being handled by others, and he placed himself on temporary relief from his responsibilities as post commander at Fort Clark, delegating his duties to Major A.E. Latimer.[29]

On September 12 Mackenzie was examined by Surgeon J.F. Hammond, medical director for the Department of Texas in San Antonio. Although the fever, redness and most severe pain had subsided, Dr. Hammond noted thickening and stiffness around the joints. "In addition," the surgeon wrote:

> his general system has lost functional vigor, from exposure, deprivations and arduous duties in a hot and more or less malarial climate, and needs recuperation. . . . As there is a danger of permanent disability, it is recommended that he be given a leave of absence for four months for the benefit of his health, with permission to go beyond the limits of the department.[30]

A thirty-day leave was granted the same day. Although extended for another three months by Assistant Adjutant General William D. Whipple, under orders from General Sherman, Mackenzie never completely recovered.[31]

William W. Belknap *(National Archives)*

CHAPTER 11

"I Brought You In. I Will Take You Out!"

The year 1874 brought more than the usual election-year intrigue. Although personally honest, President Grant was singularly inept in his appointments and was surrounded by graft and corruption. The Democrats were overjoyed. Branded as the party of secession, they had been relegated to obscurity for fourteen years. Now, with Grant's Republican administration mired in scandal, they mounted a campaign to regain control of the House of Representatives.

Much of the scandal centered on the War Department, where Secretary Belknap presided over a massive system of payoffs. Virtually any service-related position that could be sold was sold, and the secretary made sure he collected his share of the selling price. In response, the Democrats courted any well-known, reasonably untainted army officer who appeared in Washington, but any such officer in the capital without official business was automatically suspect at the War Department.

It is not known whether Mackenzie was suspect when he appeared in Washington. He had never showed any interest in politics, but he *had* applied for an extra month's leave and come to the capital. Apparently, he felt some need to assure the War Department of his innocent intentions, for he notified the adjutant general that he was visiting friends.[1]

Mackenzie may have felt he had time to relax since the western plains were reasonably quiet compared to previous years. The Kiowas had secured the parole of Satanta and Big Tree, which had temporarily given Kicking Bird's peace faction the upper hand. Trouble broke out again, however, in December 1873 when a detachment of Fourth Cavalry under Lieutenant Charles Hudson defeated a raiding party of Kiowas, Comanches and Kiowa-Apaches. Among the dead was the son of Lone Wolf, who now headed the Kiowa war faction.[2] The old chief swore revenge.

The fight in which Lone Wolf's son died was only the outward symptom of trouble stirring just under the surface. Although the Kiowa penchant for raiding was partly responsible, much of the blame must fall on white avarice and government ineptitude, aggravated by forces of nature beyond anyone's control. The War Department created its share of problems when it initiated a survey of the Kiowa-Comanche lands. The superstitious Kiowas were uneasy at the sight of the measuring equipment, and the more sophisticated Indians, who understood its uses, suspected the survey meant their land might be divided for settlement.[3]

When heavy rains interrupted the freight service bringing supplies to the reservation, Agent James M. Haworth, who had succeeded Lawrie Tatum at Fort Sill, had to put the Indians on half-rations. When the raiding season began, some of the hungry young warriors began killing cattle at random, and Haworth had to ask for troops to police the reservation.[4]

On the Cheyenne reservation at Darlington (Indian Territory), the situation was even worse. Initially the tribe prospered, continuing its traditional buffalo hunts with government sanction. But when commercial uses were found for buffalo hides, whites converted the hunt into a major industry and began a massive slaughter. Buffalo became scarce, forcing the tribe to draw rations from the agency. In addition, whisky traders had infiltrated the reservation, and alcoholism ran rampant. Warriors traded their goods for liquor while their families went hungry. When horse thieves from Kansas began making off with their stock, the Cheyennes began listening to the war talk from visiting Kiowas and Comanches. The Cheyenne chiefs informed their agent they were losing control.[5]

Throughout 1873 and early 1874 the plains tribes simmered. Reports reached the army and the agencies that the Comanches and Cheyennes were accumulating large stores of modern weapons. Even more disturbing were reports that the Comanches, who were normally indifferent to religion and ritual, had raised a prophet. His name was Isa-tai, and by the spring of 1874 he had become a powerful figure. In May he called the Comanches together for a Sun Dance, a ceremony unprecedented for that tribe. When the Sun Dance ended, delegations were sent to the Kiowas, Arapahoes and Southern Cheyennes calling for a general uprising. The Cheyenne chiefs moved most of their people closer to the agency, but the Dog Soldier faction responded to the call. Kicking Bird managed to keep most of the Kiowas in line and led them to Fort Sill, but some followers of Lone Wolf and the shadowy medicine man, Maman-ti, joined the uprising. Except for a few renegades, most of the Arapahoes ignored the call.

The lines were drawn. Even though the majority of the plains tribes had opted for neutrality, the Comanches had managed to gather enough people to mount a major rebellion.[6]

Hostilities commenced on June 27, 1874, when the Indians attacked a hide trading center at Adobe Walls in the Texas Panhandle. The superb marksmanship and high-powered rifles of the buffalo hunters ultimately drove them off, but the future looked ominous. In Chicago and Washington it appeared that the United States would have to go to war. To facilitate military action, Sheridan extended the boundary of the Department of Missouri to include that part of the Indian Territory and Texas north of the main Canadian River. The new boundaries, however, did not limit the local commanders, who were free to disregard boundaries in operations against the Indians, "either for the purpose of punishing them, or the protection of persons and property against their depredations."[7]

Mackenzie, back at Fort Clark since February 11, had performed only routine duties. With the Mexican border quiet, Sheridan recommended to General Augur that Mackenzie be moved to the war zone. On July 23 Augur ordered Mackenzie to concentrate the bulk of his regiment at Fort Concho.[8]

The army planned a four-pronged offensive, with columns under Colonel Nelson Miles, Fifth Infantry, marching south from Fort Dodge, Kansas; forces under Lieutenant Colonel John W. Davidson, Tenth Cavalry, riding west from Fort Sill; Major William R. Price's Eighth Cavalry moving east from Fort Bascom, New Mexico; and Mackenzie's Fourth Cavalry maneuvering north from Fort Concho. At his old camp on the Fresh Fork of the Brazos, Mackenzie was to be reinforced by a column under Lieutenant Colonel George P. Buell, Eleventh Infantry, from Fort Griffin. The generals expected to compress the hostile Indians into a small area of the high plains, where they could be defeated.

Augur's orders to Mackenzie were very clear.

As you are aware, the object of the proposed Campaign against the hostile Cheyennes, Comanches, Kiowas, and others from the Fort Sill Reservation, is to punish them for recent depredations along the Kansas and Texas frontiers, and you are expected to take such measures against them as will, in your judgment, the soonest accomplish the purpose. . . .

In carrying out your plans, you need pay no regard to Department or Reservation lines. You are at liberty to follow the Indians wherever they go, even to the Agencies. In this latter event great care must be exercised not to involve such friendly bands as have already gone to the Agencies and have remained peaceful.

Should it happen in the course of the Campaign, that the Indians return to the Agency at Sill, you will follow them there and assuming Command of all troops at that point, you will take such measures as will insure entire Control of the Indians there, until such time as you can report the condition of affairs to Department Headquarters. While the Indian Agent is to be consulted and to be treated with great respect, he will not be permitted to interfere in any way with the hostile bands, until the Orders of the Government for the disposition of the Indians are received.[9]

In other words, Mackenzie could do as he pleased, as long as he did not attack neutrals. As for the Quaker agents,

Christopher C. Augur
(National Archives)

they had been given their opportunity but had failed to keep the peace. This time the generals were determined to have absolute control.

General Augur joined Mackenzie at Fort Clark and accompanied him to Fort McKavett, where troops were being consolidated. From there the command moved to Fort Concho, arriving on August 21. The following day Mackenzie organized his expedition as the Southern Column, consisting of eight companies of Fourth Cavalry, four companies of the Tenth Infantry, one of the Eleventh Infantry, and scouts. The infantry would guard the camp and train while the cavalry and scouts were in the field. The scouting detachment included six white soldiers and civilians, thirteen Seminole-Negro soldiers from Fort Clark, some Lipans and twelve Tonkawas. Lieutenant William A. Thompson was named chief of scouts, and John Charlton assigned as sergeant. Henry Strong was the civilian guide. Among the scouts was the Lipan-Tonkawa, Johnson, veteran of the Remolino raid, who had been working as a Comanchero trading with Indians on the headwaters of the Red River. His thorough knowledge of the Panhandle area was to prove invaluable.[10]

While Mackenzie organized, Nelson Miles's Fifth Infantry was already in the field, having left Fort Dodge on August 14. A former clerk from Boston, Miles was self-educated and had worked his way up the ranks of the Union Army, finishing the war as a brevet major general. His promotion through the ranks made him an outsider with a deep-seated resentment of West Pointers. His marriage to Sherman's niece both helped and hindered him. Sherman disliked Miles, sometimes seeming to deliberately hold him back to avoid accusations of nepotism. Miles, vain and arrogant with a ruthless determination to advance himself, often at someone else's expense, nevertheless exploited the relationship every way he could.

Despite his faults, Miles was a superb field commander and one of the few officers on the Indian frontier who was equal to Mackenzie in daring and imagination. A bitter rivalry was to develop between the two men. Now that he was finally in the field, Miles was determined to make the most of it. If this meant encroaching on the jurisdiction of Mackenzie or anyone else who got in his way, Miles would do it if he had to.

Mackenzie was not accustomed to being challenged, and he thoroughly resented it. It was one thing for him to undermine Colonel Reynolds, his former departmental commander, but for someone else to try the same thing on him was an entirely different matter. He did not consider Miles his equal and said so. As Miles' prestige rose, it became a race to see which man would ultimately get a general's star, if one became available.[11]

For the time being, however, these officers would have to work toward a common goal—the defeat of the uprising on the Southern Plains. As far as anyone knew, the Indians had

Nelson A. Miles
(Little Bighorn Battlefield National Monument)

massed with their families on the headwaters of the Red River. Mackenzie's column moved out of Fort Concho on August 23, headed for his supply camp on the forks of the Brazos. Buell left about the same time to rendezvous with Mackenzie, while Price traveled down the main Canadian River to join Miles. Davidson was still at Fort Sill, since trouble was brewing at the agencies.[12]

By September 2 Mackenzie's column had reached the base of the caprock. He had remained behind, meeting with Augur and working out the logistics of the campaign, so the troops went into camp, drilled and accumulated supplies while they waited for him.[13] The Indians had been forced to yield ground under pressure from Miles and Price, and Davidson, whose Tenth Cavalry forces were finally able to take to the field on September 10, closed the ring. Davidson's object was "to meet Col. McKenzie, driving toward him any Indians in this part of the country, or catching those he might drive towards me."[14] Hemmed in from three sides, the majority of the Indians converged on Palo Duro Canyon, where they settled into a winter encampment that stretched for miles. Unfortunately for them, their encampment was in Mackenzie's line of march.

Mackenzie rejoined his column and, on September 17, began moving it north along the base of the caprock. One set of trails had been reported going north toward the head of the Pease River, and for four days the Seminole-Negro scouts had followed another set in the same general area. On the night of September 19 Mackenzie sent out a scouting party. At 6:15 A.M. the following day he marched out the command in column, ascending Quitaque Canyon until it emerged onto the plains. The troops were eating lunch when the scouts rode in to report they had been in a fight with about twenty

Indians. A lieutenant and some Seminole-Negro scouts were sent in unsuccessful pursuit.[15]

The Indians now knew soldiers were in the area, and every precaution against attack was taken by the troops. "A Commander against hostile Indians is never in such imminent danger as when fully satisfied that no Indians can possibly be near him," General Augur had cautioned, in a warning well-recognized by Mackenzie. Boehm was sent out, reporting back that he had found the trail of a hunting party coming from the north. The command marched in that general direction, while McLaughlen was sent to pick up the trail made by the Indians who had attacked the scouts.[16]

The troops remained in camp all day September 22, waiting for McLaughlen to return and for bad weather to subside. A storm had hit the night before, with torrents of rain and lightning like "sheets of flame." The supply train was mired in mud eight miles behind, although Lawton did manage to get one wagon through by hitching twelve mules to it. On September 24, when a wet norther blew in, the cold and miserable troops bogged down. The column did not get moving again until 4:00 P.M. and made only three miles before the order was given to halt for the night. There was better progress the following day, and the troops covered about twenty miles before the column camped at the head of Tule Canyon. McLaughlen had returned to report he had made contact with the hostiles but had lost them at nightfall. More parties were sent out. Thompson reported he had seen a large number of trails, while Strong reported seeing three Indians with a herd of about 150 horses.[17]

The next day scouts were sent out to look for the main body of Indians. Although the troops moved a few miles for better access to water, no major march was undertaken.

Mackenzie seemed to be waiting either for more information on the hostile camps or for the Indians to make the first move. That night the horses were hobbled to prevent stampede, and the troops bedded down in skirmish line. The moon was bright, and Lieutenant Charles Hatfield found he could read a copy of the New York *Herald* in the light. At about 10:15 P.M. the Indians attacked the camp.[18]

Company A took the main assault as the Indians tried to charge through and stampede the horses, but the troopers threw them back even before the other companies arrived in support. Their advance broken, the Indians withdrew to some breaks about three hundred yards away and maintained a continuous fire into the camp all night, continuing at dawn with long range fire from high points around the area. Mackenzie ordered Boehm's Company E to counterattack, and a running fight ensued for about three miles.

"The sun, rising in our rear, seemed to light up the entire line of hostiles, in their full dress of gaudy paint and feathers as they turned in their saddles to fire at us, scurrying across the prairie in rapid flight," Hatfield remembered some forty years later. "I recollect well saying to myself; now look and take it all in, for with the rapid advance of civilization and settlement on the frontier, the like of this I will never see again."[19]

Thompson's scouts, sweeping up from the flanks, spotted a Comanche warrior riding up the side of an arroyo. A Seminole-Negro jumped off his horse, leveled his carbine and killed the Indian's horse, then a Tonkawa rode the Comanche down and fired his revolver into his head from such close range that the powder burned his skin. Even in death the warrior drew admiration. A correspondent for the New York *Herald* said he was "one of the finest looking fellows" he had ever seen, while Hatfield called him "a handsome fellow in a gorgeous head dress." Mackenzie, more concerned with success of the expedition than with poetic imagery, simply referred to him as "one Indian (whose body fell into our hands)." Pursuit was broken off when the Indians disappeared in the distance, "as completely as if the ground had swallowed them." It was later learned that as many as fifteen Indians had been killed, although presumably other bodies were recovered by their comrades. The only army casualties were three horses wounded during the night firing.[20]

Mackenzie rested his men until 3:00 P.M. when he broke camp and resumed the march. A large trail was located, but lost again after the sun set. Finally, at 2:00 A.M., he gave up and allowed his exhausted troops some rest. The scouts were in the worst shape of all, having neither eaten nor slept for over twenty-four hours.[21]

They were now very close to the main Indian encampment in Palo Duro Canyon. Exactly how it was discovered is a matter of conjecture—Mackenzie credits it to following the large trail, while Hatfield said the camp was located by Johnson. However it has also been suggested that Mackenzie learned of the location from José Piedad Tafoya, a notorious Comanchero he had captured who, on interrogation, first pretended to know nothing about a main camp. When Mackenzie had him hanged from an upright wagon tongue until he almost strangled, the Comanchero discovered plenty to say. The incident, of course, would not appear in any official report which might have left Mackenzie open to charges. The officers would also keep silent about it, to avoid accusations of complicity. Mackenzie, however, later told Sheridan about "an arrangement with Jose Piedad, a Mexican Indian Trader," although he said he had made the arrangement in December.[22]

Regardless of how they learned of its location, they were now aware that the camp was in a canyon in the vicinity. Sergeant Charlton, Johnson and Job, another Tonkawa, located the trail and followed it for several miles before spotting other trails—all fresh—converging on this main one. They followed it across the totally flat terrain until the vast chasm of Palo Duro Canyon suddenly yawned in front of them. Job stayed with the horses while Charlton and Johnson crept on hands and knees to the edge, from which they could make out the dark shapes of hundreds of horses grazing on the open canyon floor, and tepis as far as the eye could see.

"Heap Injun!" Johnson grunted.

"You bet your life, old scout, and some canyon, too," Charlton whispered. They backed away and went for their horses.[23]

Meanwhile, Mackenzie had resumed the march at 4:00 A.M. from his camp about four miles from the canyon. At daybreak the troops stood looking down on the scene Charlton had reported. "Lor' men, look a de sheep and de goats down dar!" one of the Seminole-Negroes exclaimed, mistaking the horses for livestock from the great height.

Three bands of Indians had gathered together where Canyon Cita Blanca opens into Palo Duro: O-ha-ma-tai's Comanches; a small group of Southern Cheyennes under Iron Shirt; and Kiowas led by Maman-ti. The Indian camps covered about two miles, bisected by the thin little stream which forms the headwaters of the Prairie Dog Fork of the Red River. The Comanches were camped at the juncture of Cita Creek and the main stream, the Cheyennes by the main stream, and the Kiowas a good distance beyond. The succession of small campsites, of about fifteen or twenty tepis each, totaled about two hundred lodges. No one stirred, for Maman-ti had assured

THE BATTLE OF PALO DURO CANYON
SEPTEMBER 26, 1874

ONE OF THE MOST SIGNIFICANT BATTLES OF 1874-75 INDIAN CAMPAIGN. COLUMNS OF TROOPS CONVERGING FROM FIVE DIRECTIONS HARASSED INDIANS ON THE PANHANDLE PLAINS FOR OVER SIX MONTHS.

THE 4TH CAVALRY UNDER COL. RANALD S. MACKENZIE, MOVING NORTH FROM FORT CONCHO, TRACKED A LARGE BAND OF INDIANS TO THEIR SECRET CANYON CAMP.

MOVING SILENTLY AT DAWN DOWN A PERILOUS PATH ON THE SOUTH RIM, THE FIRST TROOPS REACHED THE FLOOR OF THE CANYON BEFORE THE AROUSED CAMP FLED.

SOME OF THE WARRIORS TOOK UP POSITIONS ON THE CANYON WALLS FROM WHICH THEY FIRED ON THE TROOPS, SEEKING TO GIVE THEIR FAMILIES TIME TO ESCAPE.

REALIZING HIS TACTICAL DISADVANTAGE, MACKENZIE ORDERED THE INDIAN CAMP AND SUPPLIES BURNED AND WITHDREW, TAKING ALONG 1,400 CAPTURED HORSES (1,000 OF WHICH HE LATER DESTROYED).

THE CAVALRY SUFFERED NO CASUALTIES IN THE FIGHT AND ONLY FOUR INDIAN DEAD WERE COUNTED.

HAVING LOST HALF THEIR HORSES AS WELL AS ALL THEIR SUPPLIES AND SHELTER, THE INDIANS DRIFTED BACK TO THEIR RESERVATIONS AT FORT SILL AND FORT RENO.
(1967)

Palo Duro Historical Marker
(Author photo)

Palo Duro Canyon *(Author photo)*

them that as long as they were in the canyon, they were safe from the soldiers.[24]

Mackenzie had located the camp, but the question remained of how to reach it. The canyon, about half a mile wide at this point, had sheer walls dropping over five hundred feet with little evidence, from where the soldiers stood, of any descending trail. To Hatfield, the depths looked "very black." A fifteen-minute search along the edge located a trail which the *Herald* correspondent said was "such as a goat could hardly travel."[25]

"Mr. Thompson," Mackenzie said to the chief of Scouts, "take your men down and open the fight."

First Battalion was ordered to remain on the top, while Second Battalion and the scouts dismounted and started down. Men and horses zig-zagged down the path in single file, slipping and stumbling as they went. They had gone about 150 yards when an Indian sentry spotted them, let out a whoop which echoed off the far walls, fired his rifle, waved his blanket and disappeared into the dark vastness of the canyon.

Incredibly, the Indians bedded down on the canyon floor seemed to take no notice, not stirring even when more shots rang out. When the soldiers hit, panic seized the first camps. "As far as the eye could see in the fast coming light, Indians were mounting their ponies and hurrying up the canyon," Hatfield wrote. One woman even tried to throw away the baby strapped on her back, so that she could run faster.[26]

Mackenzie's men made remarkable time to the floor of the canyon. The scouts and the two companies he had ordered to attack as soon as they reached the bottom remounted their horses and rode into the first camp. The canyon floor was still dark, smoke from the rifles further obscured vision, and many Indians fled to cover within the canyon walls. Two more companies formed line abreast and, with Mackenzie in the lead, charged in support of the first two. First Battalion was waved down from the heights.

"As we galloped along we passed village after village of Indian lodges both on the right and left, all empty and totally abandoned," Carter recalled.

The ground was strewn with buffalo robes, blankets, and every imaginable thing, in fact, that the

Indians had in the way of property—all of which had been hastily collected and a vain attempt made by the squaws to gather up and save, but finding the troops coming up so rapidly they were forced to drop their goods and chattels and suddenly take to the almost inaccessible sides of the Cañon to save themselves from capture.[27]

Moving through the camp, the soldiers found two letters of safe conduct issued by Agent Haworth at Fort Sill. One vouched for the conduct of a Kosoteka Comanche named Long Hungry. The other noted that a Kiowa named Wah-Lung was registered with the agency and asked that he not be molested unless engaged in hostilities. The letters confirmed the involvement of agency Indians, as did large amounts of government flour, sugar and other goods.[28]

As the battle continued beyond the camps, Companies H and L rode about two miles up the canyon, where they encountered Company A of the first wave returning with almost all of the Indians' pony herd. Halting and forming a line while awaiting orders, the two companies were exposed to withering fire from both sides of the canyon walls. The soldiers dismounted and dug in. One company's trumpeter received a near-fatal bullet wound, and six or eight horses were shot. Finally, Captain Sebastian Gunther ordered a squad from Company H up the walls to clear them, and the troopers had already started to move out when Mackenzie spotted them.

"Sergeant," he called to the noncommissioned in charge, "where are you going with those men?"

"To clear the bluff, sir!"

"By whose orders?"

"Captain Gunther's!"

"Take those men back to their company. Not one of them would live to reach the top," Mackenzie ordered, and rode over to tell Gunther he had countermanded the order.

In another incident, a horse assigned to a Private McGowan was shot down. Ignoring the bullets flying all around him, McGowan started rummaging through his gear.

"McGowan, get away from there or you will be hit," Mackenzie ordered.

"Yes, Sir!" came the reply, but as soon as Mackenzie wasn't looking, he started into his gear again. Twice more Mackenzie repeated the order. The third time he lost his temper.

"I told you to go away from there, are you going?" he demanded.

"D—d if I am until I get my tobacco and ammunition," McGowan replied. Mackenzie gave up and let him alone.[29]

In the midst of the smoke and noise, the captured ponies panicked and ran back and forth trying to escape, but each time they found an exit a soldier would shoot the leader to turn them. Meanwhile, the Indian warriors fought desperately, trying to cover the retreat of the women and pack animals but, under the unyielding pressure of the soldiers, had to fall back. Finally, they were forced out into the open, along the edge of the Prairie Dog Fork. The troops followed but were fired upon by snipers from the trees on each side. Now surrounded, it appeared the tables had turned on the soldiers.

"How will we ever get out of here?" one trooper asked.

"I brought you in. I will take you out!" Mackenzie snapped, and the line held. The Indians continued to withdraw but, as the fighting died down, Mackenzie noticed a band of Indians on the top of the bluff, heading toward the trail down which the soldiers had entered the canyon. Guessing they intended to cut them off, he ordered Gunther's company back to the top to hold it. The two forces raced for the spot, but Gunther got there first and secured it.[30]

By early afternoon the Indians had recovered from the initial shock and began to move back down the canyon. When three companies blocked them they settled behind some natural barriers, and skirmishing continued for several hours. Mackenzie considered the soldiers more "annoyed" by the gunfire than threatened by it. Finally he sent a detail on foot to overrun the barriers and put a stop to the sniping, while the majority of the soldiers set to work destroying the camps. As the soldiers demolished and burned, the Tonkawas and their women were allowed to loot whatever they wanted. One Tonkawa woman ran across a wounded Indian who asked for help in her language, but she killed him without hesitation. About 3:00 P.M. the destruction of the camp was finished, and Mackenzie ordered everyone back to the top.[31]

The soldiers, with almost two thousand captured ponies, now faced a long march back to their bivouac in Tule Canyon. They formed themselves into a large square with the ponies in the middle. "It was a living corral and our march was nearly 20 miles," Carter wrote.

The scouts, who had been on the move for forty-eight hours, were exhausted and began to doze off in their saddles. Charlton went to sleep only to find Mackenzie's hand shaking him by the shoulder. "Wake up, Sergeant," he ordered. "Wake up your men and look after the horses!"

The command finally reached Tule Canyon early the next morning, where Mackenzie made a decision on the captured ponies. Determined not to make the same mistake he had made at McClellan Creek, he separated all mules in the herd and allowed the scouts to cut out several hundred of the best ponies. The rest, about 1,450, were killed. For many years afterwards, the site was marked by piles of their bones.[32]

CHAPTER 12

"There Will Be Very Great Suffering among the Indians Near this Post"

As often happened after he achieved an objective, Mackenzie suffered an emotional letdown. It sometimes seemed he functioned best only when under severe stress, becoming increasingly nervous and irritable—and perhaps even irrational—once the situation stabilized. The aftermath of the Palo Duro Canyon fight was no exception, and Sergeant Charlton suffered the effects the day after the fight when Mackenzie ordered him to report himself under arrest.

"You are in arrest for disobedience of orders," Mackenzie told him. "You did not stop yesterday when I called you back."

"But we were fighting, General," Charlton protested.

"That will do," Mackenzie snapped. "Report to Lieutenant Thompson at once and in arrest." Within a couple of hours, however, Mackenzie let the matter drop.[1]

As the expedition moved across the plains to mop up, it discovered cart trails presumably left by Comancheros. Six carts loaded with dried meat were found on October 7, and the following day five men were overtaken with another cart, this one empty. Initially the men fled, but two returned. Mackenzie, determining the cart had been used to run contraband to the Indians, ordered it destroyed and the stock divided among the companies. A few days later the column came across an old campsite which Mackenzie later learned had been used by Colonel Miles. On October 14, as the command was about to go into camp, some Indians were seen in the distance. They were chased and "three broken down horses" captured. Thompson and his scouts kept on their trail and reported they were going north.[2]

The Indians no longer had a clear sense of purpose. As had been anticipated, Miles, Price, Davidson and Buell had driven them into Mackenzie's forces which, in turn, had thrown them back on Miles and the others. On October 29 Sheridan reported the pressure gave the Indians "no opportunity or security to kill game or get food for their families, grazing for their stock, or safety for their lives, so their *[sic]* are now being captured or surrendering unconditionally and there is a fair prospect of a close of our labors before long." Davidson noted, "The country from Fort Sill to the Staked Plains is swept of Indians."[3]

Although the uprising was almost over, the pressure of the campaign was beginning to tell on the military units in the field as well. Mackenzie's train had broken down and he was forming teams from captured mules; his horses were exhausted and frequent stops had to be made to rest and graze them. One of the companies of infantry with the Southern Column had marched over most of West Texas and was worn out. Its commanding officer's request to be exchanged for a fresh company was approved.[4]

On November 3 a small camp was taken, two warriors killed and nineteen women and children taken into custody. Two days later Thompson and his scouts surprised three more Indians guarding a herd of ponies. Again two were killed but the third escaped. From the women captured in the first fight, Mackenzie learned "that the Plains Indians are much frightened, and that even these Staked Plains Bands of Quohadis *[sic]* were going to the Reserve in a few days." To hurry them along and round up any recalcitrants, Mackenzie apparently made a deal with José Piedad Tafoya, the Comanchero. Tafoya was to return to New Mexico in the spring and form a new Comanchero expedition to trade with the Quahadis, then he would inform the army of their whereabouts so Mackenzie could strike.

For now, though, little could be done. Forage for the horses had not been adequate, and he did not expect them to last much longer. He would do the best he could "as long as they will last, and try to get as many through as possible." However he had already lost forty-four and needed about two hundred remounts.[5]

As usual Mackenzie suspected "someone must be much to blame" for the forage problem, since he had made his requirements known from the outset, but the army's supply procedures were simply not adequate to support the requirements of a mobile field force. Winter was setting in with its accompanying rain and mud. It was hard, and often impossible, to keep enough forage at the bases at Fort Concho and Fort Griffin, much less to support a fast-moving unit of cavalry.[6] This was a problem that plagued the army on all of its winter campaigns against hostile Indians, and one which Mackenzie would encounter two years later as part of Brigadier General George Crook's Powder River Expedition.

Burdened with broken down horses and exhausted men, Mackenzie realized he could do no more and wrote Augur asking that they be relieved. At the same time, however, he requested fresh troops in hopes for a winter campaign. His belief that he could catch the Quahadis received encouragement when a party under Lieutenant Lewis Warrington, Fourth Cavalry, skirmished with Indians on December 8. General Augur did not share his sense of mission, however, and ordered the expedition broken up. Units were returned to their posts, and Mackenzie was back at Fort Concho by late December.[7]

During the next several months as the Red River War wound down, Phil Sheridan found himself faced with a new set of problems. The separate military division in the South had been abolished and the Gulf Coast states (excepting Texas) reorganized as the Department of the Gulf. Within the new department, Louisiana was seething in Reconstruction hatreds. Political murders were rampant. Sheridan, a hard-line Reconstructionist who saw conspiracy and rebellion at every turn, was ready to grasp at any means, however nefarious, to put the state under direct military rule. On January 4, 1875, the Department of the Gulf was annexed to the Division of the Missouri, giving him a free hand. He had little confidence in Colonel William H. Emory, the departmental commander, and was determined to replace him with someone more decisive.[8] Mackenzie was his choice.

But Sheridan could only go so far in getting his way. The War Department balked at Mackenzie's youth and lack of seniority. In February Sheridan withdrew his request and nominated General Augur, who assumed command on March 27 and was replaced in the Department of Texas by Major General Edward O. C. Ord.[9] During Mackenzie's absence on leave in Washington, the Fourth was placed under the Department of Missouri and transferred to Fort Sill, which was designated Mackenzie's headquarters as commander of the entire western section of the Indian Territory.

Nelson Miles was furious. If the entire region was to be under a single command, he thought it should be his. He convinced General John Pope, departmental commander, that at a minimum the command should be divided between Mackenzie, to be given the posts at the agencies, and himself to command Camp Supply and the cantonments in the field. Mackenzie lost no time in protesting to Sheridan. From a purely military standpoint, he felt the divided command was a bad idea.

> If I simply have control of the Posts at Agencies, I will not be able to go into the field promptly and I will not have the men under my command to go with and will soon be held in no respect by the Indians. It is essential that the cantonements [sic] should be under the Control of the Commanding Officer here, and Camp Supply also should be in operations in this department.

That said, he vented his fury on Miles. Stating that he regarded Miles as "a very fine officer" and that no jealousy existed, Mackenzie nevertheless added, "I regard him not as my Superior in any way and in some particulars I am sure he is not my equal." If Mackenzie could not have total authority, he said, he would prefer to let Miles "or some other man have it," rather than to share it.

It was an inconsistent letter, see-sawing back and forth between military matters and his opinions of Miles. Mackenzie, like his men, was exhausted. Both he and they needed a rest, and he felt they could best get it by occupation of and administrative duties in the Indian Territory. He even went so far as to admit that the letter was being dictated, since writing was becoming difficult.[10]

As usual, Sheridan sustained Mackenzie and left him in charge of the western section. By now the hostile bands were coming in and surrendering their arms and ponies on a regular basis. Leaders were separated and imprisoned. When the government decided that the principal chiefs would be transported to prison at Fort Marion, Florida, Lieutenant Richard Henry Pratt, Tenth Cavalry, was given the task and prevailed on Kicking Bird to help make the selections, an involvement which was to cost Kicking Bird his life. The medicine man Maman-ti, one of those designated for transportation, placed a death spell on him. On May 4 Kicking Bird was assassinated by poison, probably in his morning coffee.

Initially Pratt was to take the prisoners as far as Fort Leavenworth but, shortly before they left on April 28, Mackenzie informed Mrs. Pratt that her husband would likely be placed in permanent charge of the prisoners once they reached Florida. He was correct.[11]

Meanwhile the Quahadi Chief Mow-way, the Kosoteka Long Hungry, and Wild Horse surrendered, accepting an invitation Colonel Davidson had sent before turning command over to Mackenzie. But many of the band were still out on the plains. Mackenzie hoped to bring them in of their own accord, without mounting an expedition, and sent Dr. J.J. Sturms to find them. Sturms, one of the Comanche interpreters used by the army on a regular basis, was married to an Indian and was respected by both Indians and soldiers. If he failed, four companies of cavalry were kept ready to go out and get them.[12]

Sturms found the Quahadis hunting out on the plains. During the negotiations which followed, Quanah Parker promised to bring them in after the hunt was completed. By May 15 Mackenzie was able to report, "Unless something unforseen [sic] takes place the entire Qua-ha-des Band will come in and their intention is I am confident to give up in good faith." Quanah kept that faith. On June 2 he led his people to Fort Sill, where they surrendered their weapons and 1,400 ponies. The Red River War was over. The days of Kiowa and Comanche military power were gone forever.[13]

In Darlington things were not going as well. Initially the Cheyennes had settled in at the agency and, by mid-March, were cooperative enough to be allowed to go hunting. At the same time, however, the leaders of the hostile faction were being rounded up quietly, placed in irons and confined. On April 6 one young warrior was being ironed when he broke loose and was shot down in his attempt to escape. Some of the shots went into the camp, from which the Indians returned fire. Many of the Cheyennes bolted, and those out hunting refused to return. A minor campaign ensued, ending on April 23 at Sappa Creek in northern Kansas where units of the Sixth Cavalry overwhelmed an Indian camp. Mackenzie had to post more of his units near Darlington to keep the Indians there under control.[14]

The administration of the western section of the Indian Territory brought wider responsibilities to Mackenzie. Aside from the cantonments, forts and agencies, he was also given control over the northernmost portion of the Texas Panhandle. Here on the Sweetwater, his command founded a cantonment which ultimately became Fort Elliott. With the establishment of Elliott, the southern plains tribes found themselves completely ringed with garrisons.

Mackenzie was also occupied with the administration required to obtain Medals of Honor for seven troopers of the Fourth and for Adam Paine, a Seminole-Negro scout, for valor during the campaign. These were finally approved by the Secretary of War on October 19, 1875.[15]

Occasionally Mackenzie found time to relax and, as usual, he spent his spare time hunting with his foxhounds. The hounds lived in the yard of his quarters at Fort Sill under the care of Private Strobel, a tough, no-nonsense Russian with definite strains of Mongol. Mackenzie and Strobel trained the hounds to hunt wildcats and bears, and they were severely punished if they chased anything else. During one hunt the baying hounds led the hunters on a long chase through rough country and heavy brush. Finally the riders caught up to the pack, which had cornered a group of feral hogs. "The rage of Strobel and the General was frightful!" one of Mackenzie's hunting companions wrote. "In the end the hounds suffered almost as much as the pigs!"[16]

On duty, Mackenzie's greatest problems were white horse thieves and inadequate food supplies for Indians interned at Sill. Discussing the former, Lieutenant James Parker, Fourth Cavalry, noted, "The ordinary horse thief who stole from whites generally received short shift; but Indian ponies were considered by the Texans fair game, whether taken from friendly or hostile Indians."[17] The troopers who followed the horse thieves into Texas got very little sympathy from civil authorities. On one occasion Parker was arrested in Denison after an altercation with some Texas cowboys over stolen ponies.[18]

Far more serious was the shortage of food. During one of Mackenzie's absences from Fort Sill, when the Indians complained about short rations, Lieutenant Colonel John Hatch, Fourth Cavalry, temporarily in command, investigated the situation and found the complaints well founded. In a report to General Pope he wrote, "This ration was established when

Mackenzie in mid-1870s
(top: Amon Carter Museum of Western Art)
(bottom: US Army Military History Institute)

the Indian could partly support himself by hunting." Now, however, the buffalo were being hunted out, and were no longer within easy distance of the agencies. Without the supplement from the hunt, the ration was not enough to prevent hunger. To make matters worse, even the short ration was not being issued in full. "There is at the agency no flour, and not over one-third the authorized amount has been issued during the present year," Hatch reported. "The beef lately issued has been shamefully bad. It is so poor that the gross is altogether out of proportion to the net weight."

Agent Haworth was absent. The acting agent told Hatch "that the beef lately issued was unfit for food. . .that was all he had for them." To remedy this Hatch, backed by Pope, ordered the Indians supplied with full rations from the post commissary. Endorsing Hatch's report to authorities in Chicago and Washington, Pope noted:

> It is idle to expect that these Indians will remain peaceably upon their reservations with the prospect of starvation in doing so. So long as this maladministration of affairs with these Indians exists the military authorities cannot be, and will not consent to be, held accountable for any outbreak which may occur. . . .[19]

Hatch's report, reflecting adversely on the Indian Bureau and the Quaker administration of the agencies, was published in the New York *Times*. In an effort to defend himself, Haworth sent his own version to Enoch Hoag, superintendent of agencies in Lawrence, Kansas, contending the Indians had been given beef "much in excess of regular rations, such a course being necessary to prevent actual suffering." He blamed their suffering, in part, on the Indian taste for buffalo, saying they could not do as well on any other kind of meat. Bacon, coffee and tobacco rations had been adequate. He acknowledged flour and sugar were short, but said the same freight conductor had both the military and agency contracts, and gave the military priority. This, in turn, created a backlog because of the large number of military installations in the territory which required supplies.[20] This letter also found its way into the *Times*, but the food situation grew steadily worse. At the overloaded Wichita Agency, where Agent Jonathan Richards had three thousand to feed, the Indians were reduced to gathering corn left in the sand after the horses were fed.[21] By the end of summer the situation in the Territory had become critical, and Mackenzie wrote Pope from Fort Sill, "I have to state that it seems very probably that there will be very great suffering among the Indians near this Post during the coming Winter unless more energy than has been recently manifested by the Interior Department can be put forth."

He pointed out that, although the weather had been good for wagon transportation during the summer, no effort had been made to deliver adequate supplies. Now there were only two months left before winter made the roads impassable. As Mackenzie saw it, Haworth was doing the best he could with the supplies on hand, but both the Indians and their agent were being failed by "some higher authority whom I do not know. . . . Can not the Interior Dept. be induced to adopt such measures as will bring their supplies here without fail [?]," he asked. As matters stood, he believed it would be useless for troops to try to control the Indians during the coming winter unless the basic needs of the Indians were met.[22]

Frustrated with the system, Mackenzie took such action as he could. Soldiers were sent to build houses for the Indians, and he continued to issue rations from military stores despite objections from the Indian Bureau. Although the bureau insisted that the tribes be taught to farm, Mackenzie knew the area was better suited for stock raising, so he bought cattle and sheep for the Indians out of his own money. As Parker noted:

> The Indians had faith in Mackenzie; they knew by his acts that he was continually endeavoring to better their condition, to make "the white man's road" of peaceful effort more acceptable. They knew he was watching the Indian agent, that he was striving with the Government at Washington to obtain them more food, clothing, comforts . . . .

They also knew that this was the man who had hunted them relentlessly. While they might have marvelled at his compassion, their admiration was tinged with fear.[23]

During his struggle to obtain adequate rations, Mackenzie suffered a near-fatal accident when he landed on his head after being thrown from a wagon. According to Dorst, "He was in a half stupor for two or three days, and it has since been learned that his mind was not entirely clear for several months."[24]

While Mackenzie slowly recovered, the War Department became increasingly frustrated with the Indian Bureau and attempted to obtain jurisdiction over it from the Department of Interior. Faced with this threat to its lucrative operation, the Indian Ring retaliated. An agent from the Board of Indian Commissioners was sent to Fort Sill and duly reported that the post:

is a sort of young Sodom, and the garrison is mostly made up of men who neither fear God nor regard man. On their grounds they have built a neat stone chapel, and it has not been used for any other purpose than a theatre and a dance hall. Drunkenness is prevalent. Evans [J.S. Evans, post trader] takes in over his bar from $200 to $300 each day, and on pay days a much larger sum.

The agent added the Indians feared the soldiers, and that the reservation should be removed "a good distance" from the military.[25]

When this letter was also published in the *Times*, the criticism of his command was too much for Mackenzie. While he had very little love or respect for individual troopers, he saw the attack on the garrison as a whole as an attack on himself as commander. In a letter of his own to the *Times*, he wrote:

Broadly, the [agent's] letter in all its spirit and inference is not true, with, some instances, just enough fact, curiously garbled, to furnish a sandy foundation. This command is not depraved or bad. I am not in favor of drunkenness or disorder, or opposed to the Christian religion. I have requested, therefore, a careful investigation of this matter, and that some one be punished, either myself or the official who wrote the communication and those who gave his statements to the press. Some one ought to be punished, for either I am a very poor officer or those other people are bad men.[26]

The request for the investigation went through channels until it reached Sherman, who had little use for newspapers. He referred the matter to the House Committee on Military Affairs, noting that he did not want his officers involved "in a newspaper controversy, because those who prepare these slips will simple repeat their inventions *ad infinitum.*" As for Mackenzie, Sherman said he was "too good an officer to be damaged in reputation by anonymous flings."[27]

The Indian Ring had good reason to be fearful, since it could no longer depend on Belknap to defend its interests. The officer corps, long disgusted with the secretary of war, finally found allies in congress. Sherman added fuel to the fire when he moved army headquarters from Washington to St. Louis to escape what he considered official and social corruption in the capital. When a series of exposés on Belknap's administration appeared in the New York *Herald,* the House Committee on Expenditures in the War Department began an investigation of Belknap.[28]

The investigation, chaired by Representative Heister Clymer, a Pennsylvania Democrat, concentrated on post traderships and army contracts. Old allegations were examined. Colonel William B. Hazen sent a deposition on the sale of the post tradership at Fort Sill. Mackenzie's earlier dispute with Colonel Reynolds, over the substandard corn delivered to Fort McKavett, was revived and testimony given by Lieutenant Colonel Alexander McCook, of Sherman's staff, and Lieutenant Robert Carter of the Fourth. Sherman, whose first loyalty was to the service, issued a perfunctory statement that he was "confident that Gen'l Reynolds will make a satisfactory explanation." Meanwhile Reynolds began a smear campaign, accusing McCook of giving false testimony to the Clymer committee.

Already sick with malaria, Mackenzie was infuriated by Reynolds and hurt by Sherman's support of Reynolds. He even wrote a letter lecturing the general-in-chief on what he felt to be improper statements.

> You must bear in mind General that with your personal character and reputation reaching everywhere, a word from you blaring hardly on me should not appear in print without better reasons than I believe myself to have been given you. I am in a difficult position, having no wish to bring into point matters which had best be otherwise settled, and having done all my duty in the premises a long time ago. . . . I have nothing in the world to care for except the respect of respectable people, and I cannot let that be taken away. By careful investigation by you of all the facts [it] would convince you that Col. Reynolds was a bad officer.[29]

A few week later he wrote Sherman again, saying, "Col. Reynolds should not to my mind be permitted to telegraph or write what he pleases uncontradicted concerning this old matter. . . ." Referring to the old court-martial proceedings which Reynolds had initiated against him, Mackenzie said, "Col. Reynolds. . . allowed me to go into the field. I was wounded, kept on with my command and was taken very ill. And then on my return these charges were placed against me."[30]

Amid this furor, the fortunes of war once again intervened on Mackenzie's behalf. In the Northern Plains the government decided to force the Sioux onto reservations; the Sioux resisted and a war ensued. Reynolds blundered during one engagement and charges were preferred against him by Brigadier General George Crook, commanding officer of the Department of the Platte. Mackenzie's old enemy was found guilty of misbehavior before the enemy and suspended from rank and command for one year.[31] In Washington, Secretary Belknap resigned to avoid impeachment.

Back in Texas, renewed raids from Mexico brought public pressure for Mackenzie's return. As Texas Adjutant General William Steele wrote to Senator Sam Bell Maxey, "Genl McKenzie is well known to our people and highly esteemed for his activity; and his action in crossing the Rio Grande after robbers has made him more popular in Texas than any other officer of the U.S. Army." Governor Richard Coke concurred, and Maxey referred the request to the War Department.

Sherman did not concur. He sent back the request with a single sentence: "Genl. Mackenzie is protecting the frontier of Texas better where he is than he could be serving in that Department."[32]

Although Sherman did not anticipate it at the moment, Mackenzie was about to be transferred again. This time he would fight the northern tribes in a bitter winter campaign.

CHAPTER 13

"The Embodiment of Courage, Skill and Dash"

As Mackenzie fretted over service politics at Fort Sill, an event occurred on the Northern Plains which again changed the face of the Indian Wars. On June 25, 1876, Lieutenant Colonel George A. Custer and five companies of the Seventh Cavalry were massacred by Sioux and Cheyenne at the Little Bighorn. The remaining combat units of the regiment, under Major Marcus Reno, were badly mauled.

The United States Army had been thoroughly humiliated. It was one thing to be defeated by British regulars or by superbly led Confederates in battles on equal terms against comparable powers. But the Little Bighorn forces, a major field expedition highly organized and well-equipped, had been brought to a standstill and one-third of its power annihilated by native tribesmen.

The Sioux Nation was composed of many individual bands, some very large. Taken together the Sioux were a powerful nation, perhaps the greatest single indigenous people north of Mexico. Their initial contacts with whites had been peaceful but, as settlement moved westward, relations grew strained. Unfair treaties and corrupt annuities systems contributed to an increase in incidents.[1]

In 1854 a misunderstanding between Indians and a rash young lieutenant led to the slaughter of an entire military detail near Fort Laramie, Wyoming. Although the officers at Laramie testified that the lieutenant, John L. Grattan, had been responsible, the government and the eastern press demanded retribution. The following year Colonel W.S. Harney retaliated by attacking a peaceful band of Sioux at Ash Hollow, on a branch of the North Platte.[2] Railroad construction and the establishment of the Bozeman Trail across Sioux lands infuriated the Indians,[3] and the United States found itself in a war which would last almost forty years.

The conflict was not continuous. After the war factions of the Northern Plains tribes, led by the great war chief Red Cloud among others, fought the federal government to a draw in 1868, the Northern Plains were quiet. In 1874, however, Custer led an expedition into the Black Hills, sacred to the Sioux and protected by treaty, where he found minute bits of gold. The region's newspapers publicized the find as a major strike, and the hills flooded with prospectors.[4] The Sioux tolerated these incursions for two years while President Grant and the War Department plotted a means to provoke a war, make the Sioux appear responsible, and expropriate the Black Hills and other Indian lands. In December 1875 the Grant Administration ordered all Sioux to the agencies, even though many bands were wandering over lands which had been recognized as theirs by treaty. When the deadline expired, those who had not reported to their agencies were declared hostile and the army was mobilized to subdue them.[5]

The early part of the U.S. military campaign was a series of mismanaged blunders, one of which resulted in Reynolds' court-martial. On June 17, 1876, after Crook suffered a tactical defeat at the hands of the Sioux and Cheyennes on the Rosebud, he abandoned his supply train to travel more rapidly and chased the Indians throughout the entire region. After the

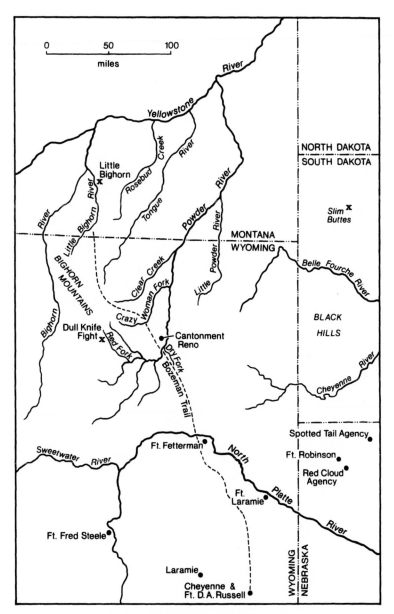

Eastern Wyoming and Montana

Little Bighorn, public opinion demanded retribution for the Custer disaster. All Indians within the war zone were removed from the authority of the Department of the Interior and placed under the War Department. Troops were pulled into the theater from throughout the entire Military Division of the Missouri, among them the Fourth Cavalry.

In August Mackenzie was ordered to Fort Robinson, Nebraska, to command the District of the Black Hills. As usual the move brought administrative problems. His troops were scattered all over the Indian Territory when the order was received, and they had to be reassembled. He started off the first two companies, then went to Chicago to confer with Sheridan. Among other matters, he requested that his men be armed with Winchester repeating rifles in place of the standard-issue, single-shot Springfield carbines.

Mackenzie first ordered his troops to wait for him at the railhead in Cheyenne, then changed his mind. "On arrival at Cheyenne, move so soon as you can get your horses off the cars and your wagons loaded, out on the Laramie road, telegraphing for instructions to the A.A.G. at Omaha," he wrote his adjutant. "Get to Laramie as soon as you properly can, taking the greatest care to have your horses and mules in good order."[6]

The movement of his companies entailed many personnel actions involving the troops and their families, such as this letter to a company commander:

> The Regimental Commander directs that you issue a Company Order reducing Blacksmith Brees to Private to enable him to be detailed on extra duty to obtain the advantages of extra duty pay for his family.

This man will continue to shoe the Horses for Company "I", and will go with the Company wherever it may be ordered.[7]

And to the divisional adjutant in Chicago:

A Mrs. Boland, wife of Trumpeter James J. Boland, Company "I", 4th Cavalry, arrived here on the 7th, inst. from Cheyenne, W.T., having been furnished transportation from St. Louis, Mo. to that place.

I request, that no more women be permitted to come to the companies of this Regiment, temporarily in the Department of the Platte, or during the Sioux troubles. And that the Commanding Officer of the post of D.A. Russell [Fort D.A. Russell at Cheyenne] be directed in case any should by accident reach that post, to send them to Sill. I have no means of having the wives of soldiers properly cared for in this Department, at present.[8]

Always there was the touchy subject of Mackenzie's personal honor. His simple request for Winchester rifles led to some sort of slight, real or imagined, from the Bureau of Ordnance, and caused him to write the Adjutant General in Washington.

I have the honor to object to the manner in which my name is used by the Chief of Ordnance in a recent Ordnance note, No. LVI, dated August 17th. 1876, and to state that the defects as noted by Captain Reilly i.e. inaccuracy and short range were not the grounds of my objection, and that the experiments which Colonel Benton [Lieutenant Colonel J.B. Benton, commander of the Springfield Arsenal] superintended do not bear in any way, directly or indirectly, on the reasons which influenced my request.

The cause of my desiring the change was my wish, officially expressed, in various ways during several years, that cavalry under my command serving against Indians be supplied with a magazine arm.

My reason for wishing for Winchesters instead of Spencers was my belief that the Spencer was no longer manufactured and that the repaired arms were likely again to get out of order. I very much regret that it has appeared judicious to the Chief of Ordnance to hold me up to the ridicule of the Army without taking the trouble to ascertain my views and I respectfully request, that that officer be directed to do me justice in this matter.

I have not objected to the Springfield Carbine as an inefficient arm, nor to its range. I have only expressed what is no caprice, but a preference of many years standing for a good magazine arm.

I do not wish the rifle cartridge for the Carbine, as in my judgment, the present Carbine cartridge is much to be preferred.[9]

Despite his problems, the new assignment brought back something of the old Mackenzie. Absorbed in the operations of a regiment, the administration of a district and preparation

for a campaign, he no longer was preoccupied with bureaucracy and plots. He was doing what he did best and thriving
on it. To John F. Finerty, correspondent for the Chicago
Times, Mackenzie seemed like "a noble specimen of the beau
sabreur, tall, well built and with a frank, handsome face."
They discussed the Indian situation and Mackenzie predicted
there would be a winter campaign.[10]

Mackenzie's command had expanded to include eighteen
companies of the Third, Fourth and Fifth Cavalry, the Fourth
Artillery, and the Ninth and Fourteenth Infantry. Some of
these units were not accustomed to the rigid discipline of the
Fourth and, with a major campaign in the immediate future,
Mackenzie clamped down on them. On Sundays the officers'
billiard room and the post trader were closed, and games of
pool and cards were forbidden. The number of courts-martial
increased. Although Mackenzie's penalties were never as severe as Custer's, they were harsh by modern standards. A
frequent punishment was to require the offender, for twelve
days, to stand on a barrel from reveille to retreat with only
half an hour's rest for each meal. During the campaign, two
soldiers who forgot courtesy spent the next hour and half
saluting a tree stump. For the more serious offense of reporting late for duty, a guard detail had to carry forage for a mile.[11]

Fort Robinson was located near the vast Red Cloud and
Spotted Tail Agencies, which had provided "not less than 500
men" to Sitting Bull and Crazy Horse's bands. Mackenzie
believed Red Cloud was largely responsible for the uprising,
but a peace commission was sent from Washington to treat
with the Sioux. The commissioners brought a letter from
General Sherman, who confided to Mackenzie, "I have little
faith in such missions but I know that the President lays much
stress on it, and has firm belief in the success of this special

Mission. . .so that it is my duty to do all that is possible to make it a success."[12]

Negotiations were underway when a message arrived from General Crook, who had been chasing Indians all over the countryside for three months with only one engagement worth noting—a minor battle at Slim Buttes on September 9. Having long since exhausted their rations, his men were starving and reduced to eating horses. Mackenzie sent his entire transportation service to Crook's support, stripping his own units. He now had fourteen companies of horses and men living on the post but unable to build shelters until the train returned. The Indians at the agencies were disgruntled, and he felt there might be trouble at any time. He called the peace commission's arrival "very unfortunate . . . it unsettles the minds of these Indians." No one had any information "or if they do don't bother to tell you."[13]

In spite of Sherman's misgivings, the commission was generally successful. The friendly chiefs agreed to cede the Black Hills and appointed a delegation to look at the Indian Territory offered them in return. Red Cloud, however, still presented an obstacle. He had left the agency about the time Mackenzie took over and was camped on Chadron Creek about twenty-three miles from Fort Robinson. Mackenzie believed both Red Cloud and Spotted Tail were sheltering other hostile Indians. In consultation with Sheridan and Crook, he drafted a letter recommending that the agencies be sealed off and that all communication be prohibited except through the military. The letter, designed to cripple the peace commission, was sent to Crook and then to Sheridan who, according to plan, wholeheartedly endorsed Mackenzie's recommendations.[14] To complete the farce, Mackenzie sent an officer to advise the runaways to return.

Mackenzie had long since determined that Indians were great talkers well able to prolong discussions to buy time for any private plans they might be making. On the other hand, they respected decisive action backed by force. Since this was clearly a case for decisive action, Mackenzie wrote Crook:

> I do not think any of the principal bands will move in unless there is some strong power brought to bear to cause them to be obedient. As I did not wish to do so until your arrival, I have told Capt. Smith to explain to them how very wrong such conduct was, and how it would meet the disapproval of the Great Father and all that sort of thing which is customary with Indians, and about as efficient as the plan which is sometimes recommended of catching birds by the use of salt.

Mackenzie had also received reports of three major camps on the Powder River, one under Crazy Horse, one of Sans Arcs Sioux and one of the Cheyenne. Passing this information on to Crook, he said, "A great many Indians have I think gone North quite recently and I wish that you would either come here or order me to get them together."[15]

As anticipated, the initial contact with the runaways failed to produce results. Crook ordered Mackenzie to bring them in and sent Colonel Wesley Merritt, Fifth Cavalry, to back him. By October 22, with Merritt close enough to provide any support he might need, Mackenzie decided to force the issue with Red Cloud. Eight companies of Fourth and Fifth Cavalry left Fort Robinson about sundown. They skirted the agency, to avoid any possible warning to the runaways, and rode for about five hours until they met a detachment of Pawnee Scouts under the brothers Frank and

Luther North. After a few minutes rest the march resumed. About 4:00 A.M. their guides told them they were nearing two camps on the creek about a mile apart. One was Red Cloud's, the other belonged to the Brulé Chiefs Red Leaf and Swift Bear. Major George A. Gordon, Fifth Cavalry, was sent to secure the Brulé camp, while Mackenzie's unit surrounded Red Cloud.[16]

The camps were seized and horses rounded up with no resistance. The women and children tried to hide in the brush but were gathered up and brought back. When the women balked at taking down the lodges, Mackenzie warned he would burn them down. The women still refused until several of the tepis were fired. The women began taking them down immediately.

No record of what was actually said when Mackenzie faced down Red Cloud has been located, but Captain Frederick Mears of the Ninth Infantry summed up the encounter for a correspondent from the *Alta California*.

> For the first time in the life of Red Cloud, he heard in plain and firm language, from General Mackenzie. . .what was expected of him in the matter of turning over the hostiles to the General, if any of them attempted to come in to the Agency and be peaceful for the Winter. I was present at the interview, and saw the effect on Red Cloud's nerves of the plain talk. Hitherto the Agent, when he tried to gain a point, and he never secured one from Red Cloud, it was done by what the Bureau called "diplomacy;" another name for "the please-do and please-don't policy." Never in Red Cloud's life had he ever been talked to by a white man, as he was in

this interview, and never in his life was he ever lifted from his lofty breech-clouted pedestal and made to feel that he stood in the presence of his superior, and the reason was this, at the beck and call of the General were eighteen companies of troops, ready at a moment's notice to carry out his orders. On the other hand, had a civil agent dared to say to Red Cloud what General Mackenzie did, Red Cloud would not only have laughed at him to his face, but probably some young buck of the tribe, burning for some distinction, would have put a bullet in Mr. Agent and settled him for this earth. [17]

Sioux Chief Red Cloud
(Smithsonian Institution, Bureau of American Ethnology)

The blunt account is understandable from the soldier's point of view. The army had suffered one humiliation after another since the Custer disaster, and morale was low. The American public, starved for good news from the plains, now heard of the defeat of Red Cloud, the chief who had previously forced the United States government to accede to his treaty terms following a bloody, exhausting war. The tables had turned. Red Cloud's camp would be dismantled under military supervision. He would be allowed only enough horses to pack and for the "old and feeble" to ride. The rest of his people would walk. The army and the press corps felt they had a right to celebrate.

At Fort Robinson that evening, the Indians were completely disarmed and their horses seized. Merritt's Yellowstone and Bighorn veterans assisted in disarming and unhorsing the Indians who had remained at the Red Cloud Agency.[18] The disarmed runaways were shocked to learn that the Arapahoes and Cut-off Sioux were allowed to keep their weapons. As Captain Mears had indicated, for years the government's civilian agents had catered to the defiant bands, trying to win them over with gifts and pleadings, expending so much effort on them that the agency Indians had been subjected to benign neglect. Now the military was in charge, and the friendly Indians were armed, hired as soldiers or scouts on the government payroll, and brought unquestionably on the side of the army.

Crook was responsible for the hiring and arming of the friendly bands. An excellent field commander when he wanted to be, his campaigns nevertheless seesawed between brilliance and stupidity. His greatest talent was diplomacy.[19] As Mackenzie marched back to the agency with Red Cloud, Crook was making even further diplomatic arrangements with the friendly Indians. First he came to an understanding with Spotted Tail, deposing Red Cloud and naming Spotted Tail chief of all the Sioux. In return, Spotted Tail and Little Wound agreed "to furnish General Crook with all the warriors he wants to go out after the northern hostiles."[20] This accord was to pay massive dividends in the coming campaign.

Crook's negotiations were a resounding success. The Sioux were divided against themselves, with some firmly in the white camp. Even Red Cloud, beginning to show a grudging respect for this general, was slowly coming around to the government's side. But from a military standpoint, Crook had accomplished little on the Northern Plains. Red Cloud, although defiant, had stopped short of going to war, but the true hostiles, Crazy Horse and Sitting Bull of the Sioux and Dull Knife of the Cheyennes, were still at liberty. They had been victorious in most encounters and were singularly unimpressed with the army's efforts to date.

From Fort Laramie, Crook decided to hit the Indians with a major attack intended to capture Crazy Horse. Determined that this time there would be no mistakes, Crook reviewed all the weaknesses of the previous expeditions. His plan was to maneuver from post to post, carrying provisions for the trail and resupplying at well-stocked bases. Thus his large force could travel lightly and move rapidly while the hostile bands, not anticipating that the troops could move in bad weather, would be settling in for the winter. The Indian scouts, who had not been available in the earlier marches, would give Crook a definite advantage.[21]

Fort Laramie "displayed a bustling activity; with troops moving in and troops moving out, officers running hither, thither and yon, changing quarters, drawing supplies and other duties," noted Crook's adjutant, Lieutenant John G. Bourke, in his diary. A total of 405 Indian ponies which Mackenzie had seized from Red Cloud and Red Leaf were sold on November 2 for an average of about five dollars apiece. Another 350 were kept for the scouts, guides and friendly Indians.

Two days later Crook issued General Order No. 7, organ-

izing the Powder River Expedition. The order named Mackenzie as chief of cavalry, with Lieutenant Colonel Richard I.
Dodge in charge of the infantry and artillery battalions. Mackenzie arrived at Fort Laramie with more than twenty companies of cavalry, artillery and infantry, and nearly 160 Indian
Scouts from Red Cloud and Spotted Tail.[22] According to
Bourke, Mackenzie:

> was looked upon by the whole army as the embodi-
> ment of courage, skill and dash in an eminent
> degree. Impetuous, headstrong, perhaps a trifle
> rash, he formed a curious contrast to his self-poised,
> cool, silent commander . . . .[23]

Early in his career, Mackenzie had served with Crook in
Virginia. The two men respected each other and got along
well. Now, at the age of thirty-six, he was serving with Crook
again in what would be Mackenzie's last major campaign.

The infantry and artillery commander, Colonel Dodge,
was almost fourteen years older than Mackenzie, senior in
service yet junior in permanent rank. Despite these disparities
and the rivalries of the period, they seemed to have worked
well together. In fact, Dodge's diary shows a certain affection
for the younger officer, whom he called "Mac" and whose
courage he openly admired. Before the campaign was over,
Dodge would help him through a severe personal crisis.

CHAPTER 14

"He Said . . . He Would Blow His Brains Out"

The Powder River Expedition left Fort Laramie for Fort Fetterman, where Mackenzie's command arrived on November 9. There it consolidated and made final preparations for the campaign. Bourke felt it was "the best equipped and best officered of any with which I have ever served; the experience of the past summer has opened the eyes of the National Legislature to the urgency of the situation and consequently appropriations for supplies have been awarded on a scale of unusual liberality."[1]

The cavalry was stronger than it had been at any time since the Civil War, with a hundred men in each of the mounted companies and fifty in dismounted companies. Recruits were "of a superior standard." The government was preparing for a hard winter campaign, and the troops were equipped accordingly with seal-skin caps, gloves, fur leggings and felt boots. Each soldier was allowed three blankets. Stores included canned soups, pressed tongue and corned beef, and there was a liberal issue of stoves and cooking utensils. Personal gear of the officers and men was crated, marked and left in the custody of the post quartermaster. Every detail had been considered. Even the rivalry between the Sioux scouts on one hand, and the Pawnees, Shoshones, Arapahoes and Crows on the other, worked to the army's advantage since it encouraged each group to outshine the other in doing its duty.[2]

But as the army prepared for its march, unsettling news arrived from the East. After a hard-fought presidential campaign, election day had not resolved the contest between Democrat Samuel Tilden and Republican Rutherford Hayes. Both parties were still claiming victory in the swing states of Louisiana, Florida and the Carolinas, and General Augur, commanding the Department of the Gulf, had been sent to Florida with infantry and artillery to counter threats of bloodshed. In his diary, Bourke noted:

> Such news is more grave than would be an intimation of hostilities with foreign nations; internecine wars are always those having an infusion of religious fanaticism. Severe as our coming experiences may be, they will be more welcome than a campaign in the sunny lands of the South against our own misguided people.[3]

Bourke was not the only officer who was worried. Dodge summed up his feelings in a single comment: "Very bad political news from the States."[4]

There is no indication Mackenzie closely followed these developments. Politics was not one of his strong points, and he had problems of his own. Aside from organizational matters, drinking was rampant in the camps. Even the normally easygoing Lawton became drunk with a trooper named Wilson and clubbed him in the face with a pistol. Mackenzie gave Lawton a thorough dressing down, and the abject lieutenant became very solicitous of Wilson.[5]

Of greatest concern to officers and men was the winter weather. On November 13 the temperature dropped to thirteen degrees below zero. But the change from the more arid climate of the Southwest seemed to invigorate Mackenzie, whose orderly, Private William Earl Smith, noted in his diary that Mackenzie was up all night with Crook. While Smith did not offer any reason, it was probably for cards. Crook was an avid whist player, and throughout the campaign would have officers over to his tent for protracted games. On his return to his own camp, Mackenzie sent word for Smith to saddle two horses.

"He come out and mounted and we started," Smith wrote. "He says to me Smith how dose your little hors run. Well I says he ollways keeps up with the rest of them. Well he says that is a good horse and we will have a [race]. Well we started. We jest flew for half of a mile. I could of past him but I did not like to." The hour's ride was substantial for Mackenzie, whose war wounds made riding painful and who did not normally ride for pleasure.[6]

The following day the expedition marched out of Fort Fetterman toward Cantonment Reno, the last post before reaching the hostile villages. Floating ice slowed the crossing of the North Platte. Dodge was in a foul humor. He and Mackenzie had not yet met, and their service rivalry led each to jockey for a head start to get the best position on the march. On this first day, Mackenzie's cavalry forded the freezing river on horseback and gained the lead, while Dodge had to cross his men in wagons to keep them warm and dry. When the day ended the infantry had covered ten miles. The cavalry had to ride four miles farther to find enough water for the horses, and that was brackish. Fuel and baled hay had to be hauled in wagons from Fort Fetterman.[7]

The Dodge-Mackenzie rivalry continued for the next two days. Invariably Mackenzie's well-drilled troopers moved out

George Crook *(National Archives)*

first, churning up the trail and leaving the infantry to slog through the mud and slush. Dodge thoroughly resented it, but their dispute was unexpectedly resolved when the two colonels discovered they had a common enemy—their commanding officer. George Crook had changed substantially from the man Mackenzie had known in the closing battles of Virginia. Like Custer, Crook had become vain and self-serving, but he was also subtle and refined. His long beard, twisted into two points, his canvas suit and white helmet, and his preference for riding a mule became his trademarks as much as Custer's buckskins. He carefully controlled the press, making sure that his news coverage was favorable. Like Custer, he surrounded himself with a staff whose devotion was total. Even Sheridan, his boyhood friend, had come to detest him, a feeling for which Crook was to repay him with a vengeance.[8]

In his own assessment of Crook, Dodge commented, "The Cavalry and Infantry are nobodies. The Indians and pack mules have all the good places. He scarcely treats McKenzie and I decently, but he will spend hours chatting pleasantly with an Indian or a dirty scout."

Because of their mutual antipathy of Crook, Dodge apparently decided to resolve his differences with Mackenzie. He was glad he did. They had a long conversation during their first meeting, and Dodge thoroughly enjoyed himself. Mackenzie gave him two orderlies and told Dodge "to call on him for any thing I want, and he would help me if he could." They also agreed to take turns in the lead on the march. From this meeting developed a bond between the two men which would last for the duration of the campaign.[9]

The days passed with a gloomy sky, chilly rain and little grass for the horses. November 17 dawned with a snow storm blowing into the faces of the soldiers, although the sky cleared up by the time the command bivouacked. Two old frontiersmen, Tom Cosgrove and Texas Bob Eckles, rode in with three Shoshones from among the hundred or so at Cantonment Reno. They told Crook that hostile Sioux trails led up toward the sources of the Crazy Woman, Clear and Tongue Rivers.

The next day the command reached Reno. Mackenzie's men camped in the shelter of a large embankment which blocked the wind, but the hay had given out and they had to cut cottonwoods to feed the horses. From Reno, Crook sent out six Arapahoes and eight Sioux to scout the Bighorn Mountains. They returned on November 21 with a young Cheyenne prisoner named Beaver Dam, who had come into their camp on Clear Creek about fifty miles west of the cantonment. Since the scouts had left all their military gear behind:

> they readily deluded the young hostile who gave them all the news of the day, where the different villages were and how many in each. By the time he had finished, half a dozen revolvers were cocked

and pointed and he told to surrender his guns. This
he did without a word, but showed much amaze-
ment when the strangers told him they were . . .
soldiers.[10]

After interrogating Beaver Dam, Crook wired Sheridan:

Scouts returned to-day and reported that Cheyennes have crossed over to the other side of the Big
Horn Mountains, and that Crazy Horse and his
band are encamped on the Rosebud near where we
had the fight with them last summer. We start out
after his band to-morrow morning.[11]

Troops were made ready. Each man was issued a hundred
rounds of ammunition and ten days rations. But on November 23 Sitting Bear, a Cheyenne Mackenzie had sent from the
Red Cloud Agency to deliver an ultimatum to the hostile
renegades, rejoined the command. He told Crook that Beaver
Dam's village of five lodges had become alarmed when he
failed to return, and had left to warn Crazy Horse. He also
reported a large Cheyenne village hidden in a canyon in the
Bighorns. Since the chance of surprising Crazy Horse was lost,
Crook immediately decided to move against the Cheyennes
instead.

Mackenzie was sent out with about eight hundred cavalrymen and nearly all the Indian scouts, including the North
brothers and their Pawnees. Henry Lawton and wagonmaster
John Sharp left twelve hours in advance to prepare crossings
over streams and ravines. As Bourke noted, "In the wintery
season, the banks of these creeks acted upon by the stem frost
offer grave obstacles to cavalry, especially with smoothly shod
animals." Scouts reported back with the location of the camp

and the warning that it had "heap ponies," meaning a large number of warriors. Their concern caused Mackenzie to order a halt while he consulted with Chief Scout Frank Grouard. The latter advised him to do what he had no doubt been planning anyway—conduct a forced night march so as to attack at daylight. Accordingly, he ordered everyone ready to move at sundown. No fires were allowed while the command rested under a projecting ledge of rocks, "lest the curling smoke betray us."[12]

The climb over the Bighorn Mountains was hard, and Smith wasn't sure how they made it. Horses gave out. "In some places we had to go in single file and that strung the [column] out five or six mil[e]s. If the hostils had [known] we were a comming they could of [killed] every man of us in some of these places," Smith wrote.

Even Luther North found the going rough, despite his familiarity with the country. "This was about the hardest march that we ever had," he wrote. "We climbed up and up, it seemed for miles, then over a ridge, and down again." The altitude affected them as well. Even though some of the Pawnees were sick to their stomachs, by and large the Indian scouts were at home in these ranges and had fewer problems. They rode past the column one or two at a time until they were all in front. Mackenzie's usual impatience was aggravated by these Indians, who kept riding back and urging him forward saying they were close to the hostile village.[13]

When Mackenzie called the column to a halt, the Indian scouts shifted their saddles from their riding ponies to their war ponies and donned their war dress and paint. To Smith they looked hideous. When they had finished, the command again moved forward. Suddenly a shot rang out in the rear, where a soldier had dispatched his exhausted horse. Mackenzie lost his temper and cut loose with a stream of profanity. "He was to mad [to be of any use]," Smith observed.

He recovered his composure and the command started down the mountainside, into a canyon leading to the valley where the Indians were camped. The Red Fork of the Powder River flowed through the valley, and the terrain was broken by gullies and washes with rocky bluffs and ridges. The village, close to the Red Fork, was bounded by high cliffs of red sandstone. The Cheyennes knew every inch of the area and had obviously picked the site for defense.

Mackenzie rode ahead with one of the Indians. In the distance the soldiers heard "in a vague but awe-inspiring sort of indistinctness the thump! thump! thump! of war drums, and the jungling of their rattles sounding the measure of a war dance," Bourke wrote. "Only a mile of distance intervened, but the light had broken in the East. The hostile drums ceased beating, a sign the Cheyenne village had finished its dance and retired to rest. Now or never!"[14]

Within a few minutes Mackenzie and the Indian returned. He ordered a halt and set the troopers to tightening their saddles for a charge. He had hoped to surround the camp and disarm the warriors, as he had done with Red Cloud, but it was getting light so a similar surprise was impossible. Company commanders were told to prepare for a dash through the village, but to hold their fire unless the Indians fired first. Against the vague possibility that the Indian scouts might be leading the soldiers into a trap, the scouts were ordered to move in first. For his part, Smith recalled the Custer disaster "and began to think what I was about to go into but I did not feel a bit shakey. I dont [k]now why eather."[15]

Sharp Nose, the Arapahoe chief, asked if Mackenzie were ready, and the response was affirmative. The order went out to gallop, "and with the thundering roar of a waterfall" the column dashed out of the canyon, into the open space toward the village. Lieutenant Hayden Delaney's Sioux, Arapahoes and Cheyennes were first, followed by the Shoshones under Lieutenant Walter Schuyler and Tom Cosgrove, and the Pawnees under Frank North. War cries, reed whistles, shouts of the soldiers, commands from the officers and the thunder of hundreds of army horses all added to the general noise and confusion. A Cheyenne sentry saw them, fired one shot, jumped on his horse and headed back into the camp, from which the sharp crack of rifle fire emerged as bullets screamed past the troopers.

As Mackenzie's force reached the village, the Indian scouts turned up the side of a hill. Thinking the scouts were the attackers, the Cheyennes concentrated their fire on them, leaving a clear field for the soldiers. The lead units dashed into the village, well ahead of the rest. Mackenzie excitedly ordered Smith back to press the others on. "As I come to each company, I told them what the Genrall sed and they dashed off at [lightning] speed. It seemed as if the horses had. . .new life. When I [got] to the last Company I turned back and I never hird such a thunder of horses in all my life, for it was all rocks where we were."[16]

In the classic Mackenzie style, the soldiers headed immediately for the enemy horse herds. One soldier's horse balked at the body of an almost naked Cheyenne boy, cut down as he ran to save the horses with his lariat still around his neck, ready to lasso the first pony he came across.[17]

Frank North's unit was positioned on the south bank of the Red Fork, in readiness to ride past the village on one side, swing around and meet the cavalry at the end, cutting off a possible escape. As the column neared the village, Mackenzie had second thoughts about dividing the command in such a way, and instead ordered North to cross over and join the others. It took time to find a crossing and, when he did, his horses mired in the mud.

When North bogged down in the Red Fork, the Cheyennes were able to maintain a steady covering fire for their screaming women and children as they fled through the rear of the village and up into the rocky heights. The soldiers deployed in line-of-battle. One warrior ran within a few yards of Mackenzie and fired but missed. He was immediately riddled with bullets by the colonel's orderlies.

The troops had been able to secure much of the Cheyenne horse herd, but the Indians seemed about to counterattack and retake it. Lieutenant John A. McKinney, Fourth Cavalry, was told to take Company A and head them off. McKinney charged across a small plain until his men were blocked by a ravine with sheer sides. He wheeled to the right and had gone a few yards when Cheyenne sharpshooters in the ravine opened fire, killing a sergeant and two troopers. McKinney was hit six times and his horse was shot from under him. Be-

John A. McKinney
(Special Collection, US Military Academy)

fore he died, he shouted, "Get out of this! You are ambus-
caded!" The soldiers, mostly recruits, panicked and fled.

Mackenzie ordered Captain John M. Hamilton's company of the Fifth Cavalry to reinforce Company A. As the
Cheyennes scattered into the washes, Captain Wirt Davis
brought up his company and, together with Hamilton's men,
charged on foot. The battle degenerated into hand-to-hand
fighting. When other Indians began closing in around both
companies, Schuyler took his Shoshones to the top of a crag
which commanded the entire village, and began a covering
heavy fire which saved Davis and Hamilton from possible
massacre. Bourke estimated twenty of the best Cheyenne
warriors were killed there. Another company of the Fifth
Cavalry charged through the length of the village and seized
two commanding knolls.[18]

While the soldiers and scouts secured the village, the
Cheyennes retreated into the surrounding rocks. As Bourke
noted, "The engagement had assumed the nature of a rifle-
duel, neither contestant caring to waste a shot. The rifle
practice of the enemy was specially fine and the number of
'close-calls' on our side was most remarkable." The cavalry
carbines were not powerful enough to dislodge the Indians
from the rocks, and Mackenzie told Bourke to send a message
to Crook asking for infantry with long rifles. The pack train,
which had been left behind the night before, arrived with
sufficient rations and ammunition to carry the troops through
any protracted battle.

Over six hundred enemy ponies were captured, along
with a village of some two hundred lodges. Mackenzie's men
counted about twenty-five bodies, and he personally believed
"a much larger number were killed." His own losses were one
officer and six men killed, five of the troopers in the battle

itself and the sixth by snipers from the rocks. There were twenty-six wounded. As they inventoried, the troopers and their allies found the grisly trophies of war: scalp locks of a little blond girl and a Shoshone girl, both about ten years old; the hand of a Shoshone woman; a necklace of human fingers; and a bag containing the right hands of twelve Shoshone babies. Several veterans of the Rosebud recognized the scalp of a Shoshone scout killed in that fight. But there was even more: a pillow case made from the silk guidon of Custer's Seventh; the guard roster of Company G, Seventh Cavalry; memorandum books of the first sergeants, Seventh Cavalry; cavalry horses branded "U.S."; saddles, canteens, nosebags and other equipment marked with company letters of the Seventh; army blouses; and a buckskin jacket which looked like one used by Tom Custer, the general's brother, who had also died at the Little Bighorn.

It was November 25, 1876, five months to the day after the Little Bighorn. Clearly, these Indians had been there.

The Shoshones and the Pawnees beat the captured Cheyenne war drums in their own victory celebration, deriding their ancient enemies who could hear them clearly from their refuge. When the Cheyennes ran up a white flag, Mackenzie did not notice it and some of the troopers sniped at it. Finally Grouard told Mackenzie the Cheyenne intended to stop shooting if the soldiers would. The order was given to cease firing, the white flag went up again, and Mackenzie sent Grouard to find out what the Cheyennes wanted.

Dull Knife, one of the two principal chiefs of the Cheyennes, called down that three of his sons had been killed in the fight. For his part he wanted to surrender, but the other chiefs were adamant in making a stand. To the Indian scouts Dull Knife shouted, "Go home! You have no business here!

Cheyenne Chief Dull Knife
(National Archives)

We can whip the white soldiers alone, but can't fight you, too."

The Cheyennes then offered to surrender if the captured ponies were returned. Mackenzie replied that was impossible. Another Indian called out, "You have killed and burned a heap of our people. You may as well stay now and kill the rest of us." Then, in an effort at bravado, the Indians shouted there was a big Sioux village nearby. They planned to go there and get help, then come back and kill the soldiers.

That afternoon the soldiers burned the lodges. The Cheyennes had accumulated large stores of cartridges and powder and, as each lodge went up, the ammunition inside exploded. Tons of buffalo meat, stored as winter rations, were dumped into the flames. Buffalo robes were sorted out, and the Indian scouts took what they wanted. The rest were fed to the fires.[19]

With the battle over, Mackenzie had time to ponder his heavy casualties. His fights had always been quick, careful and efficient. Lieutenant McKinney had been popular in the regiment, and Mackenzie had recognized his potential four years earlier when he had been a hard-drinking, irresponsible shavetail. He had watched over him and pushed him along until he could call McKinney "one of the most gallant officers and honorable men that I have ever known." Now McKinney was dead and many of the wounded were in bad condition. Mackenzie went into a severe depression.

Smith noticed it that night. He had grabbed a nap after the fight and, while he slept, his leg had frozen. As the night wore on the leg hurt, and he could hear the cries of the wounded coming from the field hospital. Sometimes he would doze off, only to wake up again. Each time he awoke he saw Mackenzie pacing back and forth. "I don't believe he slept a bit that nite," Smith wrote. "His mind must of been trubled about some thing. I don't [k]now what, for he is the bravest man I ever saw. He dont seem to think any more about [bullets] flying than I would about snowballs."

The next morning, Smith woke up early and started to fix breakfast. Mackenzie came over and accepted a cup of coffee. "While he was drinking he talked to me a good deal about the fite a[nd] seemed to feel bad about the boys that had been hirt and [killed]."[20]

Destruction of the village continued. Broken lodge poles were piled up and set on fire. Marrow, fat and tallow were piled on, and the fuel which the women had stored for daily use was added to the flames. Large implements such as axes, hatchets, pans, picks and shovels were piled on. Tin cups, coffee pots, plates and other cooking and eating utensils were split with axes.

The shooting had died out during the night. As the second day's destruction was underway, Indian scouts sent out to look for the Cheyennes found them about six miles away, moving out fast. Although the Cheyennes also saw the scouts, each side left the other alone. The scouts also found the remains of six horses butchered by the already hungry enemy.

With the destruction of the village complete, the wounded were loaded on travois and the command started back to meet General Crook. As the soldiers left, two or three Cheyennes who had remained in the rocks came down to survey the wreckage, then sat down and began wailing. They were left to mourn in peace.[21]

On November 28 Mackenzie's Indian couriers met Crook, who was coming up with the infantry in answer to Mackenzie's message. The foot soldiers had pushed more than twenty-five miles through the mountains in forced marches, sleeping in the snow and eating cold food. Satisfied with the report, Crook ordered a leisurely march back to base for a rest. Mackenzie arrived the following morning.

Lieutenant McKinney's body was retained to be returned to his family, but one trooper was buried at the battlesite. Two days later on November 30, Thanksgiving Day, the remaining five dead were buried. Heading the procession were trumpeters playing the funeral dirge, followed by Crook, Mackenzie, Dodge and two majors. The cavalry command provided mounted honors. The Episcopal service was read, Taps sounded, and salute volleys fired. After the graves were covered with rock to protect them from wolves, the soldiers obliterated all visible traces so the hostile Indians would not find the graves to take the scalps.

The funeral seems to have deepened Mackenzie's depression. When Dodge and two other officers called on him afterwards, they found him acting "more like a crazy man than the sane commander of a splendid body of cavalry." He was "very downcast—bitterly reproaching himself for what he called his failure. . . .He said to an officer that if he had courage enough he would blow his brains out." The others slowly eased themselves away, leaving him alone with Dodge, who wrote:

> Mac opened his heart to me. He said he had often done better with a third of the force at this command here—that he believed he degenerated as a soldier as he got older—that he was a fool and ought to have captured every Indian—that he regarded the whole thing as an utter failure. He even stated that he was sensitive lest someone might attribute cowardice to him—and much more of the same kind.

Mackenzie sometimes became incoherent and had to stop to collect his thoughts. Despite his ranting self-criticism, Mackenzie's tactics at Powder River were no different from those he had used at Remolino and Palo Duro, and they had achieved basically the same results. The difference was that he no longer believed in himself.

Richard I. Dodge
(Author's Collection)

Dodge "bullied him and encouraged him all I could . . . told him that he was foolish and absurd to talk so, that we all regarded the affair as a grand success and that his record was too well known for anyone to attribute cowardice to him." By the time Dodge finished, Mackenzie felt much better. Still, the incident worried Dodge to the point he felt he should report it to Crook. "The General was greatly worried and soon left my tent, I think to send for Mac and get him to play whist or something."[22]

In his own mind, Dodge had mixed feelings about the fight. Disappointed that his infantry had arrived too late, he assured himself that the victory would have been far more complete if he had been there. As it was, he felt Mackenzie could have done better. Dodge admired bravery in the field, but felt Mackenzie lacked administrative ability and "political sagacity." He kept these thoughts to himself, however, recording them only in his diary.

Although Mackenzie may have thought the battle a failure, it was one of a series of actions which, taken together, proved to be the turning point in the wars on the Northern Plains. Even Dodge admitted that "It is the first blow ever struck with effect at this tribe, the Northern Cheyennes, who have always boasted heretofore that they have never been whipped. . . . The affair stamps our campaign as a success even if nothing more is accomplished."[23]

The mortal blow to the power of the Cheyennes further eroded the power of the Sioux. The seriousness of the Indian situation hit the Cheyenne warrior Wooden Leg, who with nine companions had been absent when Mackenzie attacked. Unsuccessfully seeking Crows to kill and scalp, they had traveled to the Custer battlefield where they reminisced about their summer triumph and collected the ammunition still scattered on the field. On their way back they found their own people defeated, barefoot in the snow, cold and hungry. Many had already frozen to death on the trail. The remaining were destitute and heading to the only shelter they knew, Crazy Horse's Oglala Sioux. When they reached that camp they found little comfort, for the Oglalas had just enough for their own needs. With their resources already critically strained, before long the Oglalas sent their unwelcome Cheyenne allies on their way. "The sufferings of these Indians during the three months succeeding the battle can never be known," Dodge later wrote in his memoirs. "Numbers perished, principally women and children. . .they had received a blow far worse than a bloody defeat, and from which it would take years to recover."

The Cheyennes never forgave Crazy Horse for turning them away in their time of greatest need. In place of the old alliance arose a lasting bitterness. When the U.S. Army began to prepare its final campaign against Crazy Horse, many Cheyennes enlisted as scouts to help run him down.[24]

Dull Knife Fight by Frederic Remington

CHAPTER 15

"You Were the One I Was Afraid Of"

The next few days after the battle were frustrating for the unit commanders. Crook appeared to have a plan but confided in no one. Mackenzie, who had completely recovered his composure, was ordered to hold himself in readiness for a move but was given no reason for this order. The day after the Thanksgiving Day funeral he stopped in to discuss the situation with Dodge. The two were "rather pitching into Crook" when the general came in. On being invited to sit, Crook said, "I've only a moment to stay. You will march tomorrow and should make arrangements tonight for crossing the river."

"What river?" Dodge asked.

"This," Crook replied, apparently indicating the ·Crazy Woman where they were then camped. He also told them they were heading back to Reno. Mackenzie was about to ask a question when Crook abruptly left the tent without another word.[1]

As he waited for clarification from Crook, Mackenzie busied himself with the various details which inevitably followed a military action. He wrote Colonel C.H. Carlton at Fort Fetterman, asking him to order a coffin in which to ship McKinney's body home to Tennessee. The death left an opening for first lieutenant. Second Lieutenant Wentz Miller would have been in line for the promotion if he were not the

regimental adjutant; he resigned the adjutancy and Mackenzie promoted him accordingly. Unaware of Miller's promotion, however, the War Department promoted Second
Lieutenant Abram E. Wood, to the vacancy. In the ensuing
situation, the War Department's promotion of Wood took
precedence.[2]

The force returned to Cantonment Reno on December 2.
The post had inadequate forage or supplies for a protracted
campaign, and the animals were almost worn out. Initially
Crook planned to remain there, but then changed his mind
and had them on the march early the next morning. "He really
does not know ahead what he intends to do," Dodge groused.
"Makes up his mind at the last moment, and then acts at
once—expecting everybody to do the same." To him, it
seemed Crook had no idea of how much effort went into
organizing a march.[3]

The troops marched to Buffalo Springs on the Dry Fork
of the Powder River where they remained several days. Meanwhile news of the Dull Knife Fight, for such it came to be
called, was spreading through the country. Sherman an-
nounced Mackenzie's victory to the War Department saying:

> I can't commend too highly his brilliant achieve-
> ments and the gallantry of the troops of his com-
> mand. This will be a terrible blow to the hostiles,
> as those Cheyennes were not only their bravest
> warriors but have been the head and front of most
> all the raids and deviltry committed in this country.

To Sheridan, he cabled:

> Please convey to Generals Crook and Mackenzie
> my congratulations, and assure them that we ap-

preciate highly the services of our brave officers and
men who are now fighting savages in the most
inhospitable regions of our continent. I hope their
efforts this winter will result in perfect success and
that our troops will hereafter be spared the necessity of these hard winter campaigns.

Sheridan passed these on, adding his own congratulations.
The praise especially pleased Mackenzie, who was "quite
jolly" one day when he and Crook dropped in on Dodge.
After a short visit Mackenzie left but Crook remained. When
Mackenzie returned to Dodge's quarters, the general had
departed but had briefed Dodge on his plans. He intended to
follow the Belle Fourche down to its forks, then cross over to
the junction of the Little Powder River with the Big Powder
River. From there the Indians would scout in all directions,
and Crook would move against any village they found. Crook
was concerned about the sixty miles of desert, separating the
Belle Fourche from the Powder River area, which contained
no wood, grass or drinkable water. After studying the maps
with Dodge, Mackenzie concluded the crossing could be made
and would save ten days.[4]

As the march progressed, Mackenzie's treatment of his
officers became inconsistent. In one case Lieutenant Homer
W. Wheeler, Fifth Cavalry, found his company shut out of its
rightful place in line and sent a protest, but Mackenzie could
not be found. Wheeler's unit arrived in camp late. Furious,
Wheeler was airing his opinions "in very emphatic language"
to another officer when the colonel rode up.

"Mr. Wheeler," Mackenzie snapped, "when you have a
grievance with your commanding officer you had better be
more careful what language you use and when you use it."

Then he added, "Mr. Wheeler, I have a good place for your troop to go into camp, plenty of wood and water. You fall in, in your regular place in the morning." Yet even as he sympathized with Wheeler's problems, Mackenzie had just placed two other officers under arrest for apparently minor infractions.[5]

The command reached the Belle Fourche on December 7, marched down the river for a day, then went into camp where it remained. Bureaucratic errors had misdirected many of the supplies intended for the expedition. Crook, unable to continue, decided to send out his Indians from that point, and wait.[6] In the ensuing days there were only short marches, primarily relocations of campsites.

During the waiting period, courts-martial were held with Dodge presiding. Among the defendants was Second Lieutenant H.G. Otis, Fourth Cavalry, one of Mackenzie's officers. "The offense amounts to but little," Dodge wrote, "and Mack had much better have given the boy a good scolding or a week's arrest. It is absurd to try officers for every little offense."[7]

The newspapers arrived with still no word about any settlement of the presidential election. Finally, on December 19 the mail arrived and the soldiers learned Hayes had been named president, but many areas were still in an uproar over the results and the contention was far from over.[8]

The next day Crook, fuming that "somebody ought to be hung," went to see Mackenzie. The Indians had not yet returned and the expedition was far behind schedule. On December 22 he learned the supplies which had been destined for his command had instead been delivered to Reno. With only enough supplies to last until January 2, a decision had to be made soon. As Mackenzie was riding over to visit Crook, he met Dodge who had just left the general in a severe depression. Dodge suggested Mackenzie return with him to his tent for a visit instead. "That is the more reason for our going to see him," Mackenzie replied. "Let's go and give him some consolation and propose a game of whist." Dodge wanted to laugh. Those were almost the same words Crook had used about Mackenzie after the Dull Knife Fight.

When they arrived, Crook told them he wasn't in the mood for a game. "I have got to have a big Indian Council today and it is nearly time," he explained. "The fact is, I have made up my mind to turn back tomorrow and want to give the Indians a good talk and let them go to their reservation." He had been unable to pinpoint the hostile camp, but the failure of the spies to report indicated it was a great distance away. There was not enough food or forage, and the animals were growing thin and weak. Mackenzie observed that for the past week he had felt the command should turn back. Dodge agreed there was no chance of accomplishing anything more.[9]

December 24 was clear and sunny. The temperature was ten degrees below zero, but it felt warmer because there was no wind. That night, Christmas Eve, Crook invited Mackenzie, Dodge, and Major E.F. Townsend of the Ninth Infantry, over for hot brandy punch. For the time being Mackenzie apparently put aside his aversion to alcohol for, in Dodge's words, "We did ample justice to it and the occasion, drinking to the occasion and to our absent loved ones."

The next morning the command began the march back to Fort Fetterman. In camp that night Mackenzie invited Dodge for Christmas dinner. They talked at length about the success of the expedition and the hardships involved. Mackenzie, more accustomed to the routine battering which the

Fourth had undergone on the Texas plains, was less concerned about the sufferings of the men and animals than was Dodge.[10]

Mackenzie's column left Crook's command on December 30 and started back to Fort D.A. Russell. A day later, because of the election crisis, he was summoned East "on duty under orders of the Secretary of War at Washington, D.C." Although the presidency had tentatively been given to Hayes, the political situation in the East continued to deteriorate. Until it was resolved General Grant remained president and was therefore responsible for public order. He had already started building up military and naval forces around Washington, but was worried that additional strength would be needed to defend the capital. In Chicago, Sheridan quietly began stripping the western posts of all the men they could spare and shipping them eastward. Mackenzie, whose interest in politics was limited to his own advancement, was brought in to take command and remained in Washington until March 1, 1877. When the situation had stabilized and the Hayes election virtually assured, he started back to Fort Robinson, Nebraska, to rejoin his regiment.[11]

Crook had been at Fort Robinson since January and had dispatched Red Cloud and Spotted Tail to meet with the hostile Sioux and offer them terms for surrender. On March 7 he went to Cheyenne to meet with Sheridan and discuss a summer campaign, should one be necessary. He returned four days later accompanied by Mackenzie, Lawton and Colonel James Forsyth of Sheridan's staff. After his arrival Mackenzie learned where the Cheyennes were camped and sent runners inviting them in.[12] On April 4 the hostile chief Little Wolf arrived with the first contingent. As for the others, he told the soldiers, "They will be along; they are coming."

Observing the Cheyennes as they came in, the soldiers

realized the extent of total devastation Mackenzie had inflicted in the Dull Knife Fight. "Those who were with 'Little Wolf' were in a miserable plight and told a sad story of want and destitution after losing their village," Bourke wrote. The Cheyennes detested Crazy Horse for failing to help them after the fight and wanted to enlist as scouts against him.

On April 12 Crook, Mackenzie and Bourke drove to the Spotted Tail Agency to meet the Cheyennes who had come in there. Mackenzie's driver, a man named Paul who had explored the Badlands, kept them entertained during the forty-five mile trip with stories of the vast piles of fossilized bones in that part of the country. On arrival they visited with a chief named Turkey Legs who had been with Dull Knife during the fight. He was partially paralyzed but, according to Bourke, was "a man of acute mental powers, and a strong but concise talker."

"These are the Cheyennes," Turkey Legs told Crook and Mackenzie. "You, who have fought us know what we are. We claim for our people that they are the best fighters on the plains." But now, he continued, the Cheyennes were broken. Eighty lodges, consisting of nearly one thousand people were en route to the Red Cloud Agency to surrender. They had lost everything in the Dull Knife Fight, but had no ill-will toward Mackenzie or Crook. It was Crazy Horse they wanted, and the crippled chief reiterated Little Wolf's desire to enlist against him.[13] The Indians continued to arrive, and Spotted Tail brought in 225 Miniconju Sioux.

A few days later Crook called a council where he placed, on a pole, the guidon of Captain Myles Keogh's Company I, Seventh Cavalry, lost at the Little Bighorn and retaken at the Battle of Slim Buttes. Crook, Mackenzie and the other officers sat in one semi-circle and the chiefs sat in another, facing them.

At Crook's behest the Indians laid their weapons on the ground. Bourke noted the carbines were all government issue, "evidently from the Custer massacre." The pipe was passed around. The general promised them friendship and his personal protection, but he also warned that any government soldier they killed could be very easily replaced, and that ultimately they would be defeated. The chiefs understood and promised good behavior.

On April 21 Dull Knife led his band of 524 Cheyennes, including many widows, into the Red Cloud Agency. There were numerous cases of frozen feet and other wounds. Their lodges were made of canvas, old hides, pieces of gunny sacks and the like, "just such things as they could pick up in the old camps of General Crook's expedition." Previously a rich, powerful tribe, they had been reduced to scavengers. Crook let them settle in, arranged for army surgeons to treat the wounded, and issued them rations. They were so hungry that one died from overeating.[14]

A slushy rain mixed with snow fell the following day when Crook and Mackenzie called the chiefs into the hall for a conference. Crook spoke first, and his tone was conciliatory. When Mackenzie's turn came he chastised them, then modified his tone.

> There is no more cause for anything but good talk, and you must behave well, act in good faith, and all will be well. Gen. Crook issues you rations, not because you deserve them, but because he knows how poor you are and pities you. If you had given up when we attacked you in December, there would have been no more fighting, and you would have not suffered so long.

Then Mackenzie told them he would issue rations as well, with priority going to wounded and feeble.

Little Wolf said nothing. But Dull Knife pledged peace and good faith. Then he turned to Mackenzie and said, "You were the one I was afraid of when you came here last summer."[15] Apparently stories of an unyielding, three-fingered soldier chief had made their way from Texas to the Northern Plains even before Mackenzie's arrival.

A few days later, forty or fifty Indian women held a "squaw dance" in honor of the soldiers in front of the officers' quarters in the camp. One old woman, the mistress of ceremonies, asked Mackenzie to tell some of "the nice young men" on the porch to join in. The officers made excuses but the old woman seized Captain Clarence Mauck and, with half a dozen of her friends, started to carry him off bodily. "Poor Mauck struggled hard for freedom," Bourke wrote, "and what with begging, twisting, pleading, kicking and squirming, managed to make his escape from their clutches." The other officers took up a collection to compensate the women for their loss.[16]

The Indian Bureau sent orders that the Cheyennes who had surrendered were to be sent to the Indian Territory. Although the Southern Cheyennes had already lived there for forty years, their Northern cousins balked and Crook and Mackenzie had to call a council to persuade them to go. The first group started south with an escort headed by Lawton. Meanwhile couriers had come in from Crazy Horse, under pressure from Miles in the north, who wanted to surrender to Crook. Shortly after noon, May 6, Crazy Horse led in his band.[17]

The Fourth Cavalry was now divided, with six companies in the Department of the Platte and six in the Indian Territory. With many tours of enlistment ending, the regiment was rapidly becoming depleted. To add to Mackenzie's problems, horse theft was rampant in both areas. With the lessening of the Indian threat, the soldiers were set to chasing thieves, putting additional stress on their own horses already exhausted by the campaign.

Mackenzie found it necessary to request one hundred recruits for the companies in the Platte, and "a sufficient number of men" to fill the gaps in the Territory. "Of these," he wrote, "as large a number as possible should be old instructed soldiers, as they will probably be needed soon for Field Service." He also needed fifty horses at Fort Robinson.[18] The need for field soldiers was not as urgent as Mackenzie had anticipated, for on May 26 he was ordered back to Fort Sill.[19]

In the Territory the condition of the tribes was even worse than when he left, with the Indian Bureau still insisting they become farmers. Even if they were to go into ranching, a time-consuming upheaval would be required before they could convert from their economy based on buffalo, now being hunted out much faster than anticipated. Rations, late as usual, were insufficient when they finally arrived, and Mackenzie resumed dipping into military supplies, issuing army stores to Haworth at Sill, Agent Miles at Anadarko, and to Lawton traveling with the Cheyennes, since the Bureau had made no provision to feed them en route to the territory.[20]

The Cheyennes presented Mackenzie with a special concern. Aside from the shortage of food, they were moving from a cool, dry climate to a hot, humid one. Already weak from the privations of the past several months, they became sick and many died. If the government did not provide adequate rations and medical care, Mackenzie predicted (correctly as it turned out), that they would escape again within two years. If they did, it would be the Indians in the right and not the government. He was also concerned about the Indians who had been sent to Florida after the Red River War. They had been exiled long enough, and he felt many of them should be allowed to return.[21]

Although he may have sympathized with the defeated Cheyennes and the Indian prisoners in Florida, he found some of the Quahadis in the Territory still intractable. Mackenzie sent word that a band which had been out raiding but which had sneaked onto the Fort Sill Reservation and were camped among the other Comanches, were to be turned over to the military for confinement. A delegation of Comanche chiefs appeared at his office in response to his directive. As Horace Jones, the post interpreter, translated, "one after another of the chiefs strode forward and, with flashing eyes and haughty mien, delivered his oration, which was received with many 'ughs' of approval by the others." Mackenzie summoned Lieutenant James Parker, the acting adjutant, from the outer office and quietly told him, "Have all the troops saddle up, leaving the horses in their stalls, the men to be armed and equipped with 100 rounds of ammunition. Do this quickly but quietly, in such a manner that the preparations will not be seen by the Indians."

When Parker returned to report that everything was ready, Mackenzie stood up and picked up his hat. "Jones," he said, "tell the Indians I have listened to their talk long enough. Tell them that if they do not bring those renegade Quahadi Comanches to the guardhouse in twenty minutes," he paused and began speaking very slowly, "I will go out to their camps and kill them all. Repeat that, Jones, just as I have said it. I—will—go—out—to—their—camps—and—*kill*—them—all!" Then he walked out. The chiefs made a rush for their horses and returned shortly with the renegades.[22]

Besides his more stimulating Indian problems, Mackenzie had mundane duties such as entertaining visiting dignitaries. One of these was Captain Albert Markham of the British Royal Navy, a noted polar explorer who had mentioned to General Sheridan that he would like to hunt buffalo. Sheridan felt Fort Sill would be the best place, and Markham arrived in November 1877. Mackenzie turned him over to Lieutenant Thompson and sent him out on the plains where it didn't take the little Englishman long to become "one of the boys." The hunt was successful and Markham enjoyed himself thoroughly.[23]

For the Fourth, however, intervals like these were few. The regiment was too battle-seasoned, and its commander too skillful, to remain on garrison duty for very long. Back in the East his classmates from Williams College were following his movements with the same sense of frustration that has plagued his biographers ever since. As the class yearbook put it, "He . . . is known as the worst wounded man in the army and yet is able to dash over the Mexican border or up among the Sioux. He does not stop long enough in one place to write a letter."[24]

But while Mackenzie continued to be reticent about his personal life and wary of expressing his opinions, the generals in Washington and Chicago were making plans for a new dash over the border.

CHAPTER 16

"I Have Never Known So Bad a State of Affairs on this River Before"

By late 1877, Indian and bandit raids along the Mexican border had reached a point that the army felt it best to send Mackenzie back to Texas. General Ord, the aggressive departmental commander, had already allowed several incursions across the Rio Grande on his own responsibility, and he was promoting further actions to such an extent that Sherman felt it necessary to rein him in. The restrictions were short-lived, however; the army, under attack by the Democratic Party for its role in Reconstruction, was inclined to step-up its activities on the western frontier to gain the support of Texas Democrats. Ord himself had frequently requested Mackenzie's return to Texas, and on December 3 Sheridan ordered Mackenzie to take six companies of the Fourth from Fort Sill to San Antonio and report to departmental headquarters. The balance of the regiment, scattered about various posts, was to join as soon as duties permitted. The ultimate destination was once again Fort Clark, where Mackenzie was to assume command of the Subdistrict of the Nueces.[1]

The six companies left for San Antonio on December 17. Parker, who served as adjutant for the column, noted in his memoirs that Mackenzie had been conferring in Washington and had arrived at Fort Sill just before the scheduled departure.

He also wrote that, one day as they were riding at the head of the column, Mackenzie remarked to him, "As sure as that sun rises and sets there will be war with Mexico within six months!" indicating some sort of privy information. Mackenzie's service record does not indicate a trip to Washington during this period, so it is possible that Parker, writing his recollections fifty years later, might have confused this incident with another Washington trip.[2]

Progress toward Texas was slowed by a heavy rain which continued for days. Wagons bogged, requiring soldiers to dismount and pull them out, and it took thirteen days to cover the forty miles from Fort Sill to the Red River. On one day the column covered less than a mile before the wagons mired up to their hubs and the troops had to make camp. The crossing of the Red River, a rain-filled torrent, took three days. Food ran short, and Mackenzie had to write ahead to Fort Richardson to have eighteen hundred rations delivered to him in Henrietta. "This is essential," he wrote. "Very bad storm. If out of transportation please hire." For years afterwards, the men of the Fourth called this trip the "Mud March."[3]

On reaching Henrietta, a citizens' committee informed the troops that the community planned a banquet and ball in their honor. Mackenzie, frustrated at the delays caused by rain and mud, was in no mood for festivities, but he gave in and agreed. He was further disconcerted when he had to reply to the speeches from the various dignitaries. In an obvious reference to Mackenzie's speech impediment, Parker said he responded "with difficulty" since he "was not an orator."

His aversion to alcohol also created problems, since the mayor was continually shoving his pocket flask at him and insisting he take a drink. Finally Mackenzie made an excuse and moved to the opposite side of the table.[4]

Meanwhile the enlisted men had a celebration of their own, soaking up rotgut whisky in a local saloon. When fights broke out, the proprietor closed the saloon and ran them off. Outraged at this breach of hospitality, the troopers decided to tear down the building. When the sheriff and some citizens tried to break up the melee, the soldiers drew their revolvers and began firing. The noise attracted the attention of the officers in the ball and, at the sight of gold shoulder straps, many of the troopers fled back to camp. Some of the more belligerent had to be beaten into submission with gun butts and were bound and gagged. "Suffice it say there was no more dancing that night," Parker remarked.

The weather made further marching impossible, marooning the column in Henrietta for several days. To keep the men under control, Mackenzie directed Lieutenant H.H. Crews, the battalion quartermaster, to hire a room in town to serve as a guardroom. A noncommissioned officer and six enlisted men were detailed as guards. Courts-martial were held for several enlisted men as well as one officer, First Lieutenant Lewis Warrington, charged with "drunkenness on the line of march."[5] It seems odd that Mackenzie would see fit to charge only Warrington, when Lawton's drinking was notorious throughout the regiment. From personal loyalty, and because Lawton was one of the best supply officers in the army, Mackenzie tolerated his drinking.

The march finally resumed but the rain, snow and mud continued during the trip to Fort Richardson and Fort Griffin. At Griffin, with his supplies exhausted and shoes and clothing worn out, Mackenzie pulled rank and requisitioned supplies from the commissary over the protests of the local commanding officer. In camp, with the ground too soft to hold picket pins in place, the horses pulled them up and wandered off, requiring their roundup before resuming the march.

As the column moved further into Central Texas, both the weather and Mackenzie's disposition improved. At Fredericksburg, only 150 miles from Fort Clark, Mackenzie sent the column on while he and Parker checked into a local hotel to await the stage which would take them into San Antonio. The next morning Parker came down for breakfast and found Mackenzie outside, staring at a green and gold stagecoach with the name "General McKinzy" lettered across it. "Such is fame," he remarked to Parker with a laugh, "to have your name spelled wrong."

The "General McKinzy," less reliable than its namesake, broke down just outside of town. Another coach was sent for and they arrived at the Menger Hotel in San Antonio that night. A couple of days later Mackenzie sent Parker on to Fort Clark with the band, some soldiers' wives and various other female camp followers.[6] After conferring with General Ord, he joined his troops.

Besides his own regiment, Mackenzie's command at Fort Clark included three battalions of infantry, three batteries of light artillery and units of the Eighth Cavalry. The units were portioned out to strengthen Shafter's garrison at Fort Duncan and to establish subposts. His command also included Lt. John L. Bullis' Seminole-Negroes, who were permanently assigned to Fort Clark.[7]

His troops distributed, Mackenzie decided to contact Brigadier General A.R. Falcón, the Mexican commander in the area, to propose a joint effort to subdue the Lipans. Explaining his idea to Shafter, he said:

Any able Mexican can understand how bitterly the
Frontier people of Coahuilla *[sic]* would feel towards the Government of the United States, should
it allow a band of Comanches to camp in the
vicinity of Uvalde, or the mountains on the Nueces, and while at peace here, commit constant depredations on the other side of the river, and this is
precisely the position the Mexican authorities have
hitherto in a measure occupied regarding the Lipans.

If Falcón's response to the joint effort were positive,
Shafter was authorized to accept any prisoners as well as to
further "act at once if there is any proposition made to you
by General Falcon."[8] Mackenzie also told him to "use every
exertion" to capture revolutionaries or thieves from Mexico,
if they were on the U.S. side, and to request the Mexicans to
notify him of any probable crossing points.[9]

Falcón, however, had other ideas. Responding to Mackenzie's suggestions, he pointed out that the Lipans had
permission from the Mexican government to live near Santa
Rosa, and that he was not authorized to cooperate with U.S.
forces in suppressing them. The best he could do was to
forward the request to higher authorities in Mexico.

Mackenzie viewed this reply as a slap in the face both to
himself and to the United States. "The Mexican government
has now and has had for several months, enough troops
stationed at Piedras Negras to put a stop to all raiding of either
Indian or Mexicans if the soldiers were energetically employed
to that end," he wrote to departmental headquarters. "The
underlying reason for the continuous failure to restrain the
inhabitants is that, the Mexican frontier people have no re-

spect for the American Nation or government, and profit by the depredations committed on our territory."

The military was thus faced with two conflicting national policies, a conflict which worked to the advantage of Indians and outlaws. On the one hand, U.S. forces were ordered to pursue raiders into Mexico if necessary, but Mexican troops were ordered "to repel such pursuit by force, so that, at any time, if the orders of both governments are carefully followed, we are likely to have a war."

Mackenzie pointed out that, although personally opposed to a war or to annexation of Mexican territory, he did not see how war could be avoided unless the United States government were willing to abandon protection of its citizens in the border areas. Since he felt conflict was inevitable, he suggested "going to war so soon as troops and transportation can be got ready."[10]

He had already sent spies to Mexico who were trying to locate the Indians responsible for the most recent raids into Texas. He had also concluded that Kickapoos were involved, as well as Lipans, and suspected (erroneously) that President Porfirio Díaz was responsible. His plan was to give the Indians time to settle down more or less permanently, then attack them in heavy force, including infantry and artillery.[11]

In early May 1878, Mackenzie hired a former Comanchero who had worked with him before and who had proven himself "brave, intelligent and sagacious." The man was not known on either side of this area of the border, but had enough Indian contacts to trade with the marauders and to gather information without arousing suspicion. By the end of the month Mackenzie had learned which Indians were responsible for the raids and was convinced an expedition into Mexico was justified. "The location of their Camps is tolerably well established, but I have no guide for a small part of the route near their camps," he wrote on May 22, adding, "I expect to have one in a few days." He also wanted to wait until his Comanchero was back, which he felt would take another ten to fifteen days.[12]

In mid-May, from Fort Duncan, Mackenzie communicated with Colonel Jesús Nuncio, commander of the Mexican forces in Piedras Negras. Although Nuncio was sympathetic with the problem, the revolutionary forces again stirring in northern Mexico prevented any action by his troops against the Indians. Consequently Mackenzie saw no other option than to go ahead with his plan to take his troops across the border and settle the Indian problem himself. He only needed official approval. Perhaps reminded of the furor which had followed Remolino five years earlier, he had already written Colonel T.M. Vincent, departmental adjutant, asking General Ord to advise him if he were opposed to the strike. "If I undertake anything I do not expect to fail, so far as a human being can forsee, but the danger of Mexican interferance [sic] is considerable, and I believe the responsibility for the command should not be devolved on me alone," he explained.[13]

Ord, whose aggressiveness was causing Sheridan to consider his recall, now became cautious. Although he approved the raid, the language of his telegram was not clear enough for Mackenzie, who was in desperate need of what he called "moral support." On May 28 he wrote Vincent, "I wish General Ord to know that it appears to me that he ought to say distinctly that he wishes me to punish those raiders. I am only now waiting for the return of a man from Santa Rosa, to start." Two days later Ord replied that Mackenzie could cross the Rio Grande either in active pursuit or in following a fresh trail. In such a case, he should take advantage of any opportunity to reach the hostile camp. This reply, along with a rereading of Ord's original telegram, convinced Mackenzie that he had the backing of his superiors if, in his own judgment, crossing the border were warranted.[14]

On June 3 the Comanchero still had not returned, and Mackenzie began to believe he might have been discovered and killed. He sent another man to look for him, with orders to report back to Bullis' camp at the mouth of the Devils River by the end of the week. As soon as he returned, Captain Samuel Young, Eighth Cavalry, was to take a battalion across the border. "Col. Shafter will cross after Young has got a start and endeavor to clean up the thieves," he wrote. "I have never known so bad a state of affairs on this river before in my life."

A previous conversation with Colonel Nuncio convinced Mackenzie there might be real trouble with Mexico. The Mexican officer had reviewed for Mackenzie the orders from President Díaz to military commanders on the northern frontier: not only were they to refuse assistance to U.S. forces on Mexican territory, they were to attack if they felt they had sufficient strength. Despite this warning, Mackenzie had already begun distributing his troops for a crossing into Mexico.[15]

Mackenzie joined Young on the Devils River. Since there is no further mention of the Comanchero, it might be presumed he had finally returned safely. On June 11 they broke camp and made for a point on the Rio Grande known as Winker's Crossing, about fifteen miles below the mouth of the Devils River. The command was organized into two columns with Mackenzie and Young heading a scouting group consisting of four companies of Eighth Cavalry, two of the

Fourth and some Seminole-Negroes. Shafter headed the larger column with three battalions of infantry, three battalions of artillery, two companies of cavalry, and forty wagons with thirty days rations.[16]

On reaching Winker's Crossing, Mackenzie's column found the waters of the Rio Grande too high to cross until the afternoon of the following day. Once across the column made ten miles in blistering heat before going into dry camp. Although the guide had expected to find water at various points along the march, there was little to be had. At 4:30 P.M. June 13, the second day of the march into Mexico, enough water was located for the stock but the troops once again had to go into dry camp. The column broke camp at 2:00 A.M., to take advantage of the coolness of the early morning, and marched nine miles to Burro Mountain where the guide expected water to be plentiful. "We found barely enough for the men to make coffee, and to water the pack-mules, leaving none for the horses," Mackenzie complained.[17]

Another water hole was estimated to be about thirty-five miles away. The guide became sick and the surgeon felt he could not travel during the heat of the day, so the lead company was ordered to move ahead without its pack train and make a trail to the water hole. The main column followed considerably later. The sick guide was so confused he led the main column on a roundabout march of twelve miles to reach a point only four miles away, where it ran into the lead company.

Mackenzie became convinced he would lose all his stock from thirst before water could be reached, and sent a messenger ordering Shafter to remain on the U.S. side if he had not yet crossed, and to turn back if he was already in Mexico.

Mackenzie then turned his column back toward the border. On the return march, however, the column ran across another water hole. After drinking, the horses proved to be in better condition than he had thought, so Mackenzie decided to push on and search the country around the San Diego and San Rodrigo Rivers. New orders were sent to Shafter, who met the Mackenzie column on the San Diego on June 17. That night it rained, the ground turned soft, and the two columns covered only six miles the next day before going into camp by a water hole. At least water was now available.[18]

The expedition broke camp at 1:00 A.M. June 19 and marched to Remolino, near the scene of Mackenzie's victory five years earlier, where it met "a considerable body of troops of the Mexican Army" under Colonel Pedro Advícula Valdez.[19] This was the "Colonel Winker" Mackenzie had recommended to command Mexican forces in the district following the Remolino raid, and whom Mackenzie considered "a very Gallant but corrupt officer, but probably however not more corrupt than the average Mexican officers of high rank." Believing they could work together, Mackenzie sent a messenger asking the Mexicans to join the U.S. column in a punitive expedition.

Mackenzie's belief was ill-founded. Regardless of their mutual professional respect, "Colonel Winker" was a soldier just as determined to uphold the honor of his country as Mackenzie was to uphold that of the United States. He indicated that, although he personally would like to end the Indian trouble, his orders were to "fire on any American troops crossing the Rio Grande." The only reason he did not attack immediately was that he did not have sufficient strength to take on the American column. But, he noted, he was expecting reinforcements and would attack when they arrived unless Mackenzie had started back toward the river.

"When will you receive these reinforcements?" Mackenzie asked.

"At two o'clock."

"Very well, then, I will go into camp; at two o'clock I will advance," Mackenzie said. He added that Young's column would go into camp at one end of Remolino and the Mexicans could camp at the other. The two commanders also agreed that each would notify the other before advancing.[20]

At 1:30 P.M. Shafter and Lieutenant Crews were directed to notify Advícula Valdez that the U.S. forces had no quarrel with the Mexican government or people, and were in Mexico on a punitive expedition against outlaws and Indians who were marauding into the United States. Advícula Valdez was also warned that Mexican troops were directly in the line of march and that the American column would begin advancing at 3:00 P.M. Colonel Nuncio, arriving with additional forces, responded with a letter stating:

> You have violated and outraged the dignity of our Republic, the only manner that I can allow you to pass, as you desire to do so without an encounter is—that you will pledge your word of honor in public—to give satisfaction to my superiors and to the Nation generally.
>
> By offering to do so under solemn promise, then I will advance with my troops covering your rear guard until you cross the margin of the Bravo [the Rio Grande].[21]

Nuncio wanted an immediate answer. Mackenzie replied

that the terms were rejected and the advance would take place at 3:00 P.M. as previously stated.

At the appointed time Shafter's infantry advanced directly toward the Mexican line, down the right bank of the San Rodrigo, while Young went down the left bank to flank the Mexican position if Nuncio attempted to engage. His forces hopelessly inadequate, Nuncio withdrew without breaking camp, which Bullis' scouts looted of pots and pans. Mackenzie moved his forces nine miles down the river and camped for the night.[22]

Mackenzie realized how close he had come to starting personally a war between the two nations. Although he was a pragmatic advocate of war, he did not feel it "should be almost subject to the whim of subordinate commanders" such as himself.[23] Consequently he decided to return to Texas, and the following day turned his column toward Monclova Viejo en route back to the Rio Grande. The dust of the Mexican column was seen in the distance as it shadowed the Americans. On the morning of June 21 Lieutenant Crews was sent into Monclova Viejo to assure the townspeople that the U.S. troops meant them no harm. He returned with the information that the Mexican forces had taken up a position on the right flank, and that pickets or skirmishers were on a hill overlooking the town.

Crews was sent to tell the Mexican commander the Americans were preparing to cross the river, but would not if the Mexicans intended to attack. The commander, Colonel Nuncio, did not answer himself but sent Advícula Valdez and a major to meet with Mackenzie. They asked "as well as could be gathered some apology or reparation for the presence of our troops." Mackenzie replied that he was responsible only for his actions while in command of the troops. The presence of U.S. troops in Mexico was the responsibility of higher authorities and, consequently, "any question of apology or reparation could only be arranged through them" and not through the two commanding officers.

As he turned to ride back to his own lines, Advícula Valdez politely told Mackenzie that even though the U.S. troops were to recross the Rio Grande, they would be expected to guard themselves from attack.[24]

Mackenzie felt some sort of demonstration was in order, and sent Young with six companies of cavalry and the Seminole-Negroes to occupy the hill where the Mexican pickets were deployed. At the foot of the hill he placed the scouts and a portion of one company of cavalry as skirmishers, while the rest of Young's men turned to the west side of the hill to flank the Piedras Negras road. The Mexicans withdrew to a point about three miles away.

Mackenzie knew Nuncio would be unable to resist a march through Piedras Negras. To spare the Mexican officer the humiliation of defeat, he decided to head straight toward the river and avoid the town. Shafter, already on the Piedras Negras road, was ordered to return through Monclova Viejo and turn toward the river. Young's skirmish line covered the river crossing, which was made without incident. A final note from Colonel Nuncio assured Mackenzie that, since the crossing was obviously underway, there would be no interference.[25]

Back at Fort Clark, Mackenzie prepared his official report then sent a private letter to Ord stating his views. He told the departmental commander that the only way to put a stop to depredations was for small parties of light cavalry to hunt down the Indians in their own territory, as he had already done with the Comanches. On the border, however, "With

the absolute prohibition by the Mexican government of crossing by our troops, the case becomes singularly complicated.
A small party, which alone has any chance of overtaking the
raiders, will undoubtedly be attacked by a very superior force
if it penetrates the country any distance. A large force cannot
move with sufficient rapidity to overtake them." He then
went into a two-part indictment of the Mexican government,
blaming it for the problem of inaction, if not by actual
conspiracy.

> I will now briefly state my ideas as to what is
> necessary for the permanent settlement of this
> question. First, The entire defeat of all Mexican
> troops in the field with the occupation of the city
> of Mexico and its frontier states. Second, Peace
> with an indemnity for all past outrages secured by
> the Military occupation and government of the
> frontier states, till that indemnity is paid. . . .I wish
> in closing to say that I utterly object to any half
> measures as unworthy.[26]

Despite the dogmatic tone of his letter, Mackenzie's position was not absolute. Initially Ord wanted him to make
various demonstrations to keep Nuncio's troops in the field
awhile longer. Mackenzie responded by saying, "There is no
object in humiliating Mexican troops any further" unless the
United States were willing to go to war over it.[27]

On July 4 Mackenzie again crossed into Mexico. The river
was high again, the crossing difficult. Some of the pack mules
lost their footing and drowned. After most of the cavalry had
crossed, a courier arrived from Fort Clark with orders cancel-
ling the operation. Mackenzie returned to the post, where he
notified Ord that he had received information that Mexican

troops were being fed on stolen Texas cattle. "Moving to
Piedras Negras but driving out the Mexican troops, because
they are fed in a great measure on stolen cattle, is simply
declaring war, which is not within the scope of my orders,"
he wrote. Once again, he advocated general war and occupation of Mexico.[28] In his endorsement to Mackenzie's letter,
Ord said he did not concur with Mackenzie's views. Instead,
he felt:

> The order to follow the thieves, if maintained and
> executed, with the recovery of the stolen goods,
> and the punishment of the [protectors] of thieves—
> though they may be Mexican troops—while it may
> create quite a flow of language from Mexico, will
> result in the Mexican authorities feeding their
> troops on something else besides Texas beef.[29]

Ord's new interest in Mexico's overall national integrity
dismayed Mackenzie, who responded by applying for a transfer. Ord turned him down, saying that he was still needed,
since General Gerónimo Treviño was expected on the border
with five thousand troops and the possibility of war still
existed.[30]

In mid-August Captain Young and Lieutenant Thompson
crossed the Rio Grande to meet the *alcalde* of Villanueva, who
told them a bandit named Arreola was supplying Nuncio's
troops with beef from stolen Texas cattle. The *alcalde* had
reported it to Nuncio, and Arreola had threatened to kill him
if he reported it again. "I think we should follow Areola *[sic]*
or the stolen cattle into Piedras Negras, and humiliate Nuncio," was Young's comment on the matter.[31]

In the capitals of the two countries, however, more mod-
erate policies prevailed. Porfirio Díaz realized that his inten-

tions to stabilize Mexico and develop its industry and re-
sources would be hindered by a war with the United States.
Additionally, the problem of Indians and bandits' using
Mexico as a base, and the American reaction, were a nuisance. When General Treviño finally arrived on the border,
Ord arranged grand receptions for him and his staff in San
Antonio and Galveston, where both sides exchanged
pledges of mutual friendship and cooperation. Aside from
Ord's newfound sense of diplomacy, there can be no doubt
that Mackenzie's presence on the border, his record of
success, and his reputation for entering and leaving Mexico
as he chose were also mitigating factors in this shift of
Mexican attitude. In September Lieutenant Colonel Felipe
Vega, commanding officer at Villa de Jimenes, advised
Mackenzie that Nuncio had ordered a series of subposts "for
the purpose of persecuting smugglers and thieves." Accordingly, he asked that each side give the other notice of raids,
so that the authorities of either country could take appropriate action. This was followed by a note from Nuncio
himself, telling Mackenzie that he had revoked passports of
the Kickapoos at Santa Rosa.[32]

From his headquarters at Fort Clark, Mackenzie concentrated on the more mundane aspects of his position as
district commander. The House Subcommittee on Military
Affairs sought his opinion on a general reorganization of
the army, and he responded with a detailed reply.[33] When
President Hayes had a favorite for the position of post
trader at Fort Clark, and lined up support in the War
Department, Mackenzie rejected the proposal since he
knew of "no reasonable ground of complaint" against the
incumbent trader. The Hayes candidate, J.W. Skiles, accepted Mackenzie's rejection with good grace, but such

high-level interference with post operations could be a nuisance.[34]

Mackenzie felt some personal affront that autumn when Cheyennes bolted the reservation and headed northwest toward their traditional homeland, as he had earlier predicted they would. Several companies of the Fourth were serving near the Cheyenne Agency in the Indian Territory at the time, and their actions leading up to the outbreak and subsequent attempts to control it had been criticized in the newspapers. In a telegram to departmental headquarters in San Antonio on October 3, he said, "I am much disgusted at what I have seen in papers of action of [my] companies, though I trust it is untrue." He added that if Brigadier General John Pope, commander of the Department of the Missouri, wanted him to come up and take personal command, he would be willing to do so.[35] Headquarters replied the offer would be forwarded to Pope, but that Ord would not approve the transfer since he felt Mackenzie was still more necessary where he was.[36]

Mackenzie would not let the matter rest, and the telegrams flew back and forth throughout the next forty-eight hours. Finally Vincent told him that Ord would forward Mackenzie's request to Sheridan adding, however, that Ord also intended to point out that some five thousand Mexican regulars were headed toward the border and, due to the strained relations with Mexico, he felt Mackenzie should stay put.[37]

To Mackenzie, the movement of large numbers of Mexican forces looked like preparation for war,[38] but in actuality the Mexican troops were being transferred to the border by Díaz to clean out the Indian strongholds. An era of military cooperation between the two countries was inaugurated, culminating in the defeat of the Apache bands by coordinated effort in the 1880s. Friendly relations continued until the collapse of the Díaz regime in 1910.[39]

CHAPTER 17

"If You Will Not Go of Your Own Accord, I Will Make You Go"

With the Mexican border quiet, the government found other uses for Mackenzie. The regiment remained at Fort Clark, but someone in the War Department apparently remembered that Mackenzie had both training and field experience as an engineer, and he was ordered to Washington to serve on an evaluation board headed by Nelson Miles to consider entrenching tools and equipment. He arrived in December 1878 and remained in the East until the end of April 1879 when he returned to his command.[1]

During this interval, problems were developing with the Utes of the White River Agency in northwestern Colorado. The situation had begun earlier in the decade when silver was discovered in the San Juan Mountains, and pressure by the miners had forced the tribe to surrender four million acres of its reservation. Unsatisfied, many whites wanted the rest too, and advocated the removal of the tribe to the Indian Territory. Utes were blamed for depredations as far away as New Mexico. The government aggravated the situation in 1878 by placing Nathan C. Meeker in charge of the White River Agency. A self-righteous utopian totally unqualified for his position, Meeker was determined to convert the Indians immediately to farming.

The Indians resisted, led by the Chiefs Jack and Douglas,

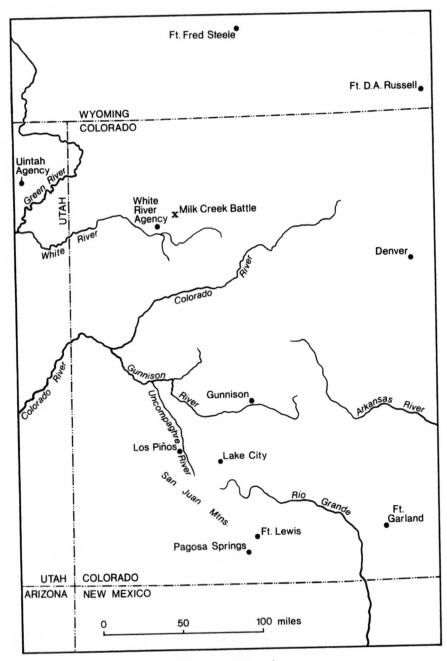

Western Colorado

and Meeker began requesting troops to force obedience.[2] General Pope, who should have known better, sided with the agent, calling the Utes "worthless idle vagabonds, who are no more likely to earn a living where they are, by manual labor, than by teaching metaphysics. . .no Utes in Colorado that I know of are kept on their Reservations, except when they choose to stay there."[3]

The showdown came in September 1879 when Meeker insisted that the Utes plow and fence the meadows where their ponies grazed. When a Ute medicine man named Johnson went to the agent's home to talk about the farming order, Meeker, recovering from injuries in a wagon accident, was in no mood to be reasonable. He told Johnson the Indians had too many ponies to begin with, and said the plowing would continue. The frustrated Ute grabbed the agent and threw him bodily out of the house. He might have been seriously injured had not his employees intervened. Not until a shot was fired at one of the plowmen did Meeker finally realize the situation was becoming dangerous and suspend plowing.[4]

Citizens of the area felt a Ute outbreak was imminent and sent word to the army asking for protection, even though the nearest military post was Fort Fred Steele, Wyoming, 175 miles away in the Department of the Platte. Despite Colorado's being in the Department of the Missouri, Major Thomas T. Thornburgh, commander at Fort Fred Steele, was ordered to take an expeditionary force to protect the White River Agency, enforce Meeker's requirements, and detain the ringleaders of Ute resistance until an investigation could be made.[5]

Thornburgh was no fool and probably knew the Utes and their country better than any other officer in the Platte,[6] but everyone had underestimated the seriousness of the situation.

The Indians had had enough of government policies. On September 29, after Thornburgh crossed the Milk River with three companies of infantry and cavalry, the Indians met him and began to parley. There was a misunderstanding and shooting broke out. The troops were surrounded and almost overwhelmed; Thornburgh and eleven men were killed, four officers and thirty-four men were wounded. Most of the animals were killed. The survivors dug in for a siege which lasted almost a week before help arrived. Enraged at the invasion of their land, the Utes killed Meeker and nine employees and captured Meeker's wife and daughter, another woman and two children. Colonel Wesley Merritt arrived with a relief column from Cheyenne and occupied the White River Agency.[7]

Ute Chief Ouray
(Author's collection)

At the Uncompahgre Ute Agency at Los Piños the Southern Utes under Chief Ouray were still quiet, and Sherman hoped Merritt's presence at White River would be enough to keep them in line. Secretary of the Interior Carl Schurz appointed General Charles Adams of Colorado as special agent to meet with Ouray "and agree upon all measures necessary to secure the guilty parties in the White River murders and to protect the innocent." Sherman ordered Sheridan to keep Merritt at White River and "collect another force preferably under McKenzie *[sic]*. . .to operate from that direction in case Agent Adams fails in his mission & makes a future requisition for military help to capture the Utes."[8]

With Colorado in an uproar, apprehension spilled over into northern New Mexico where Governor Lew Wallace asked permission to form volunteer units. Pope ordered Colonel Edward Hatch, Ninth Cavalry, commander of the District of New Mexico, to send four companies of Twenty-Second Infantry from Fort Gibson, Indian Territory, to Fort Garland, Colorado, and to have the garrison at Fort Wingate, New Mexico, ready to move toward Pagosa Springs in the Ute Country of Southern Colorado.

In Chicago, even before Sherman's order, Sheridan was already prepared to send out his favorite troubleshooter. In a message to General Ord in San Antonio, Sheridan said:

> The recent troubles with the White River Utes will, I am afraid, extend to the Southern bands of the same tribe, now very much dissatisfied, and it will be necessary to send General Pope additional troops to provide for this contingency. You are therefore directed to send Colonel Mackenzie and the six companies of his regiment by rail to the Department of the Missouri.[9]

The order was received with misgivings in Texas. General Ord complied, ordering in various companies of the Fourth from their camps to march to San Antonio where they would take the train to Fort Hays, Kansas, in preparation for their trip to Colorado. But he asked Sheridan to reconsider the

Edward O.C. Ord
(National Archives)

move if the Ute situation died down, since he felt Mackenzie was more necessary at Fort Clark. "Serious complications are likely with Mexico on account of the stream of Americans pushing for the Sierra Mojada Mines from all parts of West Texas," he explained.[10]

Ord was not the only person who had misgivings; members of the Texas delegation to Congress asked that the transfer be blocked. "I knew this protest, or remonstrances, or appeal would come from Texas," Sherman remarked, "but the orders having been made, and the necessity for troops in Southern Colorado being today more apparent & urgent than when this order was made...the order must now be obeyed." He suggested Sheridan make other arrangements for the defense of Texas and sent a letter to Senator Maxey reassuring him that the army would protect Texas. However, he said, "Mackenzie cannot be everywhere, but we promise other & excellent officers to replace him—it may be only for a short time."[11]

The first three companies of the Fourth left Fort Clark at 10:45 A.M. October 6. Mackenzie, although suffering from an infected ear which had abscessed and was draining, advised divisional headquarters that he would need twelve pack mules for each company, and five for headquarters, as well as rations and forage at Fort Hays for 450 men and four hundred horses.[12]

The news from Colorado was not good. Pope notified Chicago that the Uncompahgre Agency had been closed and the agent and employees evacuated. People in the nearby town of Animas City were greatly alarmed, and units from Fort Lewis, sixty miles away, had been ordered in to defend it.[13]

Sherman, however, was determined to give Special Agent Adams, Secretary Schurz and the Interior Department every opportunity to defuse the situation. To that end, he told Sheridan to reduce the number of troops at the White River Agency to a sufficient force to prevent the return of the hostile Utes, and to send the remaining troops back to Fort Steele. He hoped Ouray would surrender the murderers, but if they had to be fought or hunted down, the army would be ready.

> I want the troops to realize that we in Washington
> do not intend to expose them unnecessarily, but if,
> as now seems probable, these Utes have been play-
> ing the old game, they will have good reason to
> repent it for there must be no halfway measures
> this time. If necessary, I will send every man from
> the Atlantic Coast, but the trouble will be, to
> subsist and maintain troops in that quarter of the
> country.[14]

Fortunately, it appeared the southern bands would stay out of the turmoil. Since Ouray was keeping them under control, and the possibility of an outbreak there was noticeably diminishing, Pope planned to keep Mackenzie's force at Fort Garland until such time as it might be required in the field. Then, in late October, Adams managed to convince the Indians to return Mrs. Meeker and the other White River captives.[15]

Mackenzie was still suffering from his ear infection when he arrived in Kansas, and Pope questioned whether he would be able to continue the trip to Fort Garland. Within two days, however, he was ready to go. His force included six companies of the Fourth Cavalry, five companies of the Nineteenth Infantry, and two companies of the Sixteenth Infantry for a total of 637 men. Initially he was to have received two more companies of the Fourth from Fort Hays and Camp Supply, but he preferred infantry since he believed cavalry would not be as efficient "on account of transportation and operating in cold weather and in a mountainous country. . . ."[16] Besides more infantry, he asked for fifty to one hundred Cheyenne scouts as well as one, and perhaps two trains with mules which had been well broken-in to service. He suggested one mule train could be brought up from Fort Clark, where it was "not needed," but in Texas General Ord took exception saying the mules would be needed for the companies replacing the Fourth at Clark.[17]

Adams, now head of a three-man peace commission which also included Colonel Hatch and Chief Ouray, convened the commission in Lake City in an effort to obtain the surrender of the Indians guilty of the Meeker Massacre and the Thornburgh fight. Secretary Schurz was determined to send the guilty Indians under guard to Fort Leavenworth or even to Fortress Monroe in Virginia to face trial by a military commission "outside of Colorado and New Mexico."

Adams, however, apparently still feeling insecure, asked

that troops be sent from Fort Garland to Lake City. Mackenzie objected, saying the military should not become involved
"until the Peace Commission has entirely completed its labors," and Pope backed him for several reasons. Pope felt
sending troops to Lake City was militarily unsound, since it
was completely off the line of march if Mackenzie were to find
it necessary to move against the Utes. Secondly, he pointed
out that the request was apparently made by Adams alone and
not the commission as a whole. "I consider it best to wait until
the wish of the Commission is known, before making so
important a movement which may engage Mackenzie so far
as to frustrate the object for which his column was organized,"
he told Sheridan.[18]

Mackenzie's objections were also probably due to military considerations, but he personally felt the peace commission would accomplish nothing and even felt sorry for Hatch
for having to serve on it. As for the Utes, he said if they agreed
to deliver Jack and Douglas, the two chiefs, or any of the
principal warriors considered responsible for the Meeker affair, they would be:

> different from all other savages. . . .Now if these
> Indians are in a condition to be properly dealt with
> by a peace commission no troops are needed and if
> they are not in such a frame of mind no peace
> commission is needed. It should be one way or the
> other, either they or us, not half of the one and half
> of the other.

Writing to Pope, he called the commission "a farce" and
reiterated his all-or-nothing position, saying it was better for
the army to stay out of the way until the Interior Department
was ready to give it a free hand. He did not anticipate waiting

very long, since he said either the Indians or white citizens of Colorado would probably force Interior to turn the situation over to the War Department as, he pointed out, had ultimately been the case with the Southern Plains tribes in 1874 and again with the Sioux in 1876. Anticipating being placed in charge of the situation, he once again lobbied for more infantry and fewer cavalry, for hospital stewards, and for the pack trains from Fort Clark.[19]

He was uncertain whether he personally would be able to lead the expedition because the cold weather had aggravated his rheumatism. He allowed a trace of grim humor to show when he told Pope:

> Either everything will be remarkably happy and we can all go home, with a picture in our mind's eye of the bad Jack hanging to a cottonwood, while the good Ouray, in a swallow tailed coat, flanked on the right by Ned Hatch and on the left by Adams, pronounces a benediction on the faithful. Or, again there will be another state of uncertainty & delay with a prospect of most serious trouble in the spring.[20]

Negotiations continued throughout the winter with Mackenzie continuing to complain. He believed Schurz and the Indian agents were conspiring to discredit Colonel Hatch, and through him the military in the eventuality negotiations went awry. Of the opinion that the army had already made too many concessions to Schurz, he wrote Pope that someone should warn Sherman "to keep army affairs independent from those of the Interior Dept." He also felt that Adams was bungling negotiations by delivering ultimatums to the Indians without the force to back them.[21] And always he continued to complain about inadequate pack mules and insufficient forces. He told Sheridan that pack trains should be sent to him from the Platte and from Texas, a demand which neither General Crook nor General Ord appreciated.[22]

More and more as the winter progressed, Mackenzie began to envision a conspiracy against him. Under the impression he was to have been assigned command of Fort Riley, Kansas, he felt slighted because he was having to spend the winter as part

John Pope
(National Archives)

of an inactive field force at Fort Garland, a situation he did not consider appropriate for a person of his rank. Other colonels, he contended, were treated better and he even went so far as to threaten "what may be a very bitter quarrel with Genl. Pope" if his needs were not met.[23]

Then he turned on the War Department. Pressing Pope for more troops, he accused General E.D. Townsend, Adjutant General of the Army, of:

> obstructing my views in this matter which I know are indisputable in soundness. . . .I know the necessities of the entire frontier east of the mountains in

a very thorough, personal way. And knowing this,
I regard General Townsend's course in the matter
as I understand it, as wicked, both in the Military
and moral sense.[24]

His accusations against Townsend were too much. No
regimental colonel on the frontier had the right to make such
remarks about senior officers and Townsend said so, the very
same day. "This is not the first time in which that officer has
presumed to arraign the action of this office on his assumption
of facts that do not exist," Townsend lashed out in a message
to Pope. He went on to say that General Sherman was
personally directing the assignment of manpower, and considered himself a better judge of the overall situation than Mackenzie.[25]

Townsend's rebuttal heightened Mackenzie's feelings of
persecution. In a letter to a friend he wrote, "I feel that I am
so much disliked at Washington and at the same time I am not
fairly dealt with at Dept. Hdqrs. that I want to give up." He
felt much of the problem was being caused by Major E.R.
Platt, Pope's adjutant, although he admitted he had no reason
to believe that.[26]

When spring arrived and the troops were no longer
hemmed in by weather, Mackenzie was able to get his mind
off his personal problems. He sent Christopher Gilson, a
civilian employee of the Quartermaster Department, to scout
along the Uncompahgre and Gunnison Rivers. At Los Piños
he found the southern bands prepared to abandon their home-
lands for a new reservation, if that was what the government
required, but at White River he found the Indians well armed
and supplied and ready to fight.[27] To bolster the Utes and
their agents at Los Piños, Mackenzie sent them Captain Beau-

mont with four well-provisioned companies of the Fourth Cavalry. As they neared the agency after a two hundred mile march, Lieutenant Parker could well understand why the whites wanted the Uncompahgre Valley. "It was practically the only piece of land within hundreds of miles available for cultivation; could be easily irrigated, and had an inexhaustible supply of water."[28]

On May 31 Mackenzie brought his main force to join Beaumont's column, giving him several thousand infantry and cavalry troops scattered throughout the valley. He found the tribal elders were keeping the Uncompahgres under control. Although overall he found the Indians to be civil, he noted they were "very independent and richer than any Indians I have ever seen scarcely begging at all." He felt that both the Los Piños and the White River Utes would remain quiet throughout the year.

On the other hand he was furious with the government's new peace commission, which included "old Meacham and Manypenny. . .chronic commissioners."* Among other things, they had appointed one of the warriors responsible for the Meeker and Thornburgh affairs to be chief of police at White River. "Under a serious Government nothing like it has perhaps ever happened," Mackenzie fumed.[29]

With little to do, Mackenzie made sure the men maintained their drill. Regulation dress was prescribed, and competition developed over horsemanship between the cavalry

---

* Commissioners Alfred B. Meacham and G. W. Manypenny were often involved in Indian negotiations throughout the frontier. Their frequently successful arrangements with the tribes irritated officers like Mackenzie who believed in purely military solutions and viewed the commissioners as meddlers.

companies. With the rich grass available he was able to cut the issue of grain for the horses and conserve it for future hard duty, thus alleviating a potential supply problem. His only complaint was the high desertion rate, which he attributed to the high wages and the mining excitement in the surrounding country.[30]

When Sheridan arrived in late August, he was "highly pleased" with his inspection of Mackenzie's cavalry command. Mackenzie accompanied Sheridan from Los Piños to Gunnison City, and during the trip they considered potential sites for a new military post. Mackenzie felt the only way to keep Indians in line was to congregate them near posts as he had done in Texas and in the Platte. One possible location near the confluence of Surface Creek and the Gunnison River they did not consider practical because of the severity of the winters.

Sheridan had previously written Mackenzie asking for his recollections of the final days leading to the surrender at Appomattox, apparently for an impending inquiry into the actions of General Warren. Mackenzie had replied that if he were called to testify, he would like to "refresh my mind looking over the returns of my [Union Army] Command. . . ." Now, from Gunnison City, Mackenzie traveled on to Washington as a witness for the Warren Court of Inquiry.[31] On October 28, after it concluded, he took a thirty-day leave which was repeatedly extended until he was finally given permission to remain away from duty until December 31. He gave his brother Morris' home in New York as his address and gave his reasons as personal. Exactly what those personal reasons were have never been revealed but, given his overall condition and service over the past several years, he was probably exhausted.[32]

Despite his physical and mental stress, Mackenzie continued his campaign for a general's star during this period. Although his brevet rank entitled him to be called "General," his permanent rank was colonel. Given his often derogatory opinions of ranking officers, he no doubt felt a permanent promotion was long overdue, and he was particularly concerned about acquiring a permanent general's star before Nelson Miles did. The rivalry which had developed between the two officers during the Red River War had grown more intense in the succeeding years. For Mackenzie, who had far more field experience and considered himself a much better officer, the rivalry was particularly acute and Miles' achievements were piling up—first in the Red River War, then in the Sioux and Nez Percé Wars. No matter what new assignment Mackenzie accomplished, Miles seemed able to equal it. A story made its way around the army that, one night as Mackenzie was sitting in camp gazing at the stars, one officer remarked, "I'm afraid, General, there's Miles between you and that star!" Mackenzie walked away, snapping his stumps in irritation.[33]

Sherman found the Mackenzie-Miles rivalry, common knowledge throughout the service, particularly irritating. As one author has noted, he viewed the two young colonels as a pair of "vultures" hovering overhead until age or death left an opening in the higher ranks.[34] Although never obvious, some of Sherman's actions indicate he may have occasionally kept them in line by playing them off against each other. When all else failed, an impatient sentence or two in a letter to their departmental commanders was enough to tone down Miles and send off Mackenzie to sulk in silence.

Mackenzie's bid for his general's star, which intensified after August 24, 1880, when the death of Brigadier General

Albert J. Myer, chief signal officer, left a vacancy,[35] received
support from many sides. General Warren backed his nomi-
nation, recalling him as a student in West Point and as a
comrade-in-arms during the Civil War. Crook also supported
it.[36] General Augur called Mackenzie "emminently [sic] successful, not only as far as mere fighting is concerned, but in
the whole management & control of a large command thrown
upon the resources of its commander, in the midst of the great
plains."[37] Pope commented, "I know no man in the Army
better qualified or better suited by distinguished service."[38]
Sheridan endorsed each of his departments' recommendations
with the statement:

> I have known Col. R.S. Mackenzie for the past
> sixteen years, and during the war, and for the past
> ten years as a subordinate in my military division.
> He has all the qualities of a good soldier with an
> industry and intelligence which fits him for any
> command or promotion in the military service.[39]

Although it had once been remarked that Mackenzie had
"no congressmen to bow to" for a promotion, and while he
may never have catered openly to politicians, he was nevertheless aware that many congressmen were on his side. Five
members of the congressional delegation from New Jersey,
which Mackenzie still considered his home state, wrote President Hayes to urge the promotion, as did both senators and
several congressmen from Texas.[40]

His reach for a star was for naught. No amount of political
or military pressure could change the fact that Colonel William B. Hazen had eleven years seniority and an excellent
record, and on December 15 the President appointed Hazen
to the Myer vacancy. To add to the blow, Miles was elevated

to brigadier general the same day for reasons which are obscure. His supporters, however, included Major General Winfield Scott Hancock, Democratic presidential nominee, who had narrowly lost the previous month's national election to Republican James A. Garfield. It is therefore possible that the lame duck Hayes Administration promoted Miles as a peace offering to the rising Democrats.[41]

At the end of his leave Mackenzie was called to confer with Sheridan and Pope. A new administrative area, the Military Division of the Gulf comprising Texas, Louisiana, Arkansas and the Indian Territory, had just been created under the command of Major General John Schofield. Perhaps to ease the blow of not being promoted, and possibly to give him administrative experience toward the next vacancy for general, Mackenzie was placed in command of the Department of Arkansas on January 31, 1881. Since a departmental commander was expected to be a brigadier general, his brevet rank was invoked.[42]

Over the next several months Mackenzie busied himself with mundane administrative chores at his new headquarters in Little Rock, but he did not particularly care for the assignment. Although he felt he deserved a desk command, he wanted an eastern city. Arkansas was the worst of two worlds: too far removed from the frontier to keep him busy but too close to the frontier to provide the relaxation and diversion he sought.[43] In April he was mentioned as a potential commandant of the new cavalry-infantry school at Fort Leavenworth. He seems to have liked the idea—if he were to remain on the frontier, at least he would be doing something that interested him—but the position went to Colonel E.S. Otis of the Twentieth Infantry. Mackenzie's tenure in Little Rock came to an abrupt end on May 9 when President Garfield abolished the Division of the Gulf as serving absolutely no military value. The Department of Arkansas ceased to exist, and previous divisional and departmental boundaries were reestablished. Once again, Mackenzie was bound for the plains.[44]

With the Utes quiet, much of the Fourth Cavalry had wintered at Fort Riley, but with the spring rumors of new troubles the troops were ordered back to Colorado. On May 9, Mackenzie's last day as departmental commander, the band at Fort Riley struck up "The Girl I left Behind Me" as the soldiers boarded the train which would take them to Fort Garland. They left Garland immediately for the Uncompahgre, arriving on June 3, and Mackenzie joined them three days later. His command now consisted of five companies of the Fourth and six companies of the Twenty-Third Infantry, which had constructed a cantonment, sent for their families and spent the winter there.[45]

The soldiers found the Utes "sulky and semi-hostile." They were armed and many had fled into the mountains. Local citizens predicted they would not move to a new reservation without a fight, but Mackenzie was more optimistic and wrote to General Pope that he did not expect much trouble. The Uncompahgre Utes would probably move, provided their new lands were suitable for their livestock and not too close to the Uintah and White River Utes "with whom they do not wish to live." If an outbreak did occur, he speculated it would be caused by "accidental collision," in which case, however, he pointed out they were well armed and well equipped. Additionally he warned that, regardless of whether or not they were willing to live together, the various Ute bands were more closely united against the whites than ever before and their relations with the Navajo stronger than any time in history. In fact, he said, "there is probably a general understanding that in case of any difficulty between the whites and one band, that the others shall join, that if one band breaks out all will aid."[46]

Mackenzie anticipated making it through the better part of the summer without an incident. If the Utes decided the new reservation was unsuitable and became determined to remain in Colorado, the trouble would probably break out in about six weeks when they were scheduled to move. Against that possibility he wanted his medical department bolstered with more experienced senior surgeons. He also felt the companies were very weak, so weak that he would be unwilling to retain the command unless more recruits were sent. "The prospect of quiet increases with the strength of the command and also the prospect of a satisfactory solution should trouble come," he wrote.[47]

Having first made a thorough and dispassionate assessment of the military situation, Mackenzie then began to ramble in this same letter, confusing his personal problems with those of the army. He said he was confident of support from Pope and Sheridan but, unless the War Department in Washington showed more confidence in him by sending him more men, some other officer should be placed in charge. Plaintively, he continued:

> the various difficult commands which I have held during the last six years where full companies were a pressing necessity have not come to me on account of any seeking of my own. The many transfers to which I have been subject have taken place, not on account of applications of mine but through unsought orders of my superiors. Indeed, for a

275

considerable period of years, it is quite well known that I have desired duty in an eastern city to which I believed I had some claim, partially that the mental & physical relaxation would be well, and in part that in years I have found it so very difficult to procure what is essential without the risk of being regarded as captious and troublesome by the authorities in Washington. This causes immense injury to the standing of an officer.[48]

To establish the new reservation, a peace commission arrived consisting of Judge T.A. McMorris, J.J. Russell, and General Townsend, who had been succeeded as adjutant general in Washington by General R.C. Drum. The surrounding territory had already been explored, and both the government and the Utes were reasonably satisfied with a section of Utah near the junction of the Green and White Rivers. Surveying teams were sent. Mackenzie himself was satisfied that the area could support a military post, which he still felt would be needed to keep the Uintah, White River and Uncompahgre Utes under control.[49] The question, however, remained: what would happen if the Utes ultimately refused to go?

On July 12 Mackenzie wrote asking for instructions in case force became necessary. The reply he received was vague and, as he saw it, placed much of the responsibility back on his shoulders. Meanwhile Schurz instructed the commissioners that the Interior Department in Washington was to be consulted before any military action was taken, a policy Mackenzie considered "criminal." He felt immediate action would contain any trouble before it got out of hand. If the army and the commissioners had to exchange time-consuming messages with Washington, an isolated incident might have time to develop into a major insurrection.[50]

On August 2 it appeared a final decision on the removal of the Uncompahgres would be reached within the next few weeks. Mackenzie, concerned that his units were scattered in case trouble arose, suspended construction of a road to have available as many soldiers as possible.[51] He was also concerned about the timing of the move. Winter comes early in the mountains of Colorado and Utah, and unless the move were accomplished soon, he said there would be "much suffering among the tribes. . . .Indians get a large part of subsistence from their sheep and goats and cannot move fast or late in the year without great loss." To avoid this he suggested Agent W.H. Berry be ordered to get them moving immediately, then draw provisions from Salt Lake City to carry the new agency through the winter. As a soldier he was required to establish a contingency plan for a possible uprising, but he trusted the Utes and believed they would go quietly. With that in mind he recommended his troops remain on the Uncompahgre until the end of September, then go into winter quarters.

While Mackenzie worried about the move and the military force necessary to handle any trouble, the commissioners and Agent Berry were busy with the details of closing the Uncompahgre Reservation. Ouray and several other Utes had made improvements to the land, which had to be appraised and arrangements made to reimburse the Indians for the loss.[52] On Monday August 22, Berry called together the Ute leaders, who balked at being told to be ready to move on Thursday. They agreed to meet again for discussions the next day, when they told Berry and McMorris they would not move.

This was the crisis everyone had hope to avoid. Townsend, McMorris and Berry went to Mackenzie, who told them

his orders were clear—no force without approval from the
secretary of the interior. McMorris immediately telegraphed
Schurz, urging him to request military intervention, Berry
and Townsend cabled the commissioner of Indian affairs, and
Mackenzie wired Pope, asking, "Shall I take action at once or
wait for request? I think force should be used at once." While
the telegrams flashed back and forth, the Utes began entrenching themselves on a mountain top from which they could
defend their families while raiding parties went out to harass
the settlements.[53]

Contrary to Mackenzie's fears, Schurz responded immediately and told McMorris to submit a formal request that the
army take charge. Mackenzie ordered ten companies of infantry and cavalry to stand equipped, with two hundred rounds
of ammunition per man and three days of cooked rations. On
Thursday afternoon August 25, Berry told a delegation of
Indians that Mackenzie wanted to talk to them, and about
twenty of them went to the cantonment four miles away.[54]

Mackenzie met them accompanied by only a few officers,
all unarmed. Facing them were the Indians, carrying arms,
bows strung and in a foul mood. Schurz's telegram, turning
the matter over to the War Department, was read to them.
"They were told that they must move to their new agency
promptly, that it would be regretted if force were necessary
but that if they continued in their disobedience it would have
to be used."[55]

The Indians temporized, proposing various alternatives
and compromises until Sapanovero, paramount chief among
the recalcitrants, denounced the whites for taking Indian land.
As Sapanovero's oration grew more forceful, Mackenzie
stood up, hat in his hand, and told them:

It is not necessary for me to stay here any longer.
You can settle this matter by discussion among
yourselves. All I want to know is whether you will
go or not. If you will not go of your own accord,
I will make you go. When you have sufficiently
discussed this matter and have arrived at a conclusion, send for me. Remember, you are to go, at
once.[56]

With that he put on his hat, walked out and went to his
quarters. The Utes, dumbfounded, called Mackenzie back in
less than ten minutes. Sapanovero asked if their answer could
be delayed until morning, after he had a chance to consult with
his people, and Mackenzie agreed but added that all who
intended to obey were to move near the agency on Friday,
draw rations on Saturday, and begin the move on Sunday.[57]

The next day Sapanovero returned and told Mackenzie
that all had agreed to move. Reporting to Pope, Mackenzie
said, "The care of their movement rests with Mr. Berry. . . .
My own opinion and that of the Agent who is better informed, is that they will go quietly and that he will not have
to call on me for troops which are entirely ready if needed."[58]
He also notified the surveying party laying out the new
reservation that work could continue without fear of an
outbreak.[59]

Mackenzie had not been bluffing—his troops had been
ready to enforce his edicts. The agent and the commissioners
had been equally determined.[60] Through determination,
backed by military strength, the crisis was settled peacefully
despite a situation in which one wrong move could have
triggered a major war. Mackenzie considered this peaceful
victory the greatest achievement of his life.[61]

Yet his achievement was tinged with sorrow as Mackenzie watched the Utes travel down the road to their new reservation, herded along by the soldiers. Sheep were abandoned. Blankets and personal possessions were strewn along the road. Women and children wailed. This rich, proud, powerful people had been reduced to poverty by a single act of the government.

Within days, settlers were setting up homesteads and laying out towns in the rich Uncompahgre Valley.[62]

CHAPTER 18

"Two People Can Not Be in Command"

The Fourth was still on the Uncompaghre at 11:00 P.M. September 5 when a courier rode in with a telegram reporting an Apache outbreak in Arizona with a "bloody fight" at Cibicu Creek. Sherman sent orders to Pope dispatching Mackenzie with one battalion to Fort Apache, near the center of the uprising. The horses and men were loaded on trains at Gunnison City for the one-thousand mile trip which took them through Pueblo, Albuquerque and Fort Wingate. After being stalled by bad weather, they arrived at the terminus of the railroad beyond Wingate on September 21, then traveled the rest of the distance by horse.[1]

As with several other outbreaks in the closing days of the Indian Wars, the rising began with a prophet, in this case the White Mountain Apache medicine man Nok-e-da-klinne, who held dances to repopulate the country with his people and drive out the whites. The situation became serious enough for Colonel E.A. Carr, Sixth Cavalry, commander at Fort Apache, to summon the medicine man to the post and warn him to give up the dances and stop inciting the tribes. The warning, however, was too late and the dances resumed when Nok-e-da-klinne returned to his camp on Cibicu Creek.[2]

Agent J.C. Tiffany then asked Carr to send troops to

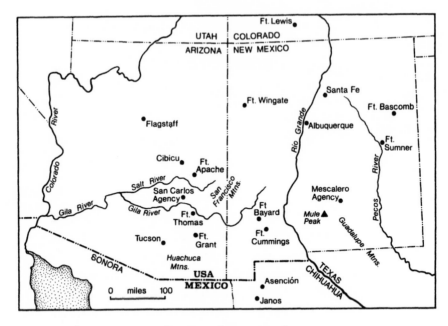

Arizona and New Mexico

arrest the medicine man. The colonel instead decided the situation had deteriorated to the point that a large show of force was necessary, and asked for more troops. None came so Carr, ordered to support the agent with the forces he had, took two companies of the Sixth and one company of Indian scouts and headed for Cibicu. His order to bring in the medicine man dead or alive was too late—the influence of Nok-e-da-klinne had already spread even among the scouts.[3]

Nok-e-da-klinne was arrested on August 30 and the expedition began the forty-mile trip back to the post, with the medicine man's followers trailing the column. When the soldiers stopped for camp that night, the Indians gathered around and Carr sent Captain E.C. Hentig to separate them from the uneasy scouts. One Indian opened fire and Hentig and his orderly were killed instantly. The scouts mutinied and joined the hostiles but Nok-e-da-klinne was also killed, shot by a bugler named Ahrens and finished off with an ax by Sergeant John Smith.

Abandoning some of his gear, Carr pushed on through the night to Fort Apache. The Indians followed, cut the telegraph wires and began firing into the post. By the time Carr's battered forces were relieved, eleven soldiers and seven civilians were dead and the Apaches were in open revolt, Nok-e-da-klinne their only casualty thus far. Colonel O.B. Willcox, who commanded the Department of Arizona as a brevet major general, called for more troops.[4]

When Mackenzie arrived at Fort Apache on September 25, his own position in the affair, as established by General Sherman, violated the usual military chain of command and created confusion. Willcox's Department of Arizona was part of the Military Division of the Pacific under Major General Irvin McDowell at the Presidio of San Francisco. As a divisional commander, McDowell was co-equal to Sheridan. Mackenzie, permanently assigned to the Department of the Missouri with a different chain of command, answered first to General Pope, then to Sheridan, and only then to Sherman. As a subordinate officer temporarily assigned to the Department of Arizona, Mackenzie should have been placed under Willcox and McDowell's command, as Willcox desired.

Sherman, senior to them all, instead decided that Willcox should retain command of the department to handle its administrative functions, but Mackenzie should have overall and independent command of forces in the field, reporting to Willcox only for administrative purposes. Sherman's odd arrangement was based on his realization that the Apache

Orlando B. Willcox
(National Archives)

ranges extended into New Mexico, under Pope's jurisdiction, where Mackenzie would have had field command anyway. The general-in-chief also wanted an energetic officer who would wind up the campaign as soon as possible.[5]

Initially Mackenzie was ordered to hold his forces on stand-by to give Willcox a chance to handle the matter himself. Willcox, pressing for troops wherever he could obtain them, was accused of packing the department with so many soldiers that even those Apaches who were still peaceful were becoming edgy, and the always suspicious Warm Springs and Chiricahua groups were nearing panic.

Most of the Apaches were associated with the San Carlos Agency, which was within the jurisdiction of Fort Thomas. A group of White Mountain Apaches under the Chiefs George and Bonito, along with a band of Chiricahuas, obeyed an agency order to report to a subagency, fifteen miles from San Carlos up the Gila River, where they were placed under parole. Five days later, three troops of cavalry rode in under orders from Willcox to terminate the parole and arrest them, but the Indians fled and went into hiding. Their escape was enough for Sherman—Willcox had had his chance and had bungled it. Mackenzie was placed in charge.[6]

Mackenzie in command was the last thing wanted by Willcox, who felt he had the situation under control. Continuing to press for troops, Willcox notified Sherman through McDowell that Mackenzie was unnecessary. En route from Fort Wingate to Fort Apache, Mackenzie was met by a courier from Willcox with a message restating that he was not needed and telling him not to enter the post. Operating under Sherman's orders, Mackenzie ignored the directive and marched in. Unable to prevent Mackenzie's presence, Willcox appointed him commanding officer of the "District of Apache," severely limiting his area of operations.[7]

The geographical limitation was absurd, since Sherman had placed Mackenzie in charge of all field operations and not just those within a single district. General Pope, unappreciative of Willcox's maneuverings, felt that Mackenzie should either be allowed to operate according to orders from Washington, or else he should be returned to Pope's jurisdiction where he was needed. In a dispatch to Sheridan, he commented:

> I have ... of this department eleven (11) companies at Apache where they are not wanted according to the repeated statements of the commanding officer of the department of Arizona himself, leaving Wingate and the whole Navajo country stripped of troops and greatly delaying if not absolutely obstructing military changes and arrangements in this department heretofore agreed on and essential to the public interests. As my troops are wholly unnecessary at Apache; as they are needed in this department and as I am powerless to traverse the

orders of the General of the Army I have the honor
urgently to request that Mackenzie be ordered back
to this department or that I be authorized to order
him back at once. There is of course much dissatis-
faction not to say embarrassment induced by this
condition of affairs.[8]

Sheridan forwarded Pope's dispatch on to the War Department with a note stating that he would also like Mackenzie returned to New Mexico as soon as the Apache situation
settled down.[9]

Sherman was not in Washington when these messages
arrived, and they caught the attention of Secretary of War
Robert Todd Lincoln. On September 28 Lincoln, aware of
Sherman's orders but apparently not totally familiar with the
situation, directed Acting Adjutant General Chauncey
McKeever to send a message to McDowell in Sherman's name,
ordering Mackenzie and all other troops belonging to the
Department of the Missouri to return to their stations.[10]

Sherman returned the same day and, finding out what had
happened, immediately countermanded the order. McDowell
was told the general-in-chief:

insists that General Mackenzie and his command
remain at Apache, not limited to a District or Post
Command, but held ready to act according to
circumstances. He wants you to ascertain and report to him (General Sherman) if all the Apaches
had surrendered and are in custody; have they
delivered up their horses and mules they gained and
saddles and equipment left by Colonel Carr on the
ground [at Cibicu?].

While Willcox was to retain departmental command, he was "to see that General Mackenzie is supplied for vigorous action. As soon as General Sherman is satisfied that the Apaches are in fact subjugated and punished adequately he will order that command back to the Department of the Missouri."

To be certain that everyone understood Sherman's position, McKeever added, "The Secretary of War has heard read [sic] the above dispatch, confirms it and modifies his orders of this morning accordingly," and also sent a copy to General Sheridan. Apparently everyone understood but Willcox. As departmental commander he had to accede to Sherman's wishes and order Mackenzie to take command in the field, but he had additional plans of his own.[11]

Meanwhile Mackenzie, at Fort Apache positioning his and Willcox's forces to handle the situation, received word on October 1 that a large group of Chiricahuas had broken out of the subagency. To keep the remaining Apaches in line he ordered Carr to San Carlos to take direct control of the agency and subagency. He further ordered Lieutenant Colonel W.R. Price, Sixth Cavalry, to report to Carr with his entire field command to arrest all hostile Indians then on the agency or who came in, to place them in double irons and send them to Fort Thomas "or such place as you wish. . . ." Price was also to hold roll call of friendly Indians twice a day. At the same time Mackenzie directed Major G.B. Sanford to take two companies of his own First Cavalry, as well as two companies of the Sixth, to help run down the Chiricahuas. Mackenzie himself planned to start for Fort Thomas the next morning, with his five companies of the Fourth and two companies of the Ninth, to try and find George and Bonito. "It seems to me very important to have a good strong force at San Carlos & if Carr does not feel strong enough with Price & his own command, will go there myself or send more troops," he said.[12]

Willcox, however, appears to have been determined to undermine Mackenzie at every turn. After placing Mackenzie in charge, he sent a new set of orders to Carr. He mentioned these orders to Mackenzie but apparently did not tell him what the new orders contained. Without advising Mackenzie, he also sent different orders to Sanford, Major James Biddle, and to Captains C.B. McLellan and W.A. Rafferty who had their Sixth Cavalry forces in the field.

Mackenzie, learning of the conflicting orders, questioned whether he would get any support from Willcox[13] and fired off a telegram to the adjutant general in Washington, sending it through the usual channels of the Department of Arizona. Reviewing his entire dispute with Willcox, he stated:

> It is evident to me that it will be impossible for me to act satisfactorily under Genl. Wilcox. I am placed in command to an extent, but at the same time he is giving orders. Such a system will not work. The case is very difficult & it is hard for me to tell what is right. Genl. Sherman must settle the matter.[14]

His frustration continued to mount as he tried to find out what was happening with the troops he was supposed to have. Wiring the adjutant at Fort Thomas, he demanded:

> Have Carr, Price, Sanford & any others in the field been ordered to report to me[?]

> Wish my position clearly defined. . . .I see Genl. Wilcox gives orders to Carr & Biddle and different

to Carr from those I have used. Two people can
not be in command. Either I must be or Genl.
Wilcox.[15]

The message to Washington, of course, went through
Willcox who forwarded it with a comment that Mackenzie
had no grounds for complaint. With some justification he
blamed Sherman for the problem, since he had circumvented
the usual structure of command and placed a separate field
commander in a department, giving the departmental commander only nominal control. He concluded by asking that
Mackenzie be relieved from duty in Arizona. The reply, from
McDowell at the Presidio but undoubtedly authored by Sherman, ordered Willcox not to interfere with Mackenzie's operations and to notify Mackenzie accordingly.[16]

Willcox, however, neglected to notify Mackenzie who,
unaware of these exchanges, transferred his headquarters to
Fort Thomas. Although still unsure of his authority,[17] he was
nevertheless preparing for deployment. Price was to remain
in command at San Carlos until Carr or Mackenzie arrived,
and was to direct the agent to keep the women and children
under control since, if they scattered, it would be more
difficult to capture the warriors. Captain E.M. Heyl, Mackenzie's long-time subordinate in the Fourth, with four companies of the Fourth and two of the Ninth, was to move from
his camp on Ash Creek to the subagency and assist Carr in
subjugating the Indians still on the reservation. Mackenzie
told Carr, "If you are not strong enough, delay till he has
arrived. There's nothing like having enough men."[18]

Mackenzie's plan was similar to that he had used with Red
Cloud in 1876. Although San Carlos itself was quiet, he
believed that George and Bonito were hiding somewhere on

the vast subagency and the large concentration of troops would allow Carr to throw a ring around the area and force them in.[19] Meanwhile there were ten companies of cavalry in pursuit of the Chiricahuas, and Mackenzie telegraphed Sanford to "take general control" of that phase of the campaign. He said the telegram would be sufficient evidence of his authority and added, "I shall leave this matter to you with great confidence & best wishes."[20]

Willcox, perhaps feeling he was out of favor in Washington and, like Custer before him, hoping to recoup his fortunes by scoring a victory, intervened. He notified Mackenzie that Sanford was sick at Fort Grant and that he intended to take personal command of the expedition against the Chiricahuas. He concluded by ordering Mackenzie to send any troops that could be spared from his quarter.[21]

Mackenzie, disgusted, replied:

> There are no troops here that can be spared, but have telegraphed Carr to find out what he can spare. I think that in case of an emergency, Carr's command can be spared, leaving Price's at the Agency. There are now 10 companies of cavalry in pursuit of the Chiricahuas & I had no intention, supposing that I was in command of the operations, of sending more.[22]

In spite of his reply, Mackenzie ordered Carr to suspend operations and send what forces he could spare to Willcox, but decided to keep Heyl under his own command for the time being. Once the matter with Willcox was settled, Carr could continue with his sweep and use Heyl—assuming the opportunity for a sweep still existed.[23]

Mackenzie was determined—once and for all—to ascer-

Joseph H. Dorst
(Special Collection, US Military Academy)

tain who was actually in command of field operations. In a message to Washington he said, "Genl. Willcox deals with me in a remarkable manner." He quoted extracts from various conflicting orders and concluded by saying, "I am, while trying to do as well as I can, in a very false position."[24]

For undisclosed reasons, this message was forwarded without the usual endorsements by Willcox or McDowell. Sherman, considering Mackenzie to have violated protocol by bypassing departmental and divisional command, was not pleased and said so in his reply. Mackenzie immediately confronted Lieutenant Joseph H. Dorst who, as adjutant, was responsible for seeing that messages went through proper channels. Dorst, contending he had followed procedure, produced the copy kept by the clerk showing that it had been properly addressed. Mackenzie passed this information on to General Drum, Adjutant General of the Army, by way of the departmental adjutant at Fort Lowell. As an additional precaution the telegraph operator was told, "Please keep carefully [the] dispatch addressed on the 6th [of October] to Gen. R.C. Drum sent by General Mackenzie."[25]

Willcox himself violated the chain of command, bypassing everyone, in an appeal he sent directly to President Arthur. The president passed the message on to Sherman, who took pains to explain the situation. After discussing the initial fight at Cibicu, he said:

> Genl. Wilcox took measures to suppress this outbreak, calling for reinforcements of Genl. McDowell, his own Division Commander, and of the neighboring Dept. & Division of the [Missouri]. Genl. Pope at Santa Fe with the sanction of Genl. Sheridan ordered Col. McKenzie of the 4th Cavalry with troops from Uncompahgre and Fort Wingate. The distance is great and the country particularly difficult and as these troops approached Arizona from the North East they were met by conflicting reports—Genl. Wilcox at one time saying reinforcement were not needed and again calling for them.
>
> Inasmuch as this particular force belonged to another command and the area of operations [is] near the line dividing Genl. McDowell's and Genl. Sheridan's Divisions, the orders necessarily emmanated [sic] from a common superior—Myself. . . .[These orders] are in my judgment not only lawful and proper, but absolutely necessary to ensure successful action on the part of Colonel Mackenzie, who is an officer of peculiar energy and fitness for the task of subduing and punishing these Apaches. . . .
>
> I believe Col. McKenzie and the existing orders will so punish them that we shall have no more such

outbreaks. It is not a question of personal honor, but of National Necessity.

When the end is reached, if Genl. Wilcox still thinks he has been wronged, I will advise that a Court of Inquiry investigate and report all the facts, so that the President may act understandingly.[26]

The president apparently understood without a court of inquiry because Sherman had the last word. Three days after the letter to Arthur, he notified McDowell that he had had enough of the matter and did not plan to discuss it further.[27]

As these exchanges were underway, the hunt for the runaways continued. On October 5 an Indian brought a note saying that "17 or 18 men" who had come onto the subagency with George in September had surrendered and would be sent to Fort Thomas. The Indian said George himself had left the agency with about fifteen men and had probably fled into the mountains. When the prisoners arrived at Fort Thomas, however, it was learned that George had only taken five men with him and was probably headed toward Fort Apache.[28]

Two days later Mackenzie was at the subagency when he received word from Biddle that nine Chiricahua scouts had deserted from Fort Thomas. A citizen had seen a trail of about fifty hostile Apaches heading toward the San Francisco Mountains, and the colonel speculated that the scouts had joined that group although he questioned whether it was as large as reported. Initially he ordered Heyl to send two companies of the Fourth in pursuit but, upon returning to San Carlos, reconsidered and cancelled the order saying, "There is no object in sending two companies after a few scattered scouts." As a precautionary measure, however, he ordered the Chiricahua scouts at Fort Apache to be disarmed.[29] Further investigation of the trail of the fifty "hostiles" revealed that it was actually made by Fourth Cavalrymen on a recent scout, and resulted in a note to Biddle telling him to sift reports from civilians more carefully before sending them on.[30]

Even though it was beginning to appear the Apache problem was not as serious as the military had originally feared, Mackenzie, with troops in the field, still had to deal with the soldier's perpetual problem of supply. His wagon train was to arrive at the railhead on October 6 to pick up 100,000 pounds of grain he would need for his horses if the outbreak continued; if it ended, he would still need the grain to get his men back to New Mexico. In a message to the chief quartermaster of the department, he said, "There is grass in the country but not enough for the mules without grain. I want the forage at Apache where it is very much needed as there is none there, except a little I brought with me and left there." The wagon train arrived at the railhead on schedule but the grain did not. He told the officer in charge that the wagon train would probably have to remain at the railhead until enough grain and stores had been sent to fill it.[31]

Elsewhere the pursuit of the Chiricahuas continued. On October 4 soldiers under Captain R.F. Bernard, First Cavalry, had a running fight for fifteen miles and took one captive. The next morning the Indians fled through Mule Pass into the Huachuca Mountains, killing their livestock and abandoning their property in order to travel faster, and eventually crossed the San Bernardino Plains and the Guadalupe Mountains into Mexico.[32]

Their flight concerned Mackenzie. No longer the bellicose officer who advocated making Mexico into a U.S. protectorate, he now wanted to avoid an international incident. Consequently, he notified Sanford, Bernard's superior:

Unless Bernard is in immediate pursuit of the Chiricahuas when they go into Mexico, he should not follow them. . . .If they should go into Mexico you should at once communicate with the nearest Mexican officer & endeavor to get Mexicans to send a large force after them or they will suffer greatly by them. It is very important not to wound the feelings of the Mexicans at the present time & their cooperation is very necessary.[33]

Sanford reported back that the Indians were, in fact, in Mexico and heading toward Janos and "old haunts" in Chihuahua.[34]

To Mackenzie the Chiricahuas were no longer his concern but Mexico's, which had demonstrated during the Victorio War a year earlier that it was now perfectly willing and capable of handling Apaches. Mackenzie now turned his attention back to San Carlos where "an Indian who is believed to be the man who killed Capt. Hentig" had been arrested. To complete the pacification, he ordered Heyl to send a unit with Agent Tiffany but added that Tiffany was to take charge with agency personnel who "would be less likely to excite suspicion." The soldiers' main purpose was control of the prisoners, who were to be turned over to the infantry with deserters "carefully guarded" until they reached Fort Thomas.[35]

The Apache rebellion was collapsing. The Indians, frustrated by the rapid arrival and deployment of reinforcements by the army, had attracted only a small number of adherents, primarily among the White Mountain and Chiricahua bands. As military pressure continued, more Indians surrendered at San Carlos. Among the prisoners were Corporal Skippy and Sergeants Dead Shot and Dandy Jim, members of the scouting

detachment which had mutinied at Cibicu. Mackenzie, learning Skippy had previously been arrested and released by
Willcox, observed Willcox had been "undoubtedly under a
misapprehension" with no evidence available against Skippy
at the time. As a precaution against any further inadvertent
releases, Mackenzie told Biddle that no prisoners were to be
released from Fort Thomas without specific orders from
Mackenzie himself.[36]

When Tiffany began to reassert himself at the agency,
Colonel Carr seems to have had misgivings about him and
went so far as to question a report the agent had submitted.
Perhaps he suspected dishonesty, for it was later determined
that Tiffany had been stealing government stores from the
Apaches. Despite Carr's misgivings, Mackenzie was impressed with Tiffany and sent a letter to the Commissioner
of Indian Affairs in Washington stating the agent was "using
his best endeavors to aid in the arrest of badly disposed
Indians & . . .has acted with courage in difficult circumstances."[37]

Upon his arrival at San Carlos, Mackenzie apparently had
second thoughts concerning the agent. He asked Tiffany for a
meeting, either at the post or at San Carlos, and by October 12
seems to have felt some urgency since he again wrote the agent
for a meeting, saying, "This afternoon will do just as well &
if you get here late at night, come to my house and wake me
up."

The next day, however, a meeting appeared less urgent
and he sent yet a third message to Tiffany indicating there was
no hurry. Mackenzie had no doubt realized he would soon be
leaving Arizona, and the agent would become Carr's problem.
He did not want to delay his departure by encumbering
himself with agency affairs.[38] With grain and stores slowly

trickling in by railroad and wagon train from Fort Wingate, he had already reported in a message to departmental headquarters on October 12 that the situation was settling down and asked that the Fourth and Ninth be returned "to their proper stations." He pointed out that several companies of the Fourth had been in the field for eighteen months and would need to refit and recruit.[39]

The same day, he wrote General Pope, saying:

> There is no considerable organized band away from the agencies, the Indians who are still out being scattered in small parties and can be eventually caught by small parties of troops aided by Indians. What is needed to secure comfort so far as the agency Indians are concerned, and those still out in the mountains, is steady management extending over a considerable period of time. The Chiricahuas can only be dealt with by cooperation with Mexican troops. . . .
>
> I have no objection whatever to controlling matters in Arizona as General Sherman seems to desire but what is left to do [can] Best be done by the Department Commander.
>
> As it stands my own position is very delicate and I do not doubt that that of Genl. Willcox is disagreeable. I now should particularly dislike to be placed in command of the dept. of Arizona as a great many unwise people would always think or say that I had come here and intrigued for Genl. Willcox place. . . .There is far more for me to do in New Mexico than here.[40]

Pope and his superiors apparently agreed, because Mackenzie was soon assigned to Santa Fe as the commander of the District of New Mexico. Before leaving he was ordered to prepare charges against the scouts Dead Shot and Skippy who, along with Dandy Jim, were court-martialed for mutiny, murder and desertion to the enemy in battle and hanged at Fort Grant on March 3, 1882.[41]

For the first time Mackenzie had administered a campaign without personally leading troops in the field. He had exercised caution and good judgment both in dealing with the Indians still on the agency and in dealing with Mexico. Although the outbreak was never really serious, any error with the agency Indians could have strengthened and prolonged it. A campaign across the border without first consulting Mexican authorities could have created an international incident which Mexico was now much more prepared to handle than before. As usual he had complained to his superiors, but without his usual self-righteousness or feelings of persecution. His complaints instead centered around a very real confusion in command and, given the circumstances, were very restrained.

Mackenzie was no longer a field commander. From now on he was to be what he had wanted to be for several years—a desk soldier.

CHAPTER 19

"I Sever My Connection with the Regiment with Deep Regret"

Mackenzie took command of the District of New Mexico on October 30, 1881, assuming the position from Colonel L.P. Bradley, Thirteenth Infantry, who returned to his regiment at Fort Wingate. As with his previous administrative assignments, Mackenzie continued to command the Fourth. This time, however, he headquartered at his district offices at Fort Marcy in Santa Fe and left field operations of the regiment to subordinate officers, particularly Lieutenant Colonel George A. Forsyth who had recently been transferred into the Fourth.[1]

The Indians of New Mexico were reasonably quiet and Mackenzie was able to concentrate on administrative affairs. Among the matters which caught his attention was a letter, seeking his assistance, from Agent Berry whom he had left at the new Ute Reservation in Utah the previous summer. As Mackenzie well knew, Berry was a competent agent who did not hesitate to stand up to the Indians yet always looked after their interests. T.B. Adams & Co., traders at the White River Military Post, were trying to have Berry removed "for their own pecuniary benefit, regardless of the Indian." The agent was indifferent to his own position but did not want to leave the Utes before they had become settled in the new reservation.

Company officers' quarters, Fort Marcy, New Mexico
(National Archives)

"I can with the assistance of the Department have all the Chiefs & principal men located upon [their] allotments next year & living in houses," Berry wrote. "As soon as this is done I am satisfied. The Indians complain of there not being sufficient quantity of grass in this country for their stock and I have all I can do to reconcile them to this place, until the Department [of the Interior] can arrange & place them upon their allotments." He asked Mackenzie to back him up.[2]

Mackenzie did. Writing to Senator N.P. Hill of Colorado, he outlined Berry's accomplishments and said if the agent were removed "very great injustice will be done, and I feel it will be very difficult to supply his place in the Utes. . . .Should any outbreak occur through bad government of the Utes the brunt of it will probably fall on Western Colorado in which from my service in that country I take some interest," he concluded.[3] Apparently Hill intervened, because nothing more was said on the matter.

Mexico was a more pressing concern. Nana's band was

still operating across the border, as were the Chiricahuas who had fled San Carlos during the outbreak. Before being relieved by Mackenzie, Colonel Bradley had sent Scout Van Smith into Mexico to watch the Chiricahuas and determine if they might cross back into New Mexico or Arizona. Smith located them in the Sierra Madres and discussed the situation with the Mexican commanders, who suggested American troops might be allowed to cross the border in pursuit. When Mackenzie received Smith's report, however, he advised departmental headquarters that caution should be used—an arrangement to cross the border in pursuit would be helpful, but U.S. forces should not enter the country in search of Apaches. Mexico had sufficient forces in the field to conduct search operations.[4]

In January 1882 a reconnaissance patrol consisting of Indian scouts and civilians under Lieutenant D.N. McDonald strayed over the border to the town of Asención. McDonald was seized by the Mexicans and escorted back to the border. General Carlos Fuero, commander of the Second Military Division in Chihuahua, protested the incursion to Mackenzie.

Reporting on the incident to Pope, Mackenzie praised the Mexican commander for "good sense and good temper in a difficult position." To defuse the situation, he said it would probably be necessary to conduct a court-martial against McDonald, despite his good service record, and to write a letter of appreciation to the Mexican commander for releasing him. He also suggested that Forsyth, Lawton or Dorst be sent to Chihuahua to deliver the letter personally and to discuss Mackenzie's views on border affairs with General Fuero. "We have no cause of complaint whatever against the Mexicans on this part of the line for affording refuge to Indians. They have done and are doing their best," he said. No serious action was taken against McDonald.[5]

Potential problems also appeared on the U.S. side of the border. In February the post trader at Fort Wingate, near the Navajo reservation, passed on a rumor that the Navajo were planning to revolt. Mackenzie suggested a mounted force be sent to the Navajo country, backed by more cavalry and by infantry sent from Fort Lewis.

> If we could be sure that the Indians would keep still in Southern New Mexico there would be perhaps sufficient troops in the District to deal with the Navajoes though the last reports give their number at 16,000. But it is not good policy in my judgment to break up the command in Southern New Mexico and then probably be obliged almost at once to send the troops back.

Consequently he asked for more cavalry "from such part of the country as can best spare them...." Mackenzie's letter made its way up the chain of command until it reached Sherman, who viewed it as alarmist and refused any additional forces.[6]

Sherman was right about the Navajos, who kept the peace despite the genuine Indian scare and numerous rumors throughout Arizona and New Mexico. One story claimed that seventy Apache scouts en route to San Carlos to draw pay and reenlist had gone on a killing spree. Another rumor claimed some of the Mescaleros were on the move. To insure better security, Mackenzie ordered additional forces to Forts Cummings and Bayard, the New Mexico posts closest to San Carlos. To insure the Indian scouts would remain under control, they were assigned six to a company and were to be accompanied by cavalry. Mackenzie himself went to the Mescalero Agency to arrange the roundup and concentration of about 150 men, women and children who had been in the mountains for the past two years. As a result, the Mescaleros remained quiet.[7]

A real threat, however, remained from Mexico from where Juh, Geronimo and Nachez, the son of the great Chiricahua Chief Cochise, were planning a war. Needing the support of Loco's Warm Springs band which had remained at San Carlos, in January they warned Loco they would return within forty days and force him and his band to join them. Anyone who refused would be killed. Word of a possible rising spread until it reached both Mackenzie and Fuero.

Discussing the problem in a letter to Mackenzie in early April, Fuero said Juh and Geronimo were camped near Janos where "they pretend to be at peace, but this will not be granted them." He indicated he had sent for additional troops from Sonora "so that I may order a vigorous pursuit, until a complete extermination is accomplished."

Fuero planned to begin his operations against the Apaches on April 20, by which time he expected the troops from Sonora. Should the Apaches break through the Mexican line and head for San Carlos, he asked that Mackenzie have troops at key points on the border to stop them there. He planned to begin marching toward Janos on April 6 and would notify Mackenzie of any movement among the Apaches. Meanwhile he had directed his troops that the Indians should "not be molested on no account," in order to lull them into a sense of security.[8]

Far from being lulled, the Apaches struck San Carlos and rounded up Loco's band on April 18. Jason Betzinez,

Geronimo's second cousin who lived on the agency with his mother, later remembered hearing one of the leaders give the order to kill anyone who refused to leave. The idea that the Apaches would do this to their own people terrified Loco's band into submission. When the raiders killed the popular agency Police Chief Albert D. Sterling and Indian officer Sagotal, the agency Apaches, afraid they would be blamed for the killings, felt they had no choice but to join the marauders.[9]

The Apaches' trail of blood left the press screaming for action against "The Red Trail of the Apache Chiefs," some even going so far as to demand the disarming of all Apaches, the disbandment of Indian scouts and police, and removal of all New Mexico Indians to the Indian Territory.[10]

Forsyth, already in the field with six companies of the Fourth following the trail of the Indians across southern New Mexico, sent ahead Lieutenant McDonald with six scouts and two enlisted men. McDonald was ambushed in a canyon and sent for help. The ensuing fight appears to have been a draw,[11] after which Forsyth withdrew to the Gila River and combined forces with several units of the Sixth Cavalry.

The trail led into Mexico where, despite the goodwill of local authorities, the U.S. forces still had no official sanction to pass. Nevertheless Forsyth crossed the border, pushing the Indians ahead and driving them into a waiting body of 250 Mexican troops. When Forsyth arrived, the Mexican commander, Colonel Lorenzo García, told him the Apaches had been preoccupied with guarding their rear against the Americans and had sent their women and children ahead—straight into a trap. Some seventy-eight Apaches had been killed, with Mexican casualties of three officers and nineteen men dead, and three officers and thirteen men wounded. García then went through the formality of presenting Forsyth with a written protest for the American incursion. Forsyth gave a written reply and the two armies parted cordially,[12] but Mackenzie was less than cheerful about the border incursion. Discussing it with Pope, he said:

> In my judgment it will be impossible to get along with the Mexicans unless our troops keep on their own side of the line. It is not that the Mexican officers care anything about it at all, but it is used as a political weapon against the General Government of Mexico and it is a powerful one. The Mexicans now have plenty of troops on their frontier and are quite willing to use them. I know very well how a high spirited man like Forsyth would feel on coming to the line, but we cannot attempt to campaign in Mexico and unless this is discontinued it will lead to much trouble.

He pointed out he had a good working arrangement with General Fuero and was afraid incursions like this could cause the Mexican general trouble with his superiors. "They were just as anxious to get the Indians as ourselves, and they have certainly been very efficient." Even so, he concluded, "Too much praise cannot be given Forsyth for energy and courage."[13]

In Chicago, a more enthusiastic Sheridan sent a dispatch to Pope:

> The Lieutenant-General commanding desires to express to you his great gratification at the successful results obtained from the indefatigable pursuit of the hostile Apaches by Lieutenant-Colonel

305

George A. Forsythe *[sic]* and his command. He
believes the result obtained is due to the careful
management of Colonel Mackenzie, commanding
the District of New Mexico, and Lieutenant Colonel Forsythe, in keeping scouts in Mexico to watch
the movements of the Indians, and by arriving at a
special understanding for co-operation with Mexican military commanders on the Border.[14]

Having excelled in his administrative duties up to this
point, Mackenzie once again began showing signs of pettiness.
In June Forsyth applied directly to departmental headquarters
for a leave of absence and Pope, thinking Mackenzie wouldn't
mind, did not bother to send it back to Santa Fe for approval.
Mackenzie, furious, contended all applications should go
through his headquarters, but Pope countered that it was his
prerogative, as departmental commander, to approve or not
approve leave applications, and he need not consult the district
commander except as a courtesy. He further cautioned Mackenzie against insubordination and presumption of too much
authority.[15]

Mackenzie's continued complaints required the intervention of Sherman, who said that a district command had no
legal standing but only existed in the army "from convenience
and necessity." Even though Pope, as departmental commander, could create or disband a district at his own discre-
tion, "While existing however, every officer therein in asking
a leave of absence should apply to the Post, District and
Department Commander, and. . .to omit the District Commander would be a breach of discipline . . . .Colonel Forsyth
should have applied for his leave through Colonel Mackenzie
and on his return, Colonel Mackenzie may so charge him."

Sherman dryly added, "But [while] Colonel Mackenzie cannot hold his superior Department Commander responsible, he can and should represent the facts to the Department Commander, and that seems to have been done. . . ."[16]

Having made his point, Mackenzie did not prefer charges against Forsyth. He did, however, prefer charges against Lieutenant Colonel R.E.A. Crofton, Thirteenth Infantry, for what he considered disobedience in arresting some Indians at the Mescalero Agency. Crofton, countering that his actions had been dictated by the circumstances, filed a grievance against Mackenzie. When the paperwork reached Fort Leavenworth, Pope disallowed the charges and suggested both Mackenzie and Crofton settle down. Mackenzie continued to resent the situation and did not hesitate to say so.[17]

Ultimately the correspondence between Santa Fe and Fort Leavenworth assumed a routine tone more beneficial to Mackenzie, for whom General McDowell's pending retirement again opened the possibility for promotion. The reshuffling in the senior ranks, with Pope moving up to Major General, left a gap among the brigadiers. As before, Mackenzie's friends rallied in his support, among them Senator Hill of Colorado and Governor L. A. Sheldon of New Mexico, but he was not the only contender. Benjamin Grierson was also in line, and he too had powerful friends who were pressuring President Arthur. General Grant intervened on behalf of his "most promising young officer," and asked the president to promote Mackenzie both as a personal favor and "as a matter of simple justice" to a man who had given so many years of distinguished service.[18] The President made his decision. On October 26 Mackenzie telegraphed to Secretary Lincoln:

I acknowledge the receipt of your telegram of this date, informing me that the President has today appointed me Brigadier General. I have the honor to accept the appointment with thanks to the President.

R.S. Mackenzie
Brigadier General[19]

The same day, a general order went out to the officers and men of the Fourth United States Cavalry:

The undersigned, having been promoted, hereby relinquishes command of the Fourth regiment of United States cavalry.

In giving up the command which he has held so many years, he feels that his promotion is greatly due to the general good conduct of the officers and enlisted men of the regiment.

He thanks his officers for their loyal support in many trying circumstances, and is much gratified at the support which they have envariably *[sic]* given each other, in dangerous or difficult positions, when his juniors have commanded detachments during the past year.

Thanking both officers and enlisted men for very much kindly consideration, running through years, though promoted, I sever my connection with the regiment with deep regret.

Ranald S. Mackenzie
Brigadier General U.S. Army.[20]

He had commanded the regiment for over twelve years, almost half its existence and longer than any other officer. From an indifferent collection of time-servers he had molded the best mobile assault force in the army and, in the process, changed the concept of plains warfare. Other units had names such as the "Dandy Fifth," the "Fighting Sixth" or the "Garryowens," but the Fourth was "Mackenzie's Raiders." Although Colonel William B. Royall assumed command on November 1, 1882,[21] the regiment by name and temperament would always be associated with Mackenzie.

Now that he had his star, Mackenzie expected an eventual change in duty assignment. Since both his mother and his sister Harriet were now living with him, he needed more time than previously to make arrangements for them. He also wanted an extended leave and asked permission to travel east to be on hand for his confirmation as brigadier general and to outfit himself. He also pointed out he had been working continuously for two years and needed a rest. Leave was granted on November 17, and he was absent from Santa Fe from November 21 until February 21, 1883.[22]

From, unfortunately, only second-hand accounts which require some guesswork, Mackenzie's mental deterioration must have been noticeable by this time. Lieutenant Dorst, who had been appointed the general's aide-de-camp on January 1, 1883,[23] would have been in a position to record Mackenzie's activities, but at the end of February he was given eight months leave in Mexico and did not resume his position with Mackenzie until November 1.[24]

The months during which Dorst was absent were critical in Mackenzie's life. Shortly after his return from the east, Chiricahuas again crossed the border and raided into both Arizona and New Mexico, killing U.S. District Judge and Mrs.

H.C. McComas and abducting their six-year-old son Charlie. Sherman transferred General Crook from the Platte to the Department of Arizona and ordered Mackenzie to cooperate with him. Crook conferred with Mackenzie then went to Mexico to coordinate the campaign with officials there. Mackenzie deployed his troops in the troubled area, but the Indians slipped back across the border into Mexico, which offered only temporary safety since public pressure in Mexico was mounting for an open border in pursuit of hostile Indians. It was, however, to remain for others—not Mackenzie—to bring the Apache Wars to their conclusion.[25]

From April 29 until May 15 Mackenzie took an unusually short leave when his mother, Catherine Mackenzie, died in Santa Fe and he accompanied the body back to New York City. Shortly afterwards, he wrote a "cordial, classmately letter" to the secretary of his class association at Williams College, but the contents were not recorded. Even more important, Mackenzie had a mental breakdown about this period, and the class association's 1884 yearbook later speculated that Catherine's death might have contributed to his instability.[26]

Writers such as Lessing Nohl and Soren Nielsen, attempting to trace Mackenzie's deterioration, have made much of the Fourth of July parade of 1883. Misreading the newspaper account, they have assumed Mackenzie rode in a carriage because he was unable to sit on a horse.[27] The parade lineup as reported in the Santa Fe newspaper states:

> *Territorial and United States civil officers in carriages.*
> *Brigadier General R.S. Mackenzie, U.S.A., and staff.*[28]

Even though Mackenzie and staff were listed separately from territorial and civil officers in carriages, there is nothing in the newspaper article to indicate whether he were astride or in a carriage.

This parade was apparently Mackenzie's last major public function as commander of the District of New Mexico. On October 13, 1883, the War Department issued the following order:

> The President, having acceded to the request of General William T. Sherman to be relieved from the command of the Army on the 1st of November, 1883, preparatory to his retirement from active service, directs the following changes and assignments to command. . . .
>
> Lieutenant-General Philip H. Sheridan will proceed to Washington and on the above-mentioned date assume command of the Army.
>
> Major-General John M. Schofield will proceed to Chicago, Ill., and will on the above-mentioned date assume command of the Military Division of the Missouri.
>
> Major-General John Pope will proceed to the Presidio of San Francisco, Cal., and will on the above-mentioned date assume command of the Military Division of the Pacific and of the Department of California.
>
> Brigadier-General Christopher C. Augur will proceed to Fort Leavenworth, and will on the above-mentioned date assume command of the Department of the Missouri.

Brigadier-General Ranald S. Mackenzie will proceed to San Antonio, Tex., and will on the above-mentioned date assume command of the Department of Texas. . . .

> Robert T. Lincoln,
> Secretary of War[29]

Mackenzie was going back to Texas.

CHAPTER 20

"His Usefulness to the Service is Destroyed"

The man who moved into the commandant's mansion, later to become part of Fort Sam Houston, was only a shadow of the Mackenzie of the Plains. Still suffering from his breakdown in New Mexico, his behavior was erratic.[1] Perhaps aware of his instability, he may have been thinking of retirement or, at the least, of a possible future outside the army with Florida Sharpe, who now lived in the old Tunstall House in San Antonio with her twelve-year-old son Red. Once again Mackenzie became a frequent caller at the house. He and Florida would reminisce, and Red became very attached to him. As the Santa Fe *New Mexican Review* would later put it, "The course of courtship ran smooth and even as the command promenade around the parade ground." The marriage was set for December 19, and Mackenzie ordered his home redecorated. Five years earlier he had initiated proceedings to purchase a ranch, and in several separate transactions he obtained sizeable holdings near Boerne, west of San Antonio, possibly with an eye toward retirement.[2]

In the first week of December he began acting strangely enough to worry Colonel Thomas Vincent, the departmental adjutant, and others of his staff. Mackenzie's feelings about alcohol were well known in the army—no one could recall ever seeing him "under the least influence"—but now he began drinking heavily to a point which Dr. Joseph Smith, medical director, felt was "worthy of the name of dipsomania." Smith, Vincent and some of the other officers began very quietly to keep an eye on him.

Unfortunately, Smith and Vincent had to leave on December 9 to inspect Fort McIntosh at Laredo, and Assistant Surgeon Passmore Middleton was left in charge of the surveillance. Two incidents occurred which should have aroused Dr. Middleton's suspicions. On December 10 Mackenzie had a conversation with the chief quartermaster of the department "which convinced that officer of his insanity." Five days later he talked with the chief commissary, and likewise "satisfied that officer of the same fact." Other people also began to leave meetings with him convinced he was "either drunk or crazy."[3]

Despite the seriousness of the incidents, Middleton did not report them to higher authorities. Mackenzie's eccentricities and moods were well known, and the surgeon decided the current problem was most likely temporary. Mackenzie was quietly put under the control of his orderlies, and business at the department proceeded as usual. Few in San Antonio suspected anything was wrong.[4]

Mackenzie's mental problems could not have gone unnoticed by Harriet, but how she felt, or whether she notified their brother Morris, is not known. No Mackenzie correspondence is available for this period; the extant records are almost entirely military and Harriet did not enter into the discussions officially until later.

Vincent and Dr. Smith returned to San Antonio on December 18. The quartermaster and commissary officer briefed Smith who, in turn, reported their stories to Vincent. The medical director's comments leave no doubt as to what he thought of the reactions of Middleton, who "either failed to comprehend the gravity of the case when he should have comprehended it, or failed in his duty to report it to higher authority in order that the necessary restraint might be exercised." Despite Middleton's diagnosis—or lack of it—Vincent recognized the immediate problem was that a key military department was under the command of a man who was no longer sane.

Vincent, as assistant adjutant general for the Department of Texas, had the duty as well as the legal authority to relieve Mackenzie, but he had to proceed carefully. He was dealing not only with a brigadier general backed by the full power of the government, but a national hero as well. He had to be completely sure of his position. On the pretext of official business that needed Mackenzie's attention, he went to the general's quarters.

At first "I found him entirely rational," Vincent wrote, but as he got up to leave, Mackenzie told him "not to hurry" and began discussing personal matters to an extent which the adjutant knew was completely out of character. Vincent immediately related the discussions to Middleton, and they agreed that Middleton would examine him at 5:00 P.M. When Middleton found Mackenzie to be much better, the two officers began to think he might be recovering.[5] They were in error.

That night, the eve of the wedding, despite a wet norther which had blown in, Mackenzie traveled into town with Chief Paymaster Terrell and Chief Ordnance Officer Arnold. They stopped by the Tunstall house where Florida Sharpe's niece, Patti Lockwood, was still up and saw them in the parlor. As Mackenzie was leaving, he patted the little girl on the head, then he and the other officers stepped out into the cold rain. Arnold made his farewells and headed back to the arsenal while Mackenzie and Major Terrell started for the military reservation. Somewhere along the way Mackenzie managed to slip away from Terrell.[6]

Although there is no official record of what happened next, Vincent and Smith carefully described the ensuing event as an "altercation" in which Mackenzie "was more or less injured." The Santa Fe *New Mexican* received a more detailed account in a letter, from San Antonio, which is generally accepted as fact. Shortly after midnight two brothers who ran a store about a mile from the military reservation were awakened by someone banging on the door and demanding "a match and then... some other trifling article. They refused to open, and the applicant went away threatening to get even."

About an hour later the stranger returned and began pounding more violently. When they ordered him away he only pounded harder, then went around to the side and "dealt some jarring blows" to the flimsy frame building. Inside, with crockery falling off the shelves, the brothers had enough and decided that one would keep the man occupied from the front while the other slipped out the back and grabbed the stranger from behind. One brother crept out the back door and around the corner, only to find himself face to face with the brawler carrying a broken chair leg which he slammed into the store-keeper's chest. The storekeeper shouted in pain and then grabbed his assailant. The other brother came running up with a pistol and tried several times to shoot the stranger, "but as often as he leveled the pistol the other [storekeeper] shouted to him to not shoot, fearful that the bullet might go amiss in the constantly changing positions."

The noise aroused the neighborhood. About a dozen neighbors ran to help but the ruffian was too powerful to be restrained and had to be beaten into submission. Bruised and bleeding, soaked to the skin and his clothes ripped to shreds, he was bound to a cart wheel. Some of the men stood guard over their unknown prisoner while others went for the police, who recognized the stranger immediately. He was Brigadier General Ranald S. Mackenzie, commander of the Department of Texas.

Mackenzie was hurried back to his quarters, chilled through with his clothes caked with blood.[7] There was now no question in Vincent's mind—Mackenzie was no longer capable of command. He ordered the general "controlled in a proper manner" until, later that morning, Dr. Smith went to see him before preparing a medical report for divisional headquarters.

"I found his mental character changed," Smith wrote. "He replies rationally to most questions, but soon runs off to discourses entirely personal and braggadocio." He felt Mackenzie had never recovered from his breakdown in New Mexico, and noted that his condition "is such as to disqualify him from command, and this disability bids fair to continue for a considerable period."[8] Vincent forwarded Smith's report to Chicago with his own endorsement, saying, "I am convinced that his present deplorable condition has impaired his usefullness [sic] for a further exercise of command in this department."[9]

At divisional headquarters Schofield accepted the findings and sent them on to Washington with the note that Mackenzie's condition was such that:

> considerable time must elapse before it would be safe to entrust him with the grave responsibilities of command. Hence I respectfully recommend that another officer be assigned to the Command of the

Department of Texas. . . . I will await further
information from the Staff Officers at San Antonio
before asking instructions respecting the future
care and medical treatment of General Mackenzie.

He had already telegraphed the War Department, saying he
had ordered Vincent to assume temporary command of the
Department of Texas and to issue all necessary orders in
Schofield's name.[10]

The situation became public knowledge in San Antonio.
"'Poor Mackenzie' is the way soldiers and civilians here
speak," the local correspondent noted to the New Mexico
papers, and back east *The Nation* reported that Mackenzie had
been temporarily relieved because of nervous prostration.[11]
Mackenzie had been relieved before, sometimes at his own
request, and outside of San Antonio and top army circles no
one seemed to realize the exact nature of the problem or how
serious it really was.

Vincent, now sending daily reports directly to the War
Department in Washington, noted on December 20 that
Mackenzie's delusions "are less numerous and he is not so
violent; a marked improvement since yesterday." The following day, however, he again became irrational. Although his
physical health remained good, by December 22 Vincent said,
"It may be necessary to send him to an asylum and that in
view I have telegraphed General Schofield as to certain preliminary arrangements."[12]

The question of how to get Mackenzie to an asylum, when
he was convinced that he was perfectly sane[13] and that the
only problem was the poor organization of the army, was a
difficult one. Since Mackenzie believed only he and Sheridan
could give the service the overhaul it needed,[14] Vincent's

1st Lt. Joseph H. Dorst
(National Archives)

1st Lt. Alexander Rodgers
(National Archives)

"certain preliminary arrangements" involved a ruse in which Schofield telegraphed the War Department suggesting Sheridan order Mackenzie to Washington to consult on the reorganization. "Early action is deemed important," he urged.[15]

A medical officer, his two aides and an orderly were detailed to accompany Mackenzie for the trip. Harriet telegraphed Sheridan personally, asking him also to detail Dr. Middleton, in whom Mackenzie seems to have had a great deal of confidence and who she felt was the only person who could control him. On Christmas Day General Drum notified Vincent that Secretary Lincoln had given the go-ahead for the arrangements. "Prevent notice of departure if possible from getting into papers," he added.[16]

When Mackenzie began to deteriorate physically as well as mentally, Dr. Middleton and the two aides, Dorst and Lieutenant Alexander Rodgers, became exhausted from the constant attention he required, so Vincent detailed a second orderly to help during the trip. Convinced he was going to consult with Sheridan, and not knowing his destination was

319

the government asylum in Washington, Mackenzie allowed himself to be prepared for travel. The Missouri Pacific Railroad provided a special Pullman Hotel Car, and at 7:30 A.M. December 26 the group, including Harriet, left for St. Louis on the first leg of the trip.[17]

In St. Louis Middleton received a telegram from Drum. "The friends of General Mackenzie" had advised he be taken to Bloomingdale Asylum in New York rather than to the government hospital. The "friends" were Admiral C.R.P. Rodgers, father of Mackenzie's aide, in consultation with two surgeons, who were worried about "publicity and disturbing influences" in Washington. Lincoln had concurred. Middleton was to take Mackenzie to New York.[18]

Harriet was furious. No one had consulted her. "Miss Mackenzie insists that the general be taken to the asylum in Washington," Middleton cabled Drum, and Harriet personally telegraphed her objections to Sheridan from Columbus, Ohio. From Pittsburgh she wired Secretary Lincoln, again asking that her brother be sent to Washington. "I am his nearest friend and know it is better for him."[19] The War Department, adamant that he go to Bloomingdale, gave Sheridan the job of telling her.

> General Mackenzie was sent to Bloomingdale after a full consultation with his friends. I join with them in thinking it the best place for him for the present.[20]

In the Mackenzie party, the bureaucracy was getting on everyone's nerves. At St. Louis, where they found they could not go straight through to New York on the Missouri Pacific, the local quartermaster tried several different accommodations, none of which satisfied Dr. Middleton until the Vandalia Railroad offered a special coach on an express to New York. Middleton felt he was receiving conflicting instructions: sometimes it appeared he was to turn Mackenzie over to friends; at other times it seemed he was personally to take him to Bloomingdale. Exasperated, he wired Drum from Indianapolis, "Am I to turn him over to friends in New York or take him to Bloomingdale [?] answer [me at] Pittsburg." He was also caught in the middle of Harriet's fight with the War Department. The route of the express can be followed by the telegraph offices the party used along the way.[21]

The train, which arrived in New York at 10:20 P.M. December 29, was met by Dr. Charles H. Nichols, superintendent of Bloomingdale, and Morris Duer, a cousin. Together with Harriet and an orderly, they helped Mackenzie into a carriage, made their farewells to the soldiers and drove to the hospital at Boulevard and 117th Street. For almost two months Mackenzie was treated at Bloomingdale. On February 22 Dr. Nichols wrote Sheridan that the prognosis was "altogether unfavorable, both as to his full recovery and of his future ability to reliably discharge any of the duties of his office."[22] Five days later Sheridan sent Nichols' report to Lincoln with a cover letter, stating:

> It is with deep regret I have the honor to report that upon December 29th, 1883, Brigadier General R.S. Mackenzie, U.S. Army, became an inmate of the Bloomingdale Asylum for the Insane in the city of New York. He has been there under charge of the medical superintendent, Doctor C.H. Nichols, with a disordered state of mind.

> I am convinced by the enclosed official letters of Dr. Nichols, as well as by other private personal

letters received, that there is no probability of General Mackenzie's recovery and that his usefulness to the service is destroyed.

I therefore respectfully request that a retiring board be ordered to meet at the Bloomingdale Asylum for the purpose of passing upon the case of General Mackenzie with a view of his retirement from active service.

The orders were issued on March 3 and the hearing was set for two days later.[23]

CHAPTER 21

"I Would Rather Die than Go in the Retired List"

The retirement board convened in Bloomingdale Asylum at 11:30 A.M. Wednesday, March 5, 1884, "to carefully inquire into and determine the facts touching the nature and occasion of any disability for performing the duties of his office, or incapacity for active service in the case of Brigadier General Ranald S. Mackenzie."[1] Members included Major General Winfield S. Hancock, commanding officer of the Military Division of the Atlantic, president; Brigadier General Samuel B. Holabird, quartermaster general; and Majors Bennett A. Clements and John H. Janeway, surgeons. Captain Thomas Ward, First Artillery, was detailed as recorder.

The board opened by asking Mackenzie if he had any objections to the officers named. He replied that he had read the order and had no objections to anyone. Captain Ward swore in the board members and was in turn sworn in by General Hancock. Ward then submitted copies of the various orders, along with a statement of Mackenzie's service and "the papers pertaining to the question of his disability," which were read.[2] The two surgeons were sworn in and testimony began.

"Have you and Surgeon Clements made a careful physical examination of Brigadier General Ranald S. Mackenzie?" Ward asked Janeway. "If so, will you state when such examination was made and the result of the same?"

"I have this day made a careful physical examination of Brigadier Ranald S. Mackenzie in conjunction with Surgeon Bennett A. Clements, and the paper I now hand to the Recorder contains the result of our examination and of our opinions in the case," Janeway replied. Ward read aloud the paper Janeway handed him and entered it as evidence.[3] It said:

> We the undersigned Medical officers of the Army and members of the Retiring Board do swear that we have carefully examined Brig. Genl. Randal *[sic]* Mackenzie of the U.S. Army and find that he is suffering from "General Paresis of the insane." And that he is in our opinion unfit for any duty and it is also our opinion that the prospect of his ultimate recovery from the disease is entirely unfavorable.

> It is also our opinion that the disease originated in the line of duty and we would therefore respectfully recommend that he be placed upon the Retired list of the Army.

> B.A. Clements
> Major & Surgeon USA
> John H. Janeway
> Major & Surgeon USA
> Bloomingdale Asylum
> New York
> March 5th 1884 [4]

If Mackenzie gave any reaction to hearing the report, it is not recorded.

Dr. Clements testified that he concurred in the statement.

Mackenzie was offered but declined the opportunity to question the two surgeons. As the other members of the board had no questions, this portion of the hearing was closed and the board asked Mackenzie if he had any statements, testimony or witnesses. He replied:

> I think that I am not insane. I think that I have served as faithfully as anybody in the Army. I would rather die than go in the retired list. The Army is all I have got to care for. I don't wish to stay here. I am treated very kindly by Doctor Nichols and Mrs. Nichols and many others.

Mackenzie had no further statement at that point and the board called Dr. Nichols, who testified, "General Mackenzie came under my charge on the 30th of December last. In my opinion he is suffering from that disease which is usually denominated 'General Paralysis of the Insane,' and is not likely to recover."

"How long have you been connected with institutions for, and studying the disease of the insane?" Ward asked.

"Nearly thirty-seven years. I was Superintendent of the Government Hospital for the insane at Washington D.C. for nearly twenty-five years."

"Have you constantly had General Mackenzie under your observation since his admission to the Bloomingdale Asylum?"

"I have," Nichols replied, at which point Mackenzie asked to make another statement.

"You all know me, and have known me a great many years," he said. "And I think it very hard if I am left out of the Army where my services have always been gallant and honest and faithful. And for a few months sickness. I think it will be very hard if I am separated from the active list of the Army."[5]

That was the end of it. The room was cleared and the board began deliberating. Presently, it returned its findings.

> Brigadier Ranald S. Mackenzie is incapacitated for active service and the duties of his office, and in the judgment of the Board, said incapacity is due to "General Paralysis of the Insane," and the Board further finds that the disability of Brigadier General Ranald S. Mackenzie was incurred from wounds received and exposure in the line of duty as an Officer of the Army.
>
> Winfield S. Hancock
> Major General, U.S. Army
> President, Retiring Board
> Thomas Ward
> Captain 1st U.S. Artillery
> Recorder, Retiring Board[6]

His career was over. He was forty-three.

Mackenzie no doubt comprehended the findings, but bureaucratic formalities required he be officially notified by General Drum via telegram, which was sent in care of Dr. Nichols who passed it on to Mackenzie. Initially Mackenzie seemed ready to acknowledge receipt of the telegram, but after several days Nichols acknowledged it himself, saying Mackenzie "does not appear likely to do it."[7]

He still did not seem to comprehend that the army would actually retire him. In his mind, retirement was entirely unjustified; he firmly believed he would recover and be restored to active duty. Meanwhile he stayed in Bloomingdale where he received friends and was allowed to go out to places of amusement.[8]

On April 4 Mackenzie wrote to Drum. His penmanship, never good, had degenerated into a nearly illegible scrawl. Acknowledging his orders of retirement, he wrote,

> I do not, considering my great military service in past years, believe, that I was treated in any other than the most unprecedented way, and that in view of my recovery, which I firmly believe will take place, that I may receive again my position in the Army....[9]

In June a court ruled Mackenzie was "lunatic and of unsound mind."[10] He apparently was considered harmless, however, for on June 14, he was discharged from the hospital and went to his boyhood home of Morristown, New Jersey, which he dutifully noted to General Drum. "There will probably not be a change in my address for some months."[11] He had a "very quiet and pleasant summer" and planned to stay another six months. Apparently feeling much better although his penmanship continued to decline, on September 1 he sent Drum another letter with a more conversational tone than those earlier in the year. "I may make a trip early in April to San Antonio to look after my interests there. Any change of address will be promptly reported."[12] He did not elaborate on his "interests"; perhaps they were the ranch near Boerne or Florida Sharpe or both. There is no evidence that he ever made the trip.[13]

On November 23, 1885, Morris Mackenzie requested copies of the records of his brother's sanity hearings, and Drum dispatched certified copies the same day. Morris did not specify the reason for his request. Perhaps Mackenzie had convinced him he would be able to return to duty, or perhaps Morris wanted to be sure in his own mind that the case was hopeless.[14]

The following year Mackenzie moved in with his cousin Morris Duer, in a large house on the corner of Lafayette and Henderson Avenues in New Brighton, Staten Island. Harriet and two attendants looked after him as he continued to decline. In November 1886, Harriet filed for power of attorney in Kendall County, Texas, in order to administer Mackenzie's ranch near Boerne.[15] What he thought of this, or whether he was even aware of it, is not known. Physically he was deteriorating; he ate well, though he was no longer able to walk without assistance. The violent streaks which had characterized his initial collapse vanished entirely. One cousin, Mrs. John J. Woodruff of Somerset, Virginia, later remembered visiting with him during this period when she was a child. In a letter to Lessing Nohl, she recalled that Mackenzie was very gentle and children adored him. In New Brighton he grew more and more childish himself, until he could no longer make himself understood. Surrounded by his doting sister and other concerned family members, he drifted into a state of oblivion.[16]

The end came on January 19, 1889. The family's notification to the army was a telegram which simply stated:

Adjutant General
War Dept., Washington
General Ranald S. Mackenzie died this morning.
M.R.S. Mackenzie[17]

There was nothing more that Morris could have said. For years he had watched his brother deteriorate and the family was undoubtedly exhausted. Two days later, the New York *Times* published Mackenzie's obituary, buried in the middle of the death notices on page five. For a newspaper which had followed his career so closely over the years, the curt brevity of the notice is nothing short of incredible.

> MACKENZIE—At New-Brighton, on the 19th of January, Brig.-Gen. RANALD SLIDELL MAC-KENZIE, United States Army, in the 48th year of his age.[18]

Although the *Times* failed to recognize his place in history, the *Army and Navy Journal* gave Mackenzie his full measure. Beginning with "The sorrow with which the Army will learn of the death of the once brilliant Ranald Slidell Mackenzie derives an additional pang from the recollection of the cloud which overshadowed his later years and consigned him to a living death," the *Journal* article reviewed his entire career, as well as his family background and his personal interests.[19]

A train pulled out of New York at 11:15 A.M. January 22, bearing the body of Ranald Slidell Mackenzie on its final trip up the Hudson River, past his boyhood home to West Point. Friends, relatives and former comrades in arms stood by at 2:00 P.M. as the coffin was lowered with full honors of war into its plot in the academy cemetery.[20]

Four days after the funeral, Assistant Adjutant General J.C. Kelton wrote to Harriet asking for the immediate cause of death for the official record. His letter contained no expression of government concern for her or regret for her brother's death. On February 1 she replied that the cause of death "was the general paresis, owing to which he was retired in March 1884."[21]

Harriet, who never married, slipped into old age known to children in the family as "Aunt Hattie Mac." Morris Robinson Slidell Mackenzie achieved the rank of rear admiral and died in 1915.[22] Florida Tunstall Sharpe remained in San Antonio; for reasons of her own she is not known to have ever discussed Mackenzie. When Colonel M.L. Crimmins interviewed her in 1940, she never mentioned him.[23]

Phil Sheridan died five months before Mackenzie. The tough little general had been diagnosed as having progressive heart disease in November 1887. After a string of heart attacks the following May, Congress rushed through his fourth star. He died on August 5, 1888.[24]

Bill Shafter proved to be much better as a subordinate than as the man in charge. Given his own commands, he became a martinet whose rule was characterized by sloppy administration and blatant favoritism, and he thus became easy to blame for the government blunders which plagued his command of the U.S. military forces in Cuba in 1898. Nothing, however, can detract from his outstanding service as a combat soldier in the deserts of Southwest Texas, where he earned the name "Pecos Bill."

The faithful Henry Lawton rose to the rank of major general and was killed in the Philippine insurrection. Good-hearted and honest to a fault, he left his family almost penniless and a nation-wide fund drive was held for their relief.

Benjamin Grierson reached the pinnacle of his Indian fighting career in his campaigns against Victorio's Apaches in West Texas. After receiving his brigadier's star, he retired in 1890, and died at his summer home in Omena, Michigan, on September 1, 1911. George Crook suffered a fatal heart attack at his residence in the Grand Pacific Hotel in Chicago on

March 21, 1890. His old enemy Red Cloud remarked, "He at least, never lied to us."[25]

With the others gone, Nelson Miles became the army's foremost Indian fighter and organized the final campaign on the plains, which culminated in the massacre at Wounded Knee. In 1894 he commanded the troops that put down the bloody Pullman strike and, in 1898, he led the U.S. forces in Puerto Rico. Promoted to lieutenant general, he was sent to put down the Philippine insurrection where, made mellow by years, he roundly criticized the army's brutal treatment of Filipino prisoners. After the government eased him into retirement, he lived another twenty-two years and died in Washington on May 15, 1925.

Sergeant John B. Charlton saw Mackenzie once more, several years after Charlton left the army in 1876. In that meeting he said Mackenzie "was not very nice. No doubt he never forgave me for going to those above him to get out of the Army, for he told me when I was discharged that he had intended to do something for me."[26] Charlton died in Uvalde, Texas, on March 5, 1922, several months after Robert G. Carter had recommended him for the Medal of Honor for his actions in Palo Duro Canyon in 1874. The application was denied on the grounds that the deadline set by federal law had expired.[27]

Carter outlasted them all. He never completely recovered from the leg injury suffered in the Blanco Canyon Fight and was officially retired on disability in 1876. From then until 1906, he was in and out of active service, answering the call whenever he was needed, eventually retiring with the permanent rank of captain and his own Medal of Honor, awarded in 1900 for valor at Blanco Canyon twenty-nine years before. He pursued a literary career and became a highly respected military historian and commentator, although much of his work is now dated. When he died in Walter Reed Hospital on January 5, 1936,[28] the Fourth Cavalry that had known Mackenzie passed into history.

Of the Indians whom Mackenzie fought, Quanah Parker fared best of all. The wily Comanche chief adapted beautifully to reservation life, using his prestige to organize and administer tribal lands according to white methods. Before long he was charging trail bosses a portion of their herds for passage across the reservation, adding immeasurably to the tribal herds and, presumably, to his own. He told one white friend that he had declined an invitation to join his white Parker relatives at Weatherford because, "As far as you can see here I am chief and the people look up to me, down at Weatherford I would be a poor half breed Indian."[29] Cowboy T.J. Burkett Sr. said, "Hundreds of cowboys knew Quannah [sic] Parker, and he had scores of friends among the white people."[30] A land speculator, financier, rancher and federal judge for Indian affairs, at the time of his death in 1911 Quanah was the wealthiest Indian in North America. Comparing the Comanche's chief's success with the fate of his own commander, Carter felt it singularly unfair that Quanah should have attained such heights while Mackenzie, "who had almost sacrificed his life in an effort to promote the settlement of. . . that now richest of rich countries," was relegated to obscurity.[31]

Carter could hardly be called impartial in his view of Quanah, but his assessment of the government's attitude toward Mackenzie was correct. Once he was retired and of no further use, official Washington lost interest in him.

The cause of Mackenzie's mental deterioration and death remains debatable. He has been dead for over a century, and

we do not have the benefit of a modern post- mortem examination. Recent authorities, working under the benefit of
medical developments within the past century, tend to attribute his case to syphilis, a theory advanced most effectively by
Lessing Nohl in his dissertation "Bad Hand." Citing Robert
W. White's *The Abnormal Personality*, and G. Zilboorg and
G.V. Henry's *A History of Medical Psychology* as his authorities, Nohl points out that in 1894, five years after Mackenzie's
death, medical authorities developed the hypothesis that general paresis originated with syphilitic infection.[32]

While this might establish a general connection between
syphilis and mental deterioration, it does not necessarily
explain Mackenzie's mental deterioration. Venereal disease
was well-known to the Army Medical Corps in the last half
of the nineteenth century, and the medical reports of virtually every western military post list numerous cases. As we
have seen, Mackenzie was thoroughly examined by post and
departmental surgeons many times during his career, as well
as by Doctors Nichols, Clements and Janeway prior to his
sanity hearing. In no instance does venereal infection appear
in the extensive medical reports currently extant in Mackenzie's personnel file. One would assume that at some point,
syphilis would have been detected and noted in his file.

A second question arises: if Mackenzie did, in fact, suffer
from syphilis, where did he contract it? One answer might
be in a student tryst either at Williams College or at West
Point. Another possibility is that, as he grew older and
became shy and uncomfortable around women, he could
have hired the services of a syphilitic prostitute or, like
Custer, received sexual favors from a captured Indian woman
who, in Mackenzie's case, might have been infected. The
nineteenth century army, however, was rife with rumors

about officers such as Mackenzie who were unpopular in certain quarters, and if there had been sexual impropriety, there should be some mention of it, somewhere. As it stands, the record indicates a person who was sexually indifferent to both men and women with the single exception of Florida Sharpe.

A careful review of Mackenzie's records, combined with new knowledge of psychoses gained from studies after the Vietnam War, shows there may have been reasons for his condition other than venereal infection. This, in turn, leads to the possibility that the army's 1884 diagnosis of service-related disability—"from wounds received and exposure in the line of duty"—may be more accurate than the more recent and revisionistic theory of syphilis.

Mackenzie's mental breakdown was not sudden; it had been progressing for years in direct proportion to wounds, stress and fatigue. To Carter, Charlton recalled:

> Once he passed me, on his way to take a swim in a little stream.

> "You may come in too, if you wish, Sergeant," he said. His scars were plainly visible and by looking, when *he* wasn't looking, I learned much of what he had suffered and would suffer until his dying day.[33]

Carter accused Mackenzie of "almost criminal neglect of his own health, in his intensity of nature and purpose in prosecuting these arduous Indian campaigns," and said it made him "more or less irritable, irascible, exacting, sometimes erratic, and frequently explosive."[34]

Nohl advanced the syphilis theory in 1962 before the United States became heavily involved in Vietnam. Since then the publication of *Diagnostic and Statistical Manual of Mental Disorders, Third Edition,* also called DSM-III, has made available later findings which allow us to see a man like Mackenzie in a new light.

Describing post traumatic stress disorder, DSM-III says, "The trauma may be experienced alone. . . or in the company of groups of people (military combat)," and frequently involves a physical problem such as malnutrition or head trauma, which might incur damage to the central nervous system. A victim of the trauma might feel detached or estranged from others, and lose the ability to feel emotions, "especially those associated with intimacy, tenderness, and sexuality." As has been seen, Mackenzie had very few friends and was ill-at-ease around women. In addition, an individual suffering from post-traumatic stress disorder might show "increased irritability. . . associated with sporadic and unpredictable explosions of aggressive behavior, upon even minimal or no provocation. [*This*] *symptom has been reported to be particularly characteristic of war veterans with this disorder.* [italics added][35]

The DSM-III characterizations of post traumatic stress disorders accurately describe Ranald Mackenzie. The symptoms of his trauma are first documented after the slaughter he observed during the Civil War. Thereafter he was aloof, nervous, irritable, often explosive, and avoided becoming close to anyone. His continual exposure to combat situations, reinforced by the Union Army backgrounds of many of the men who served under him in the Fourth Cavalry on the frontier, might have brought back recollections of the savage butchery on the fields of Virginia.

Mackenzie also showed signs of dementia. Although DSM-III lists venereal infection among possible causes, it also

lists head injury such as Mackenzie suffered with the childhood sunstroke and with the accident at Fort Sill.

In advanced cases of dementia, defined as a situation when
a severe loss of intellectual ability interferes with social or
occupational functioning, the individual becomes oblivious to
his surroundings and requires constant care.[36] In addition,
there is a specific type of dementia associated with vascular
disease: multi-infarct dementia which, in its early stages,
shows "patchy" deterioration of intellectual ability but leaves
some functions intact. Its course is erratic, with rapid, fluctu-
ating changes in memory, abstract thinking, impulse control
and personality. Another symptom of the disease, exhibited
by Mackenzie when he lost his ability to walk, is weakness in
the limbs.[37]

Finally, there was Mackenzie's mutilated right hand.
Society still has not completely learned to tolerate visible
handicaps, particularly in people holding high position. In
the twentieth century, Franklin Roosevelt's paralysis was
hidden from public view as much as possible; in the nineteenth century, the social stigma was much worse. Kaiser
Wilhelm II's obsessive concealment of his withered left arm
was completely understandable during the age in which he
lived. On a lesser scale, Major Samuel H. Starr of the Sixth
Cavalry, normally the terror of his troops, was extremely
self-conscious of the arm he lost during the Civil War and once
became visibly shaken when a sergeant had to help him spread
a map.[38]

In Mackenzie's case there was no escaping his deformity.
Being right-handed, he was reminded of his mutilation every
time he tried to eat, sign his name, shake hands, return a salute
or draw his service revolver, and every time he heard the
nicknames given him by both soldiers and Indians. Might not

his disfigurement also have contributed to the strain he was under?[39]

A review of the persona of the Indian Wars reveals a disproportionately large number of Union Army veterans with personality problems when compared with those who entered the service after the Civil War. Certainly the differences in military life after 1865, particularly in having to face an enemy—the Indian—which many judged to be less than legitimate, confounded many Civil War veterans who remained in the army. In the Seventh Cavalry alone, disorders appear in three of its most famous officers, all of whom had excellent combat records: Custer, the classic case of a man whose youth was disrupted and his life changed by early exposure to war;[40] Major Marcus Reno, who lost control at the Little Bighorn and who was ultimately dismissed from the service for indecency; and Captain Frederick Benteen, who alternated between military propriety and drunken binges. The stress factors are also present in Miles' obsession with his personal aggrandizement, and in Bullis' self-isolation with his Seminole-Negro Scouts. Mackenzie's case was similar, but more extreme.

Certainly the war did not unbalance everyone. Shafter's pomposity was inherent. Wesley Merritt remained, simply, a good soldier. Grierson was kindness personified. For all his faults, Crook never lost his humanity. Regardless of what caused Mackenzie's illness, it ended a career which friends and fellow officers agreed had only begun to reach its full potential.

What went through the dark recesses of Ranald Mackenzie's mind in those last few years?

When he had coherent thoughts, were they full of bitterness at the living hell of insanity?

BAD HAND

Or were his thoughts back on the dusty plains of Texas as a commander, showing his men how to find one last ounce of energy to win where victory was impossible?

Footnotes

PROLOGUE

1. Boatner, *Civil War Dictionary,* 500
2. *Williams College,* 1877, 14; Nohl, "Bad Hand," 335.
3. Connell, *Morning Star,* 106.
4. Carter, *Sergeant's Story,* 59.
5. Ibid., 110.
6. Thompson, "Scouting With Mackenzie," 1897.
7. Parker, *Old Army,* 45.
8. Ibid., 54.

CHAPTER 1
"Quiet, Modest to Shyness"

1. New York Public Library to Charles M. Robinson III, March 31, 1987; Sears, *Slidell,* 5-6; Roehl, "Looking Back."
2. Nohl, "Bad Hand," 5; Sears, *Slidell,* 236.
3. Roehl "Looking Back"; Meltzer, *The Mexican Struggle,* 62, 64, 68, 72; Jenkins, *Britain and the War,* 1:15.
4. Sears, *Slidell,* 21; *Army Navy Journal,* vol. 23, no. 22, January 26, 1889, 424.
5. Brooks, *Washington Irving,* 251-52.
6. Ibid., 251n. *A Year in Spain* was one of Irving's favorite books, and he reread it many times. Pierre Irving recalled that, during his uncle's last illness, the family tried to avoid reading it to him, since he grew excited over the old memories and it tired him.
7. van de Water, "Panic," 22.
8. Roscoe and Freeman, *Picture History,* entry 443.
9. Morison, *John Paul Jones,* 433.
10. Roscoe and Freeman, *Picture History,* entry 489.
11. van de Water, "Panic," 21-23; Miller, *U.S. Navy,* 128-29.
12. Lavender, "White House," 82-83.
13. Hamm, *Famous Families,* 1:127-30.
14. Dorst, "Mackenzie," 1.
15. Wallace, *Mackenzie,* 5-6; *Army Navy Journal,* vol. 23 no. 23, January 26, 1889, 424.
16. Dorst, "Mackenzie," 1.

17. Ibid.

18. Ibid., 1-2; Wallace, *Mackenzie*, 5-6.

19. *Williams College*, 1863, 57.

20. Washington Gladden, letter of July 15, 1913, quoted in Spring, *Williams College*, 205.

21. Nohl, "Bad Hand," 7-8.

22. Spring, *Williams College*, 205.

23. Dorst, "Mackenzie," 2-3.

24. Nohl, "Bad Hand," 8.

25. Spring, *Williams College*, 205; Schaff, *Old West Point*, 42.

26. *Williams College*, 1884,56.

27. Schaff, *Old West Point*, 42-43; Dorst, "Mackenzie," 3.

28. Ibid., 2-3.

29. G.K. Warren to R.C. Drum, October 29, 1880, in RG 94 3877 ACP 1873, Mackenzie, Ranald S. (Personal file from the Adjutant General's Office, now in the National Archives, hereinafter cited at "RG 94 3877 ACP" with appropriate name and date).

30. *Army Navy Journal*, vol. 23, no. 23, January 26, 1889, 424.

31. Dorst, "Mackenzie," 3-4.

32. Jenkins, *Britain and the War*, 1:14-16, 194-97; Editors of Time-Life Books, *The Blockade*, 116.

33. "Cadets Arranged in Order of Merit in their respective Classes as Determined by General Examination in June, 1862," in *Official Register of the Officers and Cadets of the U.S. Military Academy, West Point, New York, June, 1862*, 9.

CHAPTER 2
"The Noble Bravery"

1. Dorst, "Mackenzie," 4.

2. Ibid.

3. Ibid.; Medical Certificate, September 3, 1862, in RG 94 3877 ACP 1873.

4. *Williams College*, 1863; Record of Service, RG 94 3877 ACP 1873, hereinafter cited as "Record of Service."

5. Record of Service.

6. C.B. Comstock to Mackenzie, December 2, 1862, in United States Department of War, Office of the Adjutant General, *War of the Rebellion: A Compilation of the Official Records of the Union and Confederate Armies*, Series 1, vol. 51, part 1, 952, 985, 987-88 (hereinafter referred to as *Official Records*).

7. McConnell, *Five Years a Cavalryman*, 147-49.

8. Dorst, "Mackenzie," 5; Record of Service.

9. Cited by Dorst, "Mackenzie," 5.

10. Record of Service.

11. Mackenzie to Professor Peter S. Michie, West Point, May 5, 1881, in Mackenzie, Letterbook, 133-34 (typescript page numbers). Mackenzie was writing on the death of Upton, who had committed suicide after learning he was suffering from a brain tumor.

12. Record of Service; Brigadier General Emory Upton, report, September 1, 1864, in *Official Records*, Series 1, vol. 40, part 1, 492-93.

13. Nohl, "Bad Hand," 2-3; John F. Finerty, *War-Path*, 334; Carter, *Sergeant's Story*, 22.

14. Carter, *On the Border*, 459.

15. Cited in Dorst, "Mackenzie," 7.

16. Ibid.

17. Ibid.

18. Upton, report, September 1, 1864, *Official Records*, Series 1, vol. 43, part 1, 162.

19. Upton, report, ibid., 162; Mackenzie, report, September 30, 1864, ibid., 179.

20. Upton, report, ibid., 162-63.

21. Cited in Dorst, "Mackenzie," 7.

22. Upton, report, *Official Records*, Series 1, vol. 43, part 1, 163.

23. Ibid.

24. Statement of Casualties, ibid., 176.

25. Lieutenant Colonel Egbert Olcott, report, October 23, 1864, ibid., 176.

26. Cited in Dorst, "Mackenzie," 7.

27. Major General Horatio Wright, report, November 27, 1864, *Official Records*, Series 1, vol. 43, part 1, 158-59.

28. Dorst, "Mackenzie," 6; Olcott, report, ibid., 174-75.

29. Sheridan, *Memoirs*, 2:89.

30. Olcott, report, *Official Records*, Series 1, vol. 43, part 1, 175.

31. Sheridan, *Memoirs*, 2:89.

32. Sheridan, report, October 20, 1864, *Official Records*, Series 1, vol. 43, part 2, 424.

33. Record of Service.

34. Ibid.

35. Mackenzie to Major Samuel Breck, date illegible (March 26, 1865?), RG 94 3877 ACP.

36. Mackenzie to Ruggles, February 24, 1865, RG 94 3877 ACP.

37. AGO, March 10, 1865, RG 94 3877 ACP.

CHAPTER 3
"The Most Promising Young Officer"

1. Porter, *Campaigning With Grant*, 422-30.
2. Major General Edward O.C. Ord, report, April 26, 1865, *Official Records*, Series 1, vol. 50, part I, 1160; the number of men in Mackenzie's division is from Mackenzie's report, May 8, 1865, ibid., 1244.
3. Sheridan, report, ibid., 1104-5; Mackenzie to Sheridan, August 7, 1880, in Mackenzie, Letterbook, 116-17.
4. Sheridan, report, *Official Records*, Series 1, vol. 50, part I, 1104-5; Mackenzie, report, ibid., 1244-45; Mackenzie to Sheridan, August 7, 1880, in Mackenzie, Letterbook, 117.
5. Major General Wesley Merritt, report, April 20, 1865, *Official Records*, Series I, vol. 50, part I, 1116-19.
6. Mackenzie, report, ibid., 1245.
7. Merritt, report, ibid., 1119.
8. "Sharp skirmish," Mackenzie, report, ibid., 1245; "engaged more or less during the entire day," Merritt, report, ibid., 1120.
9. Merritt, report, ibid., 1119.
10. Mackenzie, report, ibid., 1245.
11. Grant, *Memoirs*, 2:465-66.
12. Ibid., 466-67.
13. Major General George Crook, report, April 18, 1865, *Official Records*, Series 1, vol. 50, part I, 1142-43; Mackenzie, ibid., 1245-46.
14. Davis, *Appomattox*, 375-76.
15. Crook, report, *Official Records*, Series I, vol. 50, part I, 1143.
16. Porter, *Campaigning With Grant*, 483-84.
17. Mackenzie report, *Official Records*, Series 1, vol. 50, part I, 1246.
18. Record of Service.
19. Grant, *Memoirs*, 2:541.

CHAPTER 4
"Scouting Parties"

1. Record of Service; Mackenzie to Brevet Major General L. Thomas, October 11, November 6, 1865, RG 94 3877 ACP 1873.
2. Dorst, "Mackenzie," 8-9; Mackenzie to Thomas, March 11, 1867, RG 94 3877 ACP 1873; Crimmins, "Mackenzie," 284.
3. Examining Surgeon's Report, Board to Examine Officers Ap-

FOOTNOTES

pointed in the Infantry of the Army, March 13, 1867; President of the Board, ibid., March 13, 1867; Headquarters of the Army, AGO, Special Orders No. 209, April 26, 1867, all in RG 94 3877 ACP 1873.

4. Carlson, "Shafter," 69.

5. Ibid., 73; Dorst, "Mackenzie," 9.

6. *Army Navy Journal*, vol. 26, no. 22, January 26, 1889, 424.

7. Brownsville *Daily Ranchero*, various issues, Summer, 1867.

8. Hunter, "The Fall of Brownsville."

9. Sides, *Fort Brown Historical*, 120.

10. *Daily Ranchero*, June 28, 1867.

11. Ibid., various issues.

12. Marcum, "Fort Brown," 179-80.

13. Post Medical Report, Fort Brown, Texas, 1867. Marcum (p. 238) says the storm struck on October 3.

14. Carlson, "Shafter," 78; McConnell, *Five Years a Cavalryman*, 213.

15. Nohl, "Bad Hand," 13. Post returns for Fort Brown are unfortunately missing for this period, and the medical report is more of a retroactive summary than a detailed monthly account. This was a vital period in the post's history, and the records might have provided much information on Mackenzie's personality.

16. Record of Service; Carter, *On the Border*, 341; Nohl, "Bad Hand," 319.

17. Quoted in "Fort McKavett Was a Frontier Post," San Angelo *Times* and reprinted in *Frontier Times*, vol. 15, June 1938, 401.

18. Post Returns, Fort McKavett, Texas, May, 1869, RG 94 M 617, Roll 687.

19. Ibid., October, 1869.

20. Ibid.

21. Ibid., May, 1869, and other months.

22. Letters Sent, Fort McKavett, Texas, July 19, 1867, RG 398, quoted in Sullivan, *Fort McKavett*, 46, 52.

23. Haley, "Racial Troubles," 453-57. Jackson was eventually tried and exhonerated before a civil court.

24. Sullivan, *Fort McKavett*, 10, 30-31.

25. Ibid. 31; Mackenzie to General W.T. Sherman, April 23, 1876, in Mackenzie, Letterbook, 49.

26. Medical History, Fort Concho, Texas, August through November, 1869.

27. Post Returns, Fort McKavett, Texas, various dates, 1870, RG 94 M 617, Roll 687.

28. Austin *Daily State Journal*, December 29, 1870.

CHAPTER 5
"Blessing to this Whole State"

1. Abstracted from *Army Navy Journal*, vol. 15, no. 52, whole no. 780, August 3, 1878, 842, Grierson, Papers (Military Correspondence, 1861-1890).

2. Nye, *Carbine and Lance*, 45.

3. Texas is unique in this respect. Since it had been a sovereign republic, its regulation of public lands was already well established before it came under American jurisdiction. As one of the conditions of annexation, the Texas government insisted on the right to administer its own territory. Therefore, the federal government has no eminent domain to speak of.

4. New York *Times*, October 30, 1867, and Nye, *Carbine and Lance*, 45-46.

5. New York *Times*, November 4, 1867, and Hamilton, "History of Fort Richardson," 95-97.

6. Myers, Papers; Muir, *Contemporary Narrative*, 168-69.

7. Parker, *Old Army*, 47; Fort Concho Medical History, July, 1870, January, 1871.

8. Nohl, "Bad Hand," 16; Herr and Wallace, *U.S. Cavalry*, 144-45; McConnell, *Five Years a Cavalryman*, 13.

9. Dorst, "Mackenzie," 9.

10. Parker, *Old Army*, 47; Nohl, "Bad Hand," 17-18; Carter, *On the Border*, 57-58.

11. Mackenzie, Journal of the Move to Fort Richardson, in Wallace, "Official Correspondence," *Museum Journal* 9: 18-19; Carter, *On the Border*, 59-65.

12. Mackenzie, Journal, in Wallace, "Official Correspondence," *Museum Journal* 9:20.

13. Ibid., 22. Actually four black teamsters were buried there, after being killed only three months earlier. One of them was Britt Johnson, a former slave who had become a local hero after he had recovered many of the hostages carried off in the Elm Creek Massacre in Young County in 1864.

14. Carter, *On the Border*, 69.

15. McConnell, *Five Years a Cavalryman*, 232.

16. Carter, On *the Border*, 69.

17. Carter, *Sergeant's Story*, 62.

18. Ibid., 69.

FOOTNOTES

CHAPTER 6
"You Will Not Hesitate to Attack"

1. Carter, *On the Border*, 58.

2. Davidson to AAG, Department of the Missouri, March 30, 1871, RG 94 1305 AGO 1871, Letters Received, Main Series, 1871-1880, arranged as received by AGO, rather than chronologically (hereinafter cited as Letters Received).

3. Hamilton, *Sentinel*, 62.

4. Carter, *Sergeant's Story*, 70.

5. Post Returns, Fort Richardson, April, 1871.

6. Tatum, *Our Red Brothers*, 25.

7. Leckie, *Unlikely Warriors*, 166, 169.

8. Post Returns, Fort Richardson, May, 1871.

9. Rister, "Indian Policy." 14-18; McConnell, *Five Years a Cavalryman*, 274; *Army and Navy Journal*. vol. 7, no. 43, Whole Number 407, June 10, 1871, 675; Post Medical Report, Fort Griffin, Texas, May, 1871.

10. Rister, "Indian Policy," 18-19.

11. Nye, *Carbine and Lance*, 128.

12. Carter, *On the Border*, 76-77.

13. Ibid., 80-81, 83; the citizens' petition is reproduced in facsimile in Hamilton, *Sentinel*, 237-43.

14. Huckaby, *Jack County*, 168.

15. Sherman to Mackenzie, May 19, 1871, in Letters Received; Strong, *Frontier Days*, 21.

16. Sherman to Colonel William H. Wood, May 19, 1871, in Letters Received.

17. Carter, *Sergeant's Story*, 69-70.

18. Mackenzie to Sherman, quoted in Huckaby, *Jack County*, 168-69; Dr. Julius Patzki to Mackenzie quoted in Nye, *Carbine and Lance*, 131; Carter, *On the Border*, 81-82.

19. J. K. Mizner to AAG Department of Texas, June 11, 1871, in Letters Received.

20. Grierson to AAG, Department of the Missouri, June 9, 1871, in Letters Received; Sherman to Sheridan, May 29, 1871, ibid.; Lawrie Tatum to Jonathan Richards, May 30, 1871, in Kiowa Agency, Federal, State and Local Court Relations, Trial of Satanta and Big Tree, hereinafter referred to as "Kiowa File."

21. Mackenzie to Sherman, June 15, 1871, in Sherman, Unofficial Papers; Grierson of AAG, Department of the Missouri, June 9, 1871, Letters Received; Carter, *Sergeant's Story*, 78-79. Charlton never forgot

Satank. In 1921 he wrote Carter that he was very proud of a collection of photographs of his service days, but added, "I don't look at Se-tank's picture after dark. *He might come and roost on the bed post.*" (*Sergeant's Story,* 81).

22. Carter, *Sergeant's Story,* 81.

23. Mackenzie to Sherman, June 15, 1871, in Sherman, Unofficial Papers; Mackenzie to Tatum, June 25, 1871, in Kiowa File.

24. Indictment quoted in Huckaby, *Jack County,* 180-81; Lanham quoted in Wilbarger, *Indian Depredations,* 563-65.

25. Jack County, Minutes of the District Court, 234-39, Cause No. 224, the State of Texas vs. Satanta and Big Tree; Mackenzie quoted in AAG Department of Texas, July 13, 1871, extract from commanding officer, Fort Richardson, in Letters Received.

26. Mackenzie to Sherman, June 15, 1871, in Sherman, Unofficial Papers.

CHAPTER 7
"One Soldier Wounded"

1. Carter, *On the Border,* 105-6.

2. Reynolds to Mackenzie, July 6, 1871 and Headquarters, Department of Texas, Special Orders No. 138, July 5, 1871, both in Wallace, "Official Correspondence," *Museum Journal* 9: 35-36.

3. Carter. *On the Border,* 108.

4. Sherman to James Culbertson McCoy, aide-de-camp, July 29, 1871, in Wallace, "Official Correspondence," *Museum Journal* 9:38.

5. Nohl, "Bad Hand," 30-31; Mackenzie to Sherman, April 30, 1876; Mackenzie to AG USA, May 11, 1876, both in Mackenzie, Letterbook, 50-51.

6. Post Returns, Fort Richardson, Texas, July, 1871.

7. Carter, *On the Border,* 114; Mackenzie to Grierson, July 31, 1871, and Mackenzie to Tatum, July 31, 1871, both in RG 391 Series 757, Fourth Cavalry Expedition Records, Letters and Endorsements Sent and Orders Issued, hereinafter referred to as "Expedition Records."

8. Carter, *On the Border,* 116.

9. Ibid., 114; Post Returns, Fort Richardson, August, 1871.

10. Carter, *On the Border;* Grierson to AAG, Department of the Missouri, June [date illegible], 1871, in Letters Received. Kicking Bird's Kiowa name, Tene-an-gopte, translates as Eagle That Strikes with Talons or Striking Eagle. The traditional rendition is used here.

11. Carter, *On the Border,* 116-22.

12. Ibid., 122-24; Grierson to AAG, Department of the Missouri, June 19, 1871, Kiowa File; Hutton, *Phil Sheridan,* 237-38; Reynolds to

Adjutant General, August 3, 1871, in Wallace, "Official Correspondence," *Museum Journal* 9:39.

13. Carter, *On the Border*, 124-27.

14. Ibid., 134-35.

15. Ibid., 139.

16. Ibid., 141, 142-43, 145, 147.

17. Mackenzie to W.H. Wood, September 6, 1871, in Expedition Records; Post Returns, Fort Richardson, September, 1871.

18. Post Returns, Fort Richardson, October, 1871; Mackenzie to Major H. Clay Wood, September 29, 1871, and Mackenzie to Colonel H. W. Wood, September 30, 1871, and AAG, Fourth Cavalry to Lieutenant William Thompson, September 30, 1871, all in Expedition Records.

19. Carter, *On the Border*, 157-64; Nohl, "Bad Hand," 40.

20. Carter, *On The Border*, 164-84; Wirt Davis to Carter, December 6, 1904, quoted in ibid., 210-11.

21. Ibid., 183.

22. Ibid., 184-85.

23. Ibid., 186.

24. Ibid., 186-203; Post Returns, Fort Richardson, November, 1871.

25. Mackenzie to AAG DT, in Wallace, "Official Correspondence," *Museum Journal* 9: 41-42.

26. Sherman to McCoy, July 29, 1871, in Wallace, "Official Correspondence," *Museum Journal* 9:38; War Department, Adjutant General's Office, General Orders No. 66, November 1, 1871, ibid., 40-41.

27. Reynolds to AG USA, November 23, 1871. The telegram is quoted in Wallace, "Official Correspondence," *Museum Journal* 9:44. The source is given as RG 94, 3877 ACP 1873. However, the microfiche of that file currently available from the National Archives (1990) does not contain the record; Nohl, "Bad Hand," 55-56.

28. Utley, *Cavalier in Buckskin*, 206-7.

CHAPTER 8
"It Is a Regular Business"

1. Strong, *Frontier Days*, 33.

2. Carter, *On the Border*, 340-41.

3. Mackenzie to AAG DT, April 19, 1872, in Wallace, "Official Correspondence," *Museum Journal* 9: 51-52.

4. Carter, *On the Border*, 338-40. Fort McKinney, Wyoming, was

named for Lieutenant McKinney, after he was killed in the Dull Knife Fight.

5. Ibid., 253-55.

6. Ibid., 255.

7. Brigadier General C. C. Augur, Annual Report, 1872, in Wallace, "Official Correspondence," *Museum Journal* 9: 137.

8. Ibid., 138; Major John P. Hatch, Fourth Cavalry, to Commanding Officer, District of New Mexico, March 31, 1872, in ibid., 45-46; Fort Concho Medical History, 54.

9. Hatch to AAG DT, April 15, 1872, and Hatch to Commanding Officer, District of New Mexico, April 16, 1872, both in Wallace, "Official Correspondence," *Museum Journal* 9: 47-51.

10. Augur, annual report, ibid., 138; Fort Concho Medical History, 54-55.

11. Sheridan to Augur, April 20, 1872, in Wallace, "Official Correspondence," *Museum Journal* 9:53.

12. Headquarters, Department of Texas, Special Orders No. 102, May 31, 1872, ibid., 71-72.

13. Mackenzie to AAG DT, June 4, 1872, and Sheridan, endorsement, June 24, 1872; Major G.W. Schofield, Tenth Cavalry, to Captain W.W. Webb, May 20, 1872, all in Wallace, "Official Correspondence," *Museum Journal* 9: 73-75; Lieutenant E.C. Gilbreath, Eleventh Infantry, to Post Adjutant, Fort Griffin, June 11, 1872, ibid., 77-78; "wherever they may be joined," Lieutenant Colonel G.P. Buell, Eleventh Infantry, to AAG DT, ibid., 87.

14. Mackenzie to Shafter, June 20, 1872, and Mackenzie to Augur, June 20, 1872, both in Expedition Records.

15. E.D. Townsend, AG USA, to Augur, July 1, 1872, and reply, in Wallace, "Official Correspondence," *Museum Journal* 9: 98.

16. Mackenzie to AAG DT, July 6, 1872, ibid., 101-2.

17. Major L.N. Bliss, Twenty-Fifth Infantry, to AAG DT, July 11, 1872, and Hatch to AAG DT, July 15, 1872, both ibid., 103-6.

18. Mackenzie to AAG DT, July 22, 1872, ibid., 110-11.

19. Mackenzie to AAG DT, August 15, 1872, ibid., 129-30,

20. Mackenzie to AAG DT, August 7, 1872, ibid., 128; Strong, *Frontier Days*, 34.

21. Mackenzie to AAG DT, September 3, 1872, in Wallace, "Official Correspondence,"*Museum Journal* 9: 133-34.

22. Mackenzie to AAT DT, September 19, 1872, ibid., 133-34.

23. Augur, Annual Report, ibid., 139.

24. Mackenzie to AAG DT, ibid., 141-42; Carter, *On the Border*, 377; Carter, *Sergeant's Story*, 82-83.

25. ". . . they have become Indians," Mackenzie to AAG DT,

October 12, 1872, in Wallace, "Official Correspondence," *Museum Journal* 9: 142-44; Strong, *Frontier Days*, 38; Carter, *On the Border*, 379.

26. Strong, *Frontier Days*, 89.

27. Mackenzie to AAG DT, October 12, 1872, in Wallace, "Official Correspondence," *Museum Journal* 9: 142, 144-45.

28. Mackenzie to AAG DT, October 12, 1872, ibid., 142-43.

29. Mackenzie to AAG DT, ibid., 143; Strong, *Frontier Days*, 39; Carter, *On the Border*, 379.

30. Schofield to AAG DT, January 17, 1873, in Wallace, "Official Correspondence," *Museum Journal* 9: 160.

31. Townsend to Commanding General, Department of Texas, November 21, 1872, ibid., 147.

CHAPTER 9
"You Must Assume the Risk"

1. Sherman to Augur February 5, 1873, in Wallace, "Official Correspondence," *Museum Journal* 9: 161-62.

2. Wilbarger, *Indian Depredations*, 650-51.

3. Day, Report of Indian Depredations in Medina County [1865-1866], *Texas Indian Papers 1860-1916*, 134.

4. H.J. Richards to E.M. Pease, May 18, 1868, ibid., 262-64.

5. E.S. Parker, Department of the Interior. to James P. Newcomb, Texas Secretary of State, ibid., May 17, 1870, ibid., 306.

6. Nohl, "Bad Hand," 77-78.

7. Ibid., 79; Wallace, *Mackenzie*, 95-96.

8. New York *Times*, May 20, 1873.

9. Ibid.; Wallace, "Mackenzie Raid," 75.

10. Carter, *On the Border*, 422.

11. Ibid., 416.

12. Ibid., 421.

13. Ibid., 422-23; Nohl, "Bad Hand," 80.

14. Carter, "Raid into Mexico."

15. Beaumont, "Over the Border," 281-82

16. Thompson, *Crossing the Border*, 9

17. Carter, *On the Border*, 425; Parker, *Old Army*, 22.

18. Affidavit of Jerome Strickland April 21, 1873, and Mackenzie to AAG, DT, April 22, 1873, both in Wallace, "Official Correspondence," *Museum Journal* 9: 162-65.

19. Carter, *On the Border*, 425; Parker, *Old Army*, 22.

20. Ibid., 426-27

21. Ibid.; Beaumont, "Over the Border," 283-84

22. Carter, *On the Border,* 429-30; Nohl, "Bad Hand," 82-83.

23. Carter, *On the Border,* 431.

24. Ibid., 433-34.

25. Ibid.

26. Ibid., 435.

27. Ibid., 436; Wallace, "Border Warrior," 101.

28. Carter, *On the Border,* 436; Nohl, "Bad Hand," 84.

29. Carter, On the Border, 437-38; Mackenzie to AAG, DT, May 23, 1873, in Wallace, "Official Correspondence." Museum Journal 9: 168.

30. Carter, *On the Border,* 438-39.

31. Mackenzie to AAG, DT, May 23, 1873, in Wallace, "Official Correspondence," *Museum Journal* 9: 169; San Antonio *Daily Express,* June 11, 1873.

32. Carter, *On the Border,* 441.

33. Ibid. Carter is one of many writers of the period who confused the name. *Remolino* means "whirlwind", which is a common occurrence in that part of Mexico. *Rey Molina* (correctly *Molino del Rey)* means "The King's Mill." In view of the fact that the average soldier did not speak Spanish, it is possible that the confusion arose over the Battle of Molino del Rey in the Mexican War, which was well-known to the nineteenth century military.

34. Ibid., 444n.

35. Ibid., 441-43.

36. Mackenzie to AAG, DT, May 23, 1873, in Wallace, "Official Correspondence," *Museum Journal* 9: 168-70.

37. Strong, *Frontier Days,* 39.

38. Carter, *On The Border,* 448-55; Wallace, *Mackenzie,* 102.

39. New York *Times,* May 23, 1873; Carter, *On the Border,* 455-56.

40. Carter, *On the Border,* 456-60. Carter does not mention this incident in his 1888 article, and Beaumont does not indicate the matter was discussed at all. Beaumont, however, was still on active service when he wrote his article and, if the incident did occur, may have thought it better to ignore.

41. Nohl, "Bad Hand," 92.

42. Mackenzie to AAG, DT, in Wallace, "Official Correspondence," *Museum Journal* 9: 169.

43. Wallace, "The Mackenzie Raid," 90.

CHAPTER 10
"Grateful Thanks of the People"

1. Schuhardt to Mackenzie, May 19, 1873, in Wallace, "Official Correspondence," *Museum Journal* 9: 175-76.

2. Sheridan to Belknap, May 22, 1873, ibid., 166.

3. Wooster, "Army and Politics," 156. Wooster speculates that the unspecified official informed in advance by Sheridan was probably Sherman, Belknap or Grant. The latter two are possible, but that Sherman was told is unlikely in view of his later comments. (see fn 17 below).

4. Mackenzie to AAG DT, May 23, 1873, in Wallace, "Official Correspondence," *Museum Journal* 9: 170.

5. New York *Times*, May 23, 1873.

6. Carter, *On the Border*, 460-62.

7. Shafter to Mackenzie, May 21, 1873, in Wallace, "Official Correspondence," *Museum Journal* 9: 177-78.

8. Mackenzie to AAG DT, May 23, 1873, and Mackenzie to Augur, May 23, 1873, both ibid., 173-75.

9. Sheridan to Belknap, May 28, 1873, ibid., 178-79.

10. Mackenzie to Augur, May 29, 1873, ibid., 179.

11. Mackenzie to Augur, May 28, 1873, ibid., 179-81; Mackenzie to Schuhardt, May 28, 1873, ibid., 183.

12. Mackenzie to Augur, May 26, 1873, ibid., 174-75.

13. Dr. Redford Sharpe's obituary, Galveston *News*, March 7, 1873; Shafter to Mackenzie, May 26, 1873, in Wallace, "Official Correspondence," *Museum Journal* 9: 183; Shafter to Mackenzie, June 27, 1873, in Wallace, "Official Correspondence," *Museum Journal* 10: 35-36.

14. Mackenzie to Schuhardt, May 22, 1873, in Mackenzie, Letterbook, 2-4.

15. Mackenzie to Williams, May 22, 1873, ibid., 1.

16. Sheridan, endorsement of June 5, 1873, to Mackenzie report of May 23, 1873, in Wallace, "Official Correspondence," *Museum Journal* 10: 171.

17. Sherman, endorsement of June 9, 1873, to Mackenzie report of May 23, 1873, ibid., 171-72. In fact, Sherman was furious about the raid, which had taken him completely by surprise. Not being on speaking terms with Belknap, he knew nothing of the conference between the latter, Sheridan and Mackenzie at Fort Clark. Although Sherman contended he did not approve of the raid into Mexico, it is hard to imagine that he would not have guessed that something like this might be afoot in view of his own letter transferring the Fourth to the border. Six years later, in 1879, Col. Nelson Miles asked permission to

raid the Sioux in Canada, citing Mackenzie's raid as a precedent. Sherman, still fuming over Remolino, denied it, calling Mackenzie's action a "bad...example" (See Hutton, *Phil Sheridan*, 224-25).

18. Belknap to Secretary of the Interior, June 24, 1873, in Wallace, "Official Correspondence," *Museum Journal* 9: 172.

19. New York *Times,* June 12, 1873; Wooster, "Army and Politics," 153.

20. Sheridan, endorsement of June 13, 1873, to Mackenzie letter of May 29,1873, in Wallace, "Official Correspondence," *Museum Journal* 9: 181.

21. Texas Legislature, Resolution, ibid., 189-90.

22. New York *Times*, July 12, 1873.

23. Mackenzie to Augur, June 6, 1873, in Wallace, "Official Correspondence," *Museum Journal* 10: 21-23; Mackenzie to Augur, June 28, 1873, ibid., 33-34.

24. Sheridan, endorsement of June 17, 1873, to Mackenzie letter of June 6, 1873, ibid., 24; Sheridan, endorsement of June 30, 1873, to Mackenzie letter of June 12, 1873, ibid., 28.

25. Augur, endorsement of July 5, 1873, to Mackienzie, letter of June 28, 1873, ibid., 34.

26. New York *Times*, July 20, 1873.

27. Ibid., July 24, 1873. Those who wonder how such a rumor could even get into print need only recall the obituary and eulogies CBS ran for Jim Brady, after he and President Reagan were shot but survived in 1981. At least the *Times* had called the initial Mackenzie story "improbable."

28. Wallace, "Official Correspondence," *Museum Journal* 10: 49n; Hutton, *Phil Sheridan*. 226.

29. L.F. Hammond, medical director, Department of Texas, medical certificate, 12 September, 1873, in RG 94 3877 ACP 1873; Shafter to Mackenzie, July 26, 1873, in Wallace, "Official Correspondence," *Museum Journal* 10: 50-51; Lee 0. Parker to Augur, August 18, 1873, ibid., 51.

30. Hammond, medical certificate, RG 94 3877 ACP 1873; Headquarters, Department of Texas, San Antonio, Texas, September 12, 1873, Special Orders No. 173, ibid.

31. Headquarters of the Army, Washington, September 26, 1873, Special Orders No. 50, ibid.; Dorst, "Mackenzie," 18.

CHAPTER 11
"I Brought You In."

1. Mackenzie to AG, January 13, 1874, in Wallace, "Official

FOOTNOTES

Correspondence," *Museum Journal* 10: 73.

2. Charles L. Hudson to Post Adjutant, Fort Clark, December 15, 1873, ibid., 67-69; J.W. Davidson to AAG DT, January 20, 1874, ibid., 74.

3. Nye, *Carbine and Lance,* 165; Haley, *Buffalo War,* 39.

4. Richardson, "Adobe Walls," 26.

5. Berthrong, *Southern Cheyenne,* 380-82.

6. Leckie, *Military Conquest,* 185; Haley, *Buffalo War,* 52-58.

7. General Order No. 4, Military Division of the Missouri, July 10, 1874, in Wallace, "Official Correspondence," *Museum Journal* 10: 77-78.

8. Record of Service, RG 94 3877 AGO 1873; Sheridan to Sherman, July 21, 1874, in Wallace, "Official Correspondence," *Museum Journal* 10: 78; Special Orders No. 113, Department of Texas, July 23, 1874, ibid., 79.

9. Augur to Mackenzie, August 28, 1874, ibid., 80-81.

10. Carter, *On the Border,* 474; Hatfield, "Campaign in Northwest Texas"; Wallace, "Official Correspondence," *Museum Journal* 10: 80n. In his *On the Border with Mackenzie,* Robert Carter narrates a seemingly first hand eyewitness account of the Fourth Cavalry's Palo Duro engagement. William G. Tudor, however, in his paper "Was Carter with Mackenzie at the Palo Duro in 1874?" quotes official military reports indicating that Carter was absent on sick leave from April-October 1874 and could not have been at the Palo Duro. Tudor believes that Carter, for his chapter on the Palo Duro, used sources such as Lt. Charles Hatfield, Sgt. John Charlton, and the unknown writer, who he believes is Lt. Joseph Dorst, of the two part article entitled "Scouting on the Staked Plains (Llano Estacado) with Mackenzie in 1874," published Sep/Oct 1885 in *The United States,* a monthly magazine devoted to the military and civil services. Tudor points out that Carter's account is almost word for word that of the author of this article.

11. Utley and Washburn, *Indian Wars,* 299-300; Haley, *Buffalo War,* 126-27; Mackenzie to Sheridan, April 17, 1875, in Mackenzie, Letterbook, 33-34; Parker, *Old Army,* 48.

12. Sheridan to Sherman, September 5, 1874, in Wallace, "Official Correspondence," *Museum Journal* 10: 90-91.

13. Carter, *On the Border,* 479-82.

14. Davidson to AAG DT, October 10, 1874 in Wallace, "Official Correspondence," *Museum Journal* 10: 131.

15. Mackenzie to AAG DT, September 19, 1874, (two letters), ibid., 92-93; Mackenzie, Memorandum of March, ibid., 119.

16. "A Commander against hostile Indians . . . ." Augur to Mackenzie, August 28, 1874, in Carter, *On the Border,* 476; Mackenzie, Memorandum of March of the 1st Column from Camp on Fresh Fork

of the Brazos, in Wallace, "Official Correspondence," *Museum Journal* 10: 119-20.

17. "sheets of flame," Carter, *On the Border*, 483-84; Mackenzie, Memorandum of March, above cited, 120-21; New York *Herald*, reprinted in Galveston *News*, October 16, 1874.

18. Carter, *On the Border*, 485; Hatfield, "Campaign in Northwest Texas"; Galveston *News*, October 16, 1874.

19. Mackenzie, Memorandum, above cited, 121-22; Hatfield, "Campaign in Northwest Texas."

20. Galveston *News*, October 16, 1874; Hatfield. "Campaign in Northwest Texas"; Mackenzie, Memorandum, above cited, 122; ". . . as completely as if the ground had swallowed them," Carter, *On the Border*, 487; Bruce Gerdes to W.G. Eustis, August 31, 1936, Gerdes Papers. Gerdes either personally interviewed or corresponded with participants on both sides of the war in the Texas Panhandle.

21. Mackenzie, Memorandum, above cited, 122.

22. Haley, "Comanchero Trade," 175. Haley gives Charles Goodnight as his source. William G. Tudor has commented that he believes this act, uncharacteristic of Mackenzie, is more probably the result of a "good old boy" story told to Haley by Goodnight. Mackenzie to Sheridan, April 17, 1875, Mackenzie, Letterbook, 34.

23. Carter, *Sergeant's Story*, 106.

24. Mackenzie, Memorandum, above cited, 122; Strong, *Frontier Days*, 59; Nye, *Carbine and Lance*, 221; Bruce Gerdes to Arline Ogden, May 24, 1935, and Hatfield to Bruce Gerdes, February 12, 1923, both in Gerdes, Papers.

25. Hatfield to Gerdes, ibid.; Galveston *News*, October 16, 1874; Mackenzie, Memorandum, above cited.

26. Carter, *Sergeant's Story*, 107; Hatfield, "Campaign in Northwest Texas"; Nye, *Carbine and Lance*, 222-23; Gerdes to Arline Ogden, May 24, 1935, above cited.

27. Mackenzie, Memorandum, above cited, 123; Carter, *On the Border*, 489.

28. Galveston *News*, October 16, 1874; Hatfield, "Campaign in Northwest Texas."

29. Mackenzie, Memorandum, above cited, 123; Carter, *On the Border*, 489-91; Dykes, "Palo Duro Canyon," 216.

30. Carter, *Sergeant's Story*, 108; Carter, *On the Border*, 491-92.

31. Mackenzie, Memorandum, above cited, 123; Gerdes to Eustis, August 31, 1936, above cited; Carter, *On the Border*, 493.

32. Hatfield, "Campaign in Northwest Texas"; Carter, *On the Border*, 493; Carter, *Sergeant's Story*, 108; Gerdes, Papers. The exact number of ponies killed is in dispute. Mackenzie's journal entry for September 26, 1874 ("Official Correspondence," *Museum Journal*

10:136) notes the destruction of 548 ponies. But the entry is vague enough to leave the impression that more may have been killed at a different location. In a report to departmental headquarters dated October 26 (ibid., 146), he states, "The ponies captured by my command on the 28th of Sept were disposed of at the time in various ways . . . .There were but a few good ponies among them and I had all killed except what I thought would satisfy these people [i.e., the Indian and civilian scouts]." Both Hatfield and Thompson claimed 1,800 ponies were destroyed. The estimate of 1,450 is from Gerdes, who arrived at that number after years of research.

CHAPTER 12
"Very Great Suffering"

1. Carter, *Sergeant's Story,* 110.

2. Mackenzie, Itinerary of the march of 1st Southern Column, in Wallace, "Official Correspondence," *Museum Journal* 10: 138-41.

3. Sheridan to General E.D. Townsend AG USA, October 29, 1874, ibid, 153; Davidson to AAG DT, October 10, 1874, ibid., 133.

4. Colonel Thomas M. Anderson, Tenth Infantry, to AAG DT, October 19, 1874, ibid., 143; Anderson to AAG DT, October 24, 1874, ibid., 145; Mackenzie, Itinerary, above cited, 141; Captain John B. Park, Company I, Tenth Infantry, to AAG DT, with endorsements, October 29, 1874, ibid., 148-50.

5. Mackenzie to AAG DT, November 9, 1874, ibid., 157-58; Mackenzie to Sheridan, April 17, 1875, in Mackenzie, Letterbook, 33-36.

6. Mackenzie to AAG DT, November 9, 1874, above cited, 157. Like most army officers on the western frontier, Mackenzie put his faith entirely in grainfed government-issue horses, which required a continuous supply of forage. He failed to appreciate the captured Indian ponies which could live on grass and bark. On the other hand, Miles successfully mounted one of his battalions on captured ponies (see Nohl "Bad Hand," 140).

7. Mackenzie to Augur, December 2, 1874, in Wallace, "Official Correspondence," *Museum Journal* 10: 179-81; Mackenzie to AAG DT, with Itinerary, January 7, 1875, ibid., 187-90; G.B. Russell, aide de camp, Department of Texas, to Mackenzie, December 5, 1874, quoted in Carter, *On the Border,* 521.

8. Hutton, *Phil Sheridan,* 264-66.

9. Ibid., 271-72, 299.

10. Record of Service, RG 94 3877 ACP 1873; Haley, *Buffalo War,* 206-7; Mackenzie to Sheridan, April 17, 1875, above cited.

11. Carter, *On the Border,* 524; Pratt, *Battlefield and Classroom,*

106-8; Nye, *Carbine and Lance,* 233.

    12. Mackenzie to Pope, May 9, 1875, Mackenzie, Letterbook, 37-38; Chamberlain, "Mackenzie's Administration," 30. Carter *(Sergeant's Story,* 113) accepts Charlton's assertion that he was ordered to accompany Sturm. However, Ms. Chamberlain, who apparently had access to Sturm's journal, disputes this. Likewise, Mackenzie's correspondence makes no reference to soldiers accompanying Sturm, and he was generally very careful to note any military involvement in such undertakings.

    13. Mackenzie to Pope, May 15, 1875, and June 3, 1875, both in Mackenzie, Letterbook, 38-41; Nye, *Carbine and Lance,* 235.

    14. Mackenzie to Pope, May 9, 1875, in Mackenzie, Letterbook, 37; Berthrong, *Southern Cheyennes,* 403-4; Carter, *Yorktown to Santiago,* 174-75.

    15. Mackenzie to AG USA, August 31, 1875, with subsequent endorsements, in Wallace, "Official Correspondence," *Museum Journal* 10: 196-98.

    16. Parker, *Old Army,* 27-28.

    17. Ibid., 67.

    18. Ibid., 72-74.

    19. Lieutenant Colonel John P. Hatch to Pope, April 19, 1875, with endorsements, New York *Times,* May 4, 1875.

    20. New York *Times,* June 12, 1875.

    21. Chamberlain, "Mackenzie's Administration," 42.

    22. Mackenzie to Pope, September 5, 1875, in Mackenzie, Letterbook, 43-45,

    23. Parker, *Old Army,* 48-49; Chamberlain, "Mackenzie's Administration," 49-50.

    24. Dorst, "Mackenzie," 18. The post medical report for Fort Sill during that period could not be located by the National Archives staff.

    25. New York *Times,* April 7, 1876. Evans was replaced later that year because of his implication in scandals surrounding Secretary Belknap (see Chamberlain, "Mackenzie's Administration," 21).

    26. Ibid., April 28, 1876.

    27. Ibid., May 27, 1876.

    28. Lewis, *Sherman,* 615; Utley, *Cavalier in Buckskin,* 158; Hutton, *Phil Sheridan,* 308.

    29. *Army and Navy Journal,* April 1, 1876, copied in Mackenzie, Letterbook, 48-49; Mackenzie to Sherman, April 23, 1876, in Mackenzie, Letterbook, 49-50; Hutton, *Phil Sheridan,* 306-7.

    30. Mackenzie to Sherman, May 11, 1876, in Mackenzie, Letterbook, 51.

    31. Schmitt, *George Crook,* 191-92, 192n.

32. William Steele, adjutant general of Texas, to S.B. Maxey, May 30, 1876, with endorsements by Maxey and Richard Coke, Governor of Texas; Sherman, endorsement to same, June 9, 1876, in Wallace, "Official Correspondence," *Museum Journal* 10: 199-200.

CHAPTER 13
"Embodiment of Courage"

1. Deland, *Sioux Wars*, 34-35, 38-40.

2. Ibid., 34-36; Grinnell, *Fighting Cheyennes*, 104-9.

3. Ibid., 43-45.

4 Ibid., 274-75.

5. Gray, *Centennial Campaign*, 30-34.

6. Mackenzie to Sheridan, August 1, 1876, in Mackenzie, Letterbook, 52; Mackenzie to Lt. W.C. Miller, August 11, 1876, RG 391 Series 757, Expedition Records, Powder River Expedition.

7. Miller to Commanding Officer, Co. 1, Fourth Cavalry, August 30, 1876, ibid. Not counting longevity pay, which was withheld until discharge, a blacksmith made $15 a month, and a private made $13 a month. However, a private could draw extra duty pay, which more than made up the $2 difference. In actual income, the private often ended up more highly paid than a blacksmith.

8. Mackenzie to Col. R.C. Drum, AAG, MilDivMo, October 10, 1876, ibid.

9. Mackenzie to AG USA, August 31, 1876, ibid. This entire incident appears to have been a gross misunderstanding. Immediately after the Little Bighorn, a story circulated that the massacre was due in part to the Springfield carbine's jamming when it overheated from continuous fire. This theory is still widely accepted, even though an early investigation of the battle site showed more than 25,000 rounds had been expended by the forces of Custer and Reno. Since Mackenzie's request for Winchesters came only five weeks after the disaster, it is possible that the commander of the Springfield Arsenal, Lt. Col. J.B. Benton, felt the request was a slur on his reputation. On August 8, 1876, seven days after the request was made, Benton wrote the Chief of Ordnance, "The most powerful Winchester rifle for frontier service carries a cartridge of 40 grains of powder and 200 grains of lead. The extreme range for which this arm is sighted is 300 yards.

'The cartridge of the Springfield carbine contains 55 grains of powder and 405 grains of lead and is sighted for an extreme range of 1,300 yards.

'The penetration of the Winchester rifle, in pine, at a distance of 100 yards, is less than one half of that of the Springfield carbine at the same distance, and not so much as the penetration of the latter arm at the distance of one half a mile." (Frasca and Hill, The .45-70 Springfield, 2)

If Mackenzie saw Benton's letter, and it is reasonable to assume he at least heard about it, then his own feeling of indignation becomes more understandable.

10. Finerty, *War-Path*, 334. In fact, Mackenzie stood about five feet, nine inches. This was a reasonable height for his time, and his lean, spare frame sometimes gave the impression of being taller.

11. Nohl, "Bad Hand," 161-62; Smith, *Sagebrush Soldier*, 36-37.

12. Mackenzie to unidentified general (presumably Crook), September 8, 1876, in Mackenzie, Letterbook, 52-53; Sherman to Mackenzie, August 22, 1875, ibid., 54-55.

13. Mackenzie to Crook, September 9, 1876, ibid., 53-54.

14. Ibid., September 30, 1876, 56-58; Gray, *Centennial Campaign*, 264-65; Nohl, "Bad Hand." 161-62.

15. Parker, *Old Army*, 48; Mackenzie to Crook, October 18, 1876, and October 13, 1876, both in Mackenzie, Letterbook, 59-60.

16. North, *Man of the Plains*, 201-3; Nohl, "Bad Hand," 164-66,

17. Wheeler, *Buffalo Days*, 116; clipping from *Alta California* pasted in Bourke, Diary, vol. 13. North calls the Brulé chief "Yellow Leaf." "Red Leaf" is the generally accepted form.

18. Wheeler, *Buffalo Days*, 117; North, *Man of the Plains*, 204; King, *Campaigning with Crook*, 140.

19. Schmitt, *George Crook*, 134; Hutton, *Phil Sheridan*, 124-28. Crook richly deserved his reputation as a superb Indian fighter. But his image as a quiet, unassuming soldier is based on his aloof, unflappable demeanor, his acute sense of public relations and the unabashed hero worship of his adjutant and biographer, Bourke. Crook hated Sheridan, and it sometimes seems as if he deliberately set out to irritate the divisional commander. Hutton is perhaps the first current scholar to examine this side of his personality in detail.

20. Cheyenne *Leader*, October 24, 1876, in Bourke, Diary,

21. Schmitt, *George Crook*, 213-19.

22. Bourke, Diary, vol. 14, November 2 and 4, 1876.

23. Bourke, *Mackenzie's Last Fight*, 3.

CHAPTER 14
"He Would Blow His Brains Out"

1. Bourke, Diary, vol. 14, November 9, 1876.

2. Ibid.

3 . Ibid., November 10-11, 1876.

4. Dodge, *Diary*, November 11, 1876.

FOOTNOTES

5. Smith, *Sagebrush Soldier*, 37-38.

6. Ibid., 39. Although Private Smith was a good narrative writer, his spelling was very imaginative, using words such as "pooty" (pretty), "boolets" (bullets), and "ciled" (killed). For the sake of convenience I have corrected the worst of it, with all corrections in [brackets]; Dodge, *Diary*, various entries.

7. Dodge, *Diary*, November 14, 1876; Bourke, Diary, vol. 14, November 14, 1876.

8. Hutton, *Phil Sheridan*, 126-29.

9. Dodge, *Diary*, November 16, 1876. Dodge spells it "McKenzie" until his entry of November 30, when he inexplicably begins using the correct spelling.

10. Smith, *Sagebrush Soldier*, 50; "They readily deluded the young hostile...." Bourke, Diary, vol. 14, November 21, 1876; Grinnell, *Fighting Cheyennes*, 362.

11. Crook to Sheridan, quoted in Bourke, Diary, vol. 14, November 21, 1876.

12. Grinnell, *Fighting Cheyennes*. 362-63; North, *Man of the Plains*, 211; Bourke, Diary, vol. 14, November 14, 1876; DeBarthe, *Frank Grouard*, 326.

13. Smith, *Sagebrush Soldier*, 64; North, *Man of the Plains*, 211-12.

14. Smith, *Sagebrush Soldier*, 65-66, 72; "in a vague but awe-inspiring sort of indistinctness . . . .", Bourke, Diary, vol. 14, November 30, 1876.

15. Smith, *Sagebrush Soldier*, 66.

16. Bourke, Diary, vol. 14, November 30, 1876; Smith, *Sagebrush Soldier*, 72.

17. Bourke, Diary, vol. 14, November 30, 1876.

18. North, *Man of the Plains*, 213; DeBarthe, *Frank Grouard*, 327-28; Bourke, *Mackenzie's Last Fight*, 31-32; Bourke, Diary, vol. 14, November 30, 1876.

19. Smith, *Sagebrush Soldier*, 79-80; Mackenzie to AAG, Powder River Expedition, November 26, 1876, in Expedition Records. Bourke (Diary, vol. 14 November 30, 1876) gives the body count at about thirty.

20. Smith, *Sagebrush Soldier*, 88, 91; "one of the most gallant officers . . . .", Mackenzie to AAG, Powder River Expedition, November 26, 1876, in Expedition Records.

21. Bourke, Diary, vol. 14, November 30, 1876; Bourke, *Mackenzie's Last Fight*, 40-42.

22. Wheeler, *Buffalo Days*, 142-43; Dodge, *Diary*, November 27-30, 1876.

23. Smith, Sagebrush Soldier, 130; Dodge, Diary, November 29, 1876.

24. Connell, *Morning Star,* 340-41; Dodge, *Our Wild Indians,* 499-500; De Barthe, *Frank Grouard,* 331; Grinnell, *Fighting Cheyennes,* says on page 382 that Crazy Horse's band treated the Cheyennes "very kindly and supplied most of their needs." This is indeed possible. But most authorities agree that the Oglalas were relieved to see them go.

CHAPTER 15
"You Were the One"

1. Dodge, *Diary,* November 30-December 1, 1876.

2. Mackenzie to AG, USA, November 29, 1876; Mackenzie to Colonel C.H. Carleton, December 1, 1876; Mackenzie to AG, USA, December 32, 1876, all in Expedition Records.

3. Dodge, *Diary,* December 3, 1876.

4. Ibid., December 5, 1876; text of the telegrams in Bourke, *Mackenzie's Last Fight,* 44.

5. Wheeler, *Buffalo Days,* 149-50.

6. Dodge, *Diary,* December 6-9, 1871.

7. Ibid., December 14, 1876.

8. Ibid., December 17 and 19, 1871.

9. Ibid., December 20-21, 1871.

10. Ibid., December 24-25, 1871.

11. Record of Service, RG 94 3877 ACP 1873; Hutton, *Phil Sheridan,* 279; Dorst, "Mackenzie," 18.

12. Bourke, Diary, vol. 19, March 7, 1877; Grinnell, *Fighting Cheyennes,* 399.

13. Bourke, Diary, vol. 19, April 4 and 12, 1877.

14. Ibid., April 14-15, 1877; "just such things . . . .", ibid., April 21-22, 1877.

15. Ibid., April 22, 1877; Chicago *Tribune,* April 23, 1877; New York *Tribune,* April 23, 1877.

16. Bourke, Diary, vol. 20, April 29, 1877.

17. Grinnell, *Fighting Cheyennes,* 400; Bourke, *On the Border,* 412-13; Bourke, Diary, vol. 19, April 23, 1877.

18. Mackenzie to Colonel R.C. Drum, AAG, Military Division of the Missouri, March 27, 1877, in Expedition Records; Parker, *Old Army,* 67.

19. Record of Service, RG 94 3877 ACP 1873.

20. Chamberlain, "Mackenzie's Administration," 63.

21. Nohl, "Bad Hand," 235-37; Grinnell, *Fighting Cheyennes,* 401.

22. Parker, *Old Army,* 49-50.

23. Ibid., 55-66. Markham later became an admiral, and gained

FOOTNOTES

notoriety when his flagship rammed and sank the battleship HMS *Victoria* during peacetime maneuvers in the Mediterranean.
24. Williams College, 1877.

CHAPTER 16
"So Bad a State of Affairs"

1. Headquarters, MilDivMo, General Order No. 10, December 3, 1877, in Wallace, "Official Correspondence," Museum Journal 10: 201-2; Wooster, "Army and Politics," 157-58; Cresap, *Appomattox Commander*, 319; Record of Service, RG 94 3877 ACP 1873.

2. Parker, *Old Army*, 86; Record of Service, RG 94 3877 ACP 1873.

3. Mackenzie to Commanding Officer, Fort Richardson, December 22, 1877, in Expedition Records; Parker, *Old Army*, 86-88.

4. Parker, *Old Army*, 89-90.

5. Mackenzie to AAG DT (three letters), December 30, 1877, Expedition Records; Parker, *Old Army*, 90-91.

6. Ibid., 92-98.

7. Ibid., 99-100.

8. Mackenzie to Shafter, February 25, 1878, in Wallace, "Official Correspondence," *Museum Journal* 10: 202-3.

9. Mackenzie to Shafter, February 26, 1878, ibid., 203.

10. Nohl. "Bad Hand," 244-45; Mackenzie to T.M. Vincent, AAG DT, April 26, 1878, in Mackenzie, Letterbook, 77-79.

11. Mackenzie to Vincent, April 26, 1878, ibid.

12. Mackenzie to Shafter, May 9, 1878, and Mackenzie to Vincent, May 9, 1878, and Mackenzie to Vincent, May 18, 1878, all in Mackenzie, Letterbook, 76, 80-81.

13. Mackenzie to Vincent, May 18, 1878, and May 28, 1878, ibid., 80-83.

14. Ibid., May 28, 1878; Nohl, "Bad Hand," 246-47; Wooster, "Army and Politics," 161.

15. Mackenzie to unnamed general (Ord?) June 3, 1878, in Mackenzie, Letterbook, 83.

16. Mackenzie to AAG DT, June 23, 1878, in Wallace, "Official Correspondence,"*Museum Journal* 10: 204; ibid., 204n.

17. Ibid., 205.

18. Ibid.

19. Ibid., 205-6; Parker, *Old Army*, 106.

20. "Gallant but corrupt," Mackenzie to Augur, June 6, 1873, in Wallace, "Official Correspondence," *Museum Journal* 10: 21; Mackenzie to AAG DT, June 23, 1878, ibid., 206; Parker, *Old Army*, 106-7.

21. Jesus Nuncio to Mackenzie, June 19, 1878, copy enclosed with Mackenzie to AAG DT, June 23, 1878, in Wallace, "Official Correspondence," *Museum Journal* 10: 209.

22. Ibid., 206-7; Parker, *Old Army*, 107.

23. Mackenzie to Ord, July 1, 1878, in Mackenzie, Letterbook, 86.

24. Mackenzie tc AAG DT, June 23, 1878, in Wallace, "Official Correspondence," *Museum Journal* 10: 207-8.

25. Ibid.

26. Mackenzie to Ord, July 1, 1878, in Mackenzie, Letterbook, 85.

27. Nohl, "Bad Hand," 255-56; Mackenzie to AAG DT, June 25, 1878, in Wallace, "Official Correspondence," *Museum Journal* 10: 210.

28. Parker, *Old Army*, 109; Mackenzie to AAG DT, August 19, 1878, in Wallace, "Official Correspondence," *Museum Journal* 10: 214-15, and 214n.

29. Ord, endorsement to Mackenzie to AAG DT, August 19, 1878, ibid., 215-16.

30. Cresap, *Appomattox Commander*, 320.

31. Young to Mackenzie, August 16, 1878; Thompson to AAG District of the Nueces, August 16, 1878, ibid., 216-17.

32. Felipe Vega to "Lieutenant Colonel Commanding," September 7, 1878, ibid., 218-19; Nuncio to Mackenzie, September 25, 1878, ibid, 220-21; Cresap, *Appomattox Commander*, 320.

33. Mackenzie to Subcommittee of Military Affairs, House of Representatives, February 25, 1878, in Mackenzie, Letterbook, 66-75.

34. "no reasonable ground. . . .", Mackenzie to Secretary of War George W. McCrary, February, 9, 1878, and various letters, December 1877 through February 1878, all in Mackenzie, Letterbook, 63-65.

35. Mackenzie to unnamed general (apparently Pope), October 1, 1878; Mackenzie to AAG DT, October 3, 1878, ibid., 88.

36. AAG DT to Mackenzie, October 4, 1878, ibid., 88.

37. Mackenzie to AAG DT, October 4, 1878 (two telegrams); Vincent to Mackenzie, October 5, 1878, ibid., 89-90.

38. Mackenzie to AAG DT, October 19, 1878; R.B. Myers to Mackenzie, October 19, 1878, ibid,, 90-93.

39. Parker, *Old Army*, 109.

CHAPTER 17
"I Will Make You Go"

1. Record of Service, RG 94 3877 ACP 1873.

2. Riddle, "Milk Creek," 282-83.

3. Pope to AAG MilDivMo, September 13, 1879, RG 393, Special

File, Military Division of the Missouri, hereinafter referred to as "Special File."

4. Riddle, "Milk Creek," 282-84; Meeker to Governor Frederick W. Pitkin of Colorado, September 10, 1879, Special File.

5. AAG Department of the Platte to Sheridan, September 14, 1879, and J.W. Steele to Sheridan, September 15, 1879, and AG USA (E.D. Townsend) to Sheridan, September 16, 1879, all in Special File.

6. Price R. Williams, AAG Department of the Platte to Sheridan, October 4, 1879, ibid.

7. Williams to Crook, October 1, 1879; Sherman to Sheridan, two letters, October 8 and October 26, 1879, ibid.; Riddle, "Milk Creek," 290.

8. Sherman to Sheridan, three letters, October 8, October 14 and October 17, 1879, Special File.

9. AG USA to commander, MilDivMo (Sheridan), September 18, 1879; Pope to Sheridan, October 3, 1879, ibid.; Sheridan to Ord, October 3, 1879, in Wallace, "Official Correspondence," Museum Journal 10: 223.

10. Ord to Sheridan, October 4, 1879, Special File. Mackenzie's Record of Service (RG 94 3877 ACP 1873) states he was a "witness before civil court in Kansas to October 27, 1879; commanding regiment and post of Fort Garland, Colo. and Column of Ute Expedition to May 19, 1880." Other writers have taken this to indicate he traveled from Kansas to Colorado to join his regiment. However, his own correspondence and various other letters in the Special File show that he had already returned to Texas and traveled with the regiment at least from San Antonio to Fort Garland, via Fort Hays, Kansas.

11. C. Upson to George W. McCrary, secretary of war, October 4, 1879, with endorsement by Sherman, and Sherman to S.B. Maxey, October 17, 1879, all in Wallace, "Official Correspondence," Museum Journal 10: 224-26.

12. Ord to Sheridan, October 4, 1879, and Ord to AG MilDivMo, October 6, 1879, and Mackenzie to AG MilDivMo, October 8, 1879, all in Special File.

13. Pope to AAG MilDivMo, October 10, 1879, ibid.

14. Sherman to Sheridan, October 18, 1879; Sherman to Col. W.D. Whipple, AG MilDivMo, December 29, 1879, ibid.

15. Sherman to Sheridan, October 13, 1879, and Pope to Sheridan, October 15, 1879, and Sherman to Sheridan, October 26, 1879, ibid.

16. Pope to Sheridan, October 19, 1879, and Pope to AG MilDiv-Mo, October 26, 1879, and Pope to AG MilDivMo, October 31, 1879, and Mackenzie to AAG, Department of the Missouri, October 30, 1879, ibid.

17. Mackenzie to AAG, Department of the Missouri, October 30,

1879, and Ord to AG MilDivMo, November 3, 1879, ibid.

18. Schurz to Secretary of War, December 10, 1879, and Macken-zie to Pope, November 2, 1879, and Pope to Sheridan, November 3, 1879, ibid.

19. Mackenzie to Hatch, November 7, 1879, and Mackenzie to Pope, November 12, 1879, both in Mackenzie, Letterbook, 98-104.

20. Mackenie to Pope, ibid.

21. Mackenzie to Dunn, November 17, 1879, and Mackenzie to Pope, November 21, 1879; Mackenzie to Pope, November 24, 1879, ibid., 104-8.

22. Mackenzie to Sheridan, December 25, 1879, ibid., 108-9.

23. Mackenzie to Dunn, December 27, 1879, ibid., 109-10.

24. Mackenzie to Pope, February 19, 1880, ibid., 112-13.

25. AG USA to Pope, February 19, 1880, quoted in Nohl, "Bad Hand," 268.

26. Mackenzie to Dunn, March 26, 1880, Mackenzie, Letterbook, 111-12.

27. Nohl, "Bad Hand," 269-70.

28. Parker, *Old Army*, 127-28.

29. Ibid., 129-30; Mackenzie to Pope, June 29, 1880, Mackenzie, Letterbook, 113-15.

30. Parker, *Old Army*, 130; Mackenzie to Pope, June 29, 1880, ibid.

31. Parker, *Old Army*, 131; Mackenzie to Sheridan, August 7, 1880, Mackenzie, Letterbook, 117-18; Mackenzie to AAG, Department of the Missouri, August 2, 1881, Expedition Records; Record of Service, RG 94 3877 ACP 1873.

32. R.C. Drum, AG USA, to Mackenzie, October 14, 1880, and Pope to Drum, October 26, 1880, and E.R. Platt, AAG, Department of the Missouri, to Mackenzie, November 21, 1880, and Mackenzie to Drum, November 21, 1880, and Drum to Mackenzie, November 27, 1880, all in RG 94 3877 ACP 1873. The Court of Inquiry found in favor of General Warren.

33. Parker, *Old Army*, 48.

34. Hutton, *Phil Sheridan*, 135.

35. Nohl, "Bad Hand," 276.

36. G.K. Warren to Drum, October 26, 1880, and Crook to Drum, October 29, 1880, RG 94 3877 ACP 1873.

37. Augur to AG USA, December 4, 1880, ibid.

38. Pope to Sheridan, November 11, 1880, ibid.

39. Sheridan, endorsements to various recommendations by departmental commanders in the Military Division of the Missouri, ibid.

40. Albuquerque *Evening Review*, October 27, 1882; New Jersey

delegation to the President (R.B. Hayes), December 10, 1880, and Texas delegation to the President, December 9, 1880, RG 94 3877 ACP 1873.

41. Pohanka, *Miles*, 123; Nohl, "Bad Hand," 277-78.

42. Record of Service, RG 94 3877 ACP 1873; Nohl, "Bad Hand," 278; Dorst, "Mackenzie," 13.

43. Various entries, Mackenzie, Letterbook; Mackenzie to Pope, June 10, 1881, ibid., 134-38; Nohl, "Bad Hand," 279.

44. Nohl, "Bad Hand," 279; Record of Service, RG 94 3877 ACP 1873.

45. Parker, *Old Army*, 133-34; Record of Service, RG 94 3877 ACP 1873.

46. "sulky and semi-hostile," Parker, *Old Army*, 134; Mackenzie to Pope, June 10, 1881, Mackenzie, Letterbook, 135.

47. Mackenzie to Pope, ibid. Among the surgeons who had been recommended to Mackenzie was Dr. Passmore Middleton. It was Dr. Middleton who, less than three years later, would accompany Mackenzie on his last trip east, to an insane asylum.

48. Mackenzie to Pope, ibid.

49. Mackenzie to Pope, July 1, 1881, Mackenzie, Letterbook, 138; Mackenzie to AAG, Department of the Missouri, August 2, 1881, Expedition Records.

50. Mackenzie to Pope, August 14, 1881, Expedition Records.

51. Mackenzie to AAG, Department of the Missouri, August 2, 1881, ibid.

52. Mackenzie to AAG, Department of the Missouri, August 6, 1881; Mackenzie to Pope, August 14, 1881, ibid.

53. Mackenzie to Pope, August 23, 1881; Mackenzie to AAG Department of the Missouri, September 2, 1881, ibid,; Parker, *Old Army*, 51-52.

54. Mackenzie to Pope, August 23, 1881; Mackenzie to AAG, Department of the Missouri, September 2, 1881, Expedition Records; Dorst, "Mackenzie," 14. Dorst and Parker were both present during the confrontation.

55. Mackenzie to AAG, Department of the Missouri, September 2, 1881, ibid.; Dorst, "Mackenzie," 14-15.

56. Dorst, "Mackenzie," 15; Parker, *Old Army*, 52.

57. Dorst, "Mackenzie," 15; Mackenzie to AAG, Department of the Missouri, September 2, 1881, Expedition Records.

58. Mackenzie to Pope, August 26, 1881, ibid.

59. Mackenzie to J.R. Mershon, August 26, 1881, ibid.

60. Mackenzie to Pope, August 26, 1881, and Mackenzie to AAG, Department of the Missouri, September 2, 1881, ibid.

61. Dorst, "Mackenzie," 15.

62. Parker, *Old Army*, 53.

CHAPTER 18
"Two People Can Not Be in Command"

1. Parker, *Old Army*, 134-35; Mackenzie to AAG, Department of Arizona, October 15, 1881, in Expedition Records; Record of Service,

RG 94 3877 ACP; Mackenzie to Pope, September 21, 1881, Mackenzie, Letterbook, 8-9.

2. Wellman, *Death in the Desert*, 218-19.

3. Ibid., 219; Carter, *Yorktown to Santiago*, 210-11.

4. Carter, *Yorktown to Santiago*, 215-19; Wellman, *Death in the Desert*, 219-21; Sherman to the President (Chester A. Arthur), October 7, 1881, RG 393, 5778 AGO 1881 (filed with 4327 AGO 1881).

5. C.M. McKeever, AAG USA to Sheridan, September 28, 1881, RG 393 5590 ACP 1881; Sherman to the President, ibid.; Smith, "Apache Problem," 57-61.

6. Thrapp, *Conquest of Apacheria*, 231-32; Sherman to Major General Irvin McDowell, September 19, 1881, RG 393 5590 AGO 1881.

7. Pope to Sheridan, September 27, 1881, RG 393 5590 AGO 1881.

8. Ibid.

9. Sheridan to General R.C. Drum, September 28, 1881, ibid.

10. McKeever to McDowell, (first dispatch), September 28, 1881, ibid.

11. McKeever to McDowell, (second dispatch), September 28, 1881, ibid,; Mackenzie to AAG, Fort Thomas, October 1, 1881, Expedition Records.

12. Mackenzie to AAG, Fort Thomas, October 1, 1881 (two dispatches), Expedition Records.

13. Mackenzie to AAG, Fort Thomas, from Fort Apache, October 1, 1881, ibid.

14. Mackenzie to Brig. Gen. R.C. Drum, AG USA, October 1, 1881, ibid. Mackenzie generally spelled the name "Wilcox."

15. Mackenzie to AAG Fort Thomas, October 1, 1881, ibid.

16. Willcox to AG USA, October 1, 1881, RG 393 5590 AGO 1881; McDowell to Willcox, October 5, 1881, RG 393 5590.

17. Mackenzie to AAG, Willcox Station, Arizona, October 4, 1881, Expedition Records.

18. Mackenzie to Lt. Col. W.R. Price, October 1, 1881, and

Mackenzie to Heyl, October 4, 1881; Mackenzie to Carr, October 4, 1881, ibid.

19. Mackenzie to AAG, Willcox Station, October 4, 1881, Expedition Records; Smith, 69-70.

20. Mackenzie to AAG, Willcox Station, October 4, 1881; Mackenzie to Major G.B. Sanford, October 4, 1881, Expedition Records.

21. Smith, "Apache Problem," 71; AAG, Department of Arizona, October 4, 1881, quoted by Mackenzie in Expedition Records.

22. Mackenzie to AAG, Willcox Station, October 4, 1881, ibid.

23. Mackenzie to Carr, October 4, 1881, and October 5, 1881, ibid.

24. Mackenzie to Drum, October 6, 1881, ibid.

25. Smith, "Apache Problem," 65; Mackenzie to AAG, Fort Lowell, October 7, 1881, and Mackenzie to telegraph operator, Fort Thomas, October 7, 1881, both in Expedition Records.

26. Sherman to the President, October 7, 1881, RG 393 AGO 1881.

27. Smith, "Apache Problem," 66.

28. Mackenzie to Ezra Hoag, subagent, October 5, 1881, and Mackenzie to AAG, Willcox Station, October 5, 1881, and Mackenzie to Cochran, October 5, 1881, all in Expedition Records.

29. Mackenzie to AAG Subagency, October 7, 1881, and Dorst to Heyl, October 6, 1881, and Mackenzie to Biddle, October 7, 1881, and Mackenzie to Cochoran, October 6, 1881, ibid.

30. Mackenzie to AAG, Fort Lowell, October 8, 1881, and Mackenzie to Biddle, October 8, 1881, ibid.

31. Mackenzie to Chief Quartermaster, Department of Arizona, October 5, 1881, and October 6, 1881, and Mackenzie to C. McKibben, October 7, 1881, ibid.

32. AAAG, Fort Thomas, to Heyl, October 5, 1881, ibid.; Carter, *Yorktown to Santiago*, 227.

33. Mackenzie to Sanford, October 7, 1881, Expedition Records.

34. Mackenie to AAG, Fort Lowell, October 7, 1881, ibid.

35. Mackenzie to AAG, Department of Arizona, October 7, 1881; Mackenzie to Heyl, October 7, 1881, ibid.

36. Mackenzie to AAG, Fort Lowell, October 9, 1881, and Dorst to Biddle, October 9, 1881, ibid; Carter, *Yorktown to Santiago*, 227-28.

37. Mackenzie to Carr, October 6, 1881, and Mackenzie to Commissioner of Indian Affairs, October 10, 1881, Expedition Records.

38. Mackenzie to Tiffany, October 11 and October 12, ibid.; Smith, "Apache Problem," 76-78; Bourke, *On the Border*, 438-42. In 1882, a federal grand jury in Arizona accused Tiffany of theft and corruption. He died before he came to trial. Carr was instrumental in

the investigation.

39. Mackenzie to McKibben, October 8, and Mackenzie to AAG, Department of Arizona, October 12, 1881, both Expedition Records.

40. Mackenzie to Pope, October 12, 1881, Mackenzie, Letterbook, 9-10.

41. Record of Service, RG 94 3877 ACP; Carter, *Yorktown to Santiago*, 228.

CHAPTER 19
"I Sever My Connection"

1. Record of Service, RG 94 3877 ACP; Smith, "Apache Problem," 80; Nohl, "Bad Hand," 302.

2. H. Berry to Mackenzie, December 26, 1881, Mackenzie, Letterbook, 17.

3. Mackenzie to H.P. Hill, January 12, 1882, ibid., 15-16.

4. Smith, "Apache Problem," 87-89.

5. Ibid., 89-90; Mackenzie to Pope, January 20, 1882, Mackenzie, Letterbook, 11-12.

6. Mackenzie to Pope, February 16, 1882, ibid., 12-14; Nohl, "Bad Hand," 303.

7. Albuquerque *Daily Review*, March 15, 1882; Albuquerque *Evening Review*, March 18, 1882, March 30, 1882, April 6, 1882.

8. Thrapp, *Conquest of Apacheria*, 235; General Carlos Fuero to Mackenzie, April 5, 1882, RG 393 1831 AGO 1882.

9. Thrapp, *Conquest of Apacheria*, 235-36; Betzinez, *I Fought with Geronimo*, 56-57.

10. Albuquerque *Evening Review*, March 30, 1882; Albuquerque *Daily Review*, April 25, 1882, May 19, 1882.

11. Thrapp, *Conquest of Apacheria*, 240-45.

12. Ibid., 247-49; Albuquerque *Daily Review*, May 16, 1882.

13. Mackenzie to Pope, May 6, 1882, Mackenzie, Letterbook, 17-18.

14. Robert Williams, AAG, MilDivMo, to Pope, quoted in Albuquerque *Daily Review*, May 9, 1882.

15. Nohl, "Bad Hand," 309-11.

16. Drum to Commanding General, Department of the Missouri (Pope), August 10, 1882, RG 393 5666 AGO 1882.

17. R.C. Emmet, aide-de-camp, Department of the Missouri, to Commanding Officer, District of New Mexico (Mackenzie), August 1, 1882, RG 393 5160 AGO 1882, Mackenzie to AAG, Department of the Missouri, August 8, 1882, RG 393 5566 AGO 1882.

18. L.A. Sheldon to the President, October 4, 1882, and N.P. Hill to the President, October 5, 1882, RG 94 3877 ACP; Grierson, Military Papers, various letters, 1882; Dorst, "Mackenzie," 18.

19. Mackenzie to Lincoln, October 26, 1882, RG 94 3877 ACP.

20. Albuquerque *Evening Review*, November 3, 1882.

21. Nohl, "Bad Hand," 314.

22. Mackenzie to Drum, November 2, 1882, RG 94 3877 ACP; Record of Service; Special Orders No. 234, Department of the Missouri, November 17, 1882, RG 393 7819 ACP 1882.

23. Fourth Cavalry, Order No. 1, Fort Bayard, N.M., January 1, 1883, Dorst Papers.

24. Drum to Dorst, January 30, 1883, and Department of Texas, General Orders No. 27, November 1, 1883, ibid.

25. Nohl, "Bad Hand," 315-16; Thrapp, *Conquest of Apacheria*, 274-75. Charlie McComas is alleged to have been killed later, but this has never been proven.

26. *Williams College*, 1884, 56; Nohl, "Bad Hand," 317; Joseph R. Smith to AG, USA, December 19, 1883, RG 94 3877 ACP (see also Chapter 20, note 8).

27. Nohl, "Bad Hand," 317; Nielsen, "Ranald S. Mackenzie," 150.

28. Santa Fe *New Mexican Review*, July 7, 1883.

29. Washington, D.C., *Messages and Papers of the Presidents*, 7:4753-54.

CHAPTER 20
"His Usefulness is Destroyed"

1. Joseph Smith to AAG DT, December 19, 1883, in RG 94 3877 ACP.

2. Santa Fe *New Mexican Review*, April 1, 1884; Nohl, "Bad Hand," 318, 320-21; Wallace, *Mackenzie*, 191; Nielsen, "Ranald S. Mackenzie," 150.

3. Thomas Vincent, endorsement to Smith, and Smith to AAG DT, December 19, 1883, above cited.

4. Smith to AAG DT, ibid.; Santa Fe *New Mexican Review*, above cited.

5. Smith to AAG DT with endorsement, above cited.

6. Vincent, endorsement to Smith, above cited; Nohl, "Bad Hand," 322.

7. Smith to AAG DT with endorsement, above cited; *New Mexican Review*, above cited.

8. Smith to AAG DT. Apparently Dr. Smith had not been in-

formed that Mackenzie had previously suffered from mental problems. In his report to Vincent, he wrote, "I learn from good authority that Genl. Mackenzie had some sort of an attack of cerebral trouble in New Mexico . . . ." indicating that he was notifying the AAG for the first time, and had only recently learned of it himself.

9. Vincent, endorsement to Smith, above cited.

10. Major General J.M. Schofield, endorsement to Smith and Vincent, December 24, 1883, and Schofield to Adjutant General of the Army, December 19, 1883, both in RG 94 3877 ACP.

11. Santa Fe *New Mexican Review* above cited; *The Nation*, January 3, 1884.

12. Vincent to Drum, December 22, 1883, and Vincent to AG USA, December 21, 1883, and Vincent to AG USA, December 22, 1883, all in RG 94 3877 ACP.

13. Proceedings of the Army retiring board convened at Bloomingdale Asylum, New York City, in accordance with the following orders: Headquarters of the Army Adjutant General's office, Washington: March 3d 1884, Special Orders No. 52:7, in RG 94 3877 ACP.

14. Nohl, "Bad Hand," 324.

15. Schofield to Drum, December 24, 1883, in RG 94 3877 ACP.

16. Harriet Slidell Mackenzie to Sheridan, December (day illegible), and Drum to Vincent, December 25, 1883, ibid.

17. Vincent to AG USA, December 26, 1883, ibid.

18. Drum to Middleton, December 27, 1883, and notation on Harriet Mackenzie to Sheridan, December 29, 1883, with attachment by C.R.P. Rodgers, ibid.

19. Middleton to Drum, December 28, 1883, and Harriet S. Mackenzie to Sheridan, December 29, 1883, and Harriet S. Mackenzie to Lincoln, December 29, 1883, ibid.

20. Sheridan to Harriet S. Mackenzie, December 29, 1883, ibid.

21. Nohl, "Bad Hand," 327-28; various telegrams, RG 94 3877; Middleton to AG USA, December 28, 1883, ibid.

22. C.H. Nichols to Drum, December 31, 1883, and Nichols to Sheridan, February 22, 1884, ibid.

23. Sheridan to Secretary of War, February 28, 1884, and Drum to Major General W.S. Hancock, March 3, 1884, ibid.

CHAPTER 21
"I Would Rather Die"

1. See chapter 20, note 13.

2. Ibid., 5.

3. Ibid., 5-6.

4. Ibid., Exhibit B.

5. Ibid., 6-9.

6. Ibid., 9-10.

7. Nichols to Drum, March 11, 1884, RG 94 3877 ACP 1873.

8. Nichols to Drum, April 4, 1884, ibid.

9. Mackenzie to Drum, April 4, 1884, ibid.

10. Nielsen, "Ranald S. Mackenzie," 151.

11. Mackenzie to Drum, June 16, 1884, ibid.

12. Mackenzie to Drum, September 1, 1884, ibid.

13. Nohl, "Bad Hand," 333.

14. Drum to Lt. Cmdr. M.R.S. Mackenzie USN, November 23, 1885, in RG 95 3877 ACP 1873.

15. Nielsen, "Ranald S. Mackenzie," 156.

16. Nohl, "Bad Hand," 333, 335-36.

17. M.R.S. Mackenzie to Adjutant General, January 19, 1889, in RG 94 3877 ACP 1873.

18. New York *Times*, January 21, 1889.

19. *Army Navy Journal*, vol. 26, no. 23, January 26, 1889, 423-24.

20. New York *Times*, January 21, 1889; Dorst, "Mackenzie," 19.

21. J.C. Kelton to Harriet S. Mackenzie, January 26, 1889, and Harriet S. Mackenzie to Adjutant General, February 1, 1889, both in RG 94 3877 ACP 1873. Mackenzie's death certificate (Register No. 2568, City of New York) gives the cause of death as "scarletina." This disease cannot be identified in any of the medical dictionaries consulted. The closest reference is "scarlatina," scarlet fever, normally a disease of childhood, but Mackenzie did not show any symptoms of that disease during his years of decline. It is possible, but not probable, that a case of scarlet fever contracted during the last weeks of his life may have been the immediate cause of death.

22. Nohl, "Bad Hand," 336, Wallace, *Mackenzie*, 5.

23. Nohl, "Bad Hand," 336.

24. Hutton, *Phil Sheridan*, 370-72.

25. O'Neal, *Fighting Men*, 123-24, Bourke, *On the Border*, 486-87.

26. Carter, *Sergeant's Story*, 53.

27. Ibid., 211, 185-86, 195-201.

28. John M. Carroll, introduction to 1982 edition, ibid.

29. Quoted in Hunter, *Trail Drivers of Texas*, 775.

30. Ibid., 927.

31. Carter, *On the Border*, 214-17.

32. Nohl, "Bad Hand," 329-30. Mackenzie is not the only histori-

cal figure who has been, perhaps, unfairly branded with venereal disease. With the "new morality" of the 1960s, it was fashionable to examine the illnesses of long-dead notables and determine that they had syphilis. Among those so diagnosed was King Henry VIII of England. Recently, however, British medical historians reevaluated Henry's symptoms and determined he was more probably scorbutic or, as the Manchester *Guardian* reported in its headline, "Henry was a scurvy knave."

33. Carter, *Sergeant's Story*, 63.

34. Ibid., 18.

35. *Diagnostic and Statistical Manual of Mental Disorders*, Third Edition, 236-38. When applied to the military, post-traumatic stress disorder is commonly called Vietnam syndrome.

36. Ibid., 109-10.

37. Ibid., 127.

38. Major Starr's embarrassment over his missing arm appears in McConnell, *Five Years a Cavalryman*, 78-79.

39. On March 4, 1988, I presented my theory on Mackenzie to the Texas State Historical Association, in a paper entitled "New Ideas on Brig. Gen. Ranald S. Mackenzie's Insanity and Death." In his commentary on my paper, Franklin Smith of the National Park Service pointed out the social stigma of disfigurement in the nineteenth century, and discussed the problems it would have caused Mackenzie in his daily life.

40. Utley, *Cavalier in Buckskin*, 210.

Bibliography

Research into the personal and private life of Ranald Mackenzie is a difficult task. His personal correspondence was minimal, and what little there was has been lost. Research into his public life is almost as difficult, since his official correspondence involved numerous expeditions under several different departmental commands, each with its own filing system. The departments, in turn, came under the divisions, which had both general files and special files. Finally there are the War Department files. The problems of research are further complicated by the passage of time since Mackenzie's death more than a century ago, and by the fact that many of the records of United States Army Continental Commands and Mobile Units are only partially catalogued. Some of the records available to previous researchers could not now be located. On the other hand, I discovered some records which they apparently did not.

The primary sources on the man Mackenzie are, of course, the recollections of men who served under him, such as Robert Carter, John Charlton and James Parker. At times these have been called into question; nowadays, it is particularly fashionable in some academic circles to criticize Carter and Charlton as being inaccurate. Certainly their views were distorted by their emotions. As the years went by their memories became faulty and they exaggerated their own roles, a trait common to every soldier's memoirs from Caesar to Douglas MacArthur. No matter how they embroider their stories, however, they were there and they ran a very real risk of getting killed. The Indian service was no different.

Anyone who writes about Mackenzie owes a great debt to the pioneering work of Ernest Wallace, who made a lifetime study of Mackenzie's career and whose work is the foundation on which subsequent research is built. Wallace also compiled the official correspondence pertaining to Mackenzie's career in Texas into two volumes of the West Texas Museum Association's *Museum Journal*, in 1965 and 1966. These letters and reports were drawn from many different sources, including the Fourth Cavalry Expedition Records in the National Archives. In cases where the *Museum Journal* published material from the Expedition Records, I have cited the *Journal* in my notes, since it is more readily accessible to the average reader.

Another pioneer is Lessing Nohl, whose brilliant dissertation on Mackenzie the soldier is unlikely to be equaled in the foreseeable future.

Hopefully, I too have been able to contribute some knowledge of Mackenzie the man.

ABBREVIATIONS

AAAG	Acting Assistant Adjutant General
AAG	Assistant Adjutant General
ACP	Appointments, Commissions and Personnel Branch
AG	Adjutant General
AGO	Office of the Adjutant General
DT	Department of Texas
MilDivMo	Military Division of the Missouri
Record Group (RG) 94	Files of the Office of the Adjutant General
RG 391	Records of Army Mobile Units
RG 393	Records of the U.S. Army Continental Commands
USA	United States Army

BOOKS, ARTICLES, MANUSCRIPTS

American Heritage, eds. *The American Heritage Book of Indians.* New York: American Heritage Publishing Co., 1961.

American Psychiatric Association, eds. *Diagnostic and Statistical Manual of Mental Disorders DSM-III-R.* Washington: American Psychiatric Association, 1987.

Beaumont, E.B. "Over the Border with Mackenzie." *United Service* 12, no. 3 (March 1885): 281-88.

Berthrong, Donald J. *The Southern Cheyennes.* Norman: University of Oklahoma Press, 1963.

Betzinez, Jason, with Wilbur Sturtevant Nye. *I Fought with Geronimo.* 1959. Reprint. Lincoln: University of Nebraska Press, 1987.

Boatner, Mark Mayo III. *The Civil War Dictionary.* New York: David McKay Company, 1959.

Bourke, John Gregory. Diary. Original in U.S. Military Academy Library, West Point, New York; microfilm copy in possession of East Texas State University, Commerce, Texas.

_____. "Mackenzie's Last Fight with the Cheyennes." Vol. 11, *Journal of the Military Service Institution of the U.S.* 1890. Reprint. New York: Argonaut Press, 1966.

_____. *On the Border with Crook.* 1891. Reprint. Alexandria, Va.: Time-Life Books, 1980.

Brooks, Van Wyck. *The World of Washington Irving.* New York: E.P. Dutton & Co., 1944.

Carlson, Paul H. "William R. Shafter: Military Commander in the American West." PhD. diss., Texas Tech University, Lubbock, 1973.

Carter, Robert G. "A Raid into Mexico." *Outing* 12, no. 1 (April 1888): 1-9.

_____. *The Old Sergeant's Story: Fighting Indians and Bad Men in Texas From 1870 to 1876.* 1926. Reprint. Mattituck, NY, and Bryan, Tex.: J.M. Carroll and Company, 1982.

_____. *On the Border with Mackenzie.* 1935. Reprint. New York: Antiquarian Press, 1961.

Carter, W.H. *From Yorktown to Santiago with the Sixth U.S. Cavalry.* 1900. Reprint. Austin: State House Press, 1989.

Chamberlain, Cynthia Ann. "Colonel Ranald Slidell Mackenzie's Administration of the Western Section of Indian Territory, 1875-1877." MA Thesis, Texas Tech University, 1971.

Connell, Evan S. *Son of the Morning Star.* San Francisco: North Point Press, 1984.

Cresap, Bernard. *Appomattox Commander: The Story of General E.O.C. Ord.* San Diego: A.S. Barnes & Co. Inc., 1981.

Crimmins, M.L. "General Ranald S. Mackenzie." *Frontier Times.* Vol. 15, no. 7 (April 1938).

Davis, Burke. *To Appomattox, Nine April Days, 1865.* New York: Rinehart & Company, 1959.

Day, James M. and Dorman Winfrey, eds. *Texas Indian Papers 1860-1916.* Austin: Texas State Library, 1961.

De Barthe, Joe. *The Life and Adventures of Frank Grouard.* 1894. Reprint. Alexandria, Va.: Time-Life Books, 1982.

Deland, Charles Edmund. "The Sioux Wars." Vol. 15, *South Dakota Historical Collections.* Pierre: State Department of History, 1930.

Dodge, Richard Irving. "Diary of the Powder River Campaign, 1876-1877." Everett D. Graff Collection, The Newberry Library, MS 1110.

_____. *Our Wild Indians: Thirty-Three Years' Personal Experience Among the Red Men of the Great West.* Hartford: A.D. Worthington and Co., 1882.

Dorst, Joseph H. Papers. U.S. Military Academy Library, West Point, New York.

_____. "Ranald Slidell Mackenzie." *Twentieth Annual Reunion of the Association Graduates of the United States Military Academy, at West Point, New York, June 12th, 1889.*

Dykes, J.C. "The Battle of Palo Duro Canyon." *Great Western Indian Fights.* Potomac Corral of the Westerners, comps. Lincoln: University of Nebraska Press, 1966.

Finerty, John F. *War-Path and Bivouac: The Big Horn and Yellowstone Expedition.* 1890. Reprint. Lincoln: University of Nebraska Press, 1966.

Frasca, Albert J., and Robert H. Hill. *The .45-70 Springfield.* Northridge, Calif.: Springfield Publishing Company, 1980.

Gerdes, Bruce. Papers. Panhandle-Plains Historical Society, Canyon, Texas.

Grant, U.S. *Personal Memoirs.* New York: Charles A. Webster & Co., 1885.

BIBLIOGRAPHY

Gray, John S. *Centennial Campaign: The Sioux War of 1876.* Norman: University of Oklahoma Press, 1988.

Grierson, Benjamin. Military Papers. Southwestern Collection, Texas Tech University.

Grinnell, George Bird. *The Fighting Cheyennes.* 1915. Reprint. Norman: University of Oklahoma Press, 1956.

Haley, J. Evetts. "The Comanchero Trade." *Southwestern Historical Quarterly.* Vol. 38, No. 3 (January, 1935).

_____. "Racial Troubles on the Conchos." *The Black Military Experience in the American West.* John M. Carroll, ed. New York: Liveright, 1971.

Haley, James L. *The Buffalo War.* 1976. Reprint. Norman: University of Oklahoma Press, 1985.

Hamilton, Allen Lee. "Military History of Fort Richardson, Texas." MA Thesis, Texas Tech University. 1973.

_____. *Sentinel of the Southern Plains: Fort Richardson and the Northwest Texas Frontier.* Fort Worth: Texas Christian University Press, 1988.

Hamm, Margherita Arlina. *Famous Families of New York.* Vol. 1. New York: Heraldic Publishing Co., 1970.

Hatfield, Charles A.P. "The Comanche, Kiowa and Cheyenne Campaign in Northwest Texas and MacKenzie's Fight in the Palo Duro Canon, September 26 *[sic],* 1874." Typescript. Panhandle-Plains Historical Society, Canyon, Texas.

Herr, John K., and Edward S. Wallace. *The Story of the U.S. Cavalry.* 1953. Reprint. New York: Bonanza Books, 1984.

Huckaby, Ida Lasater. *Ninety-Four Years in Jack County.* Austin: Steck Company, 1948.

Hunter, John Marvin, ed. *The Trail Drivers of Texas.* 1925. Reprint. Austin: University of Texas Press, 1985.

Hunter, John Warren. "The Fall of Brownsville on the Rio Grande, November, 1863." Lower Rio Grande Valley Historical Society, Harlingen, Texas.

Hutton, Paul Andrew. *Phil Sheridan and His Army.* Lincoln: University of Nebraska Press, 1985.

Jenkins, Brian. *Britain and the War for the Union.* Vol. 1. Montreal: McGill-Queen's University Press, 1974.

King, Charles. *Campaigning With Crook.* 1890. Reprint. Norman: University of Oklahoma Press, 1964.

Lavender, David. "How to Make it to the White House Without Really Trying." *American Heritage.* Vol. 18, No. 4 (June, 1967).

Leckie, William H. *The Military Conquest of the Southern Plains.* Norman: University of Oklahoma Press, 1963.

Leckie, William H. and Shirley A. Leckie. *Unlikely Warriors: General Benjamin H. Grierson and His Family.* Norman: University of Oklahoma Press, 1984.

Lewis, Lloyd. *Sherman, Fighting Prophet.* New York: Harcourt, Brace & Co., 1932.

McConnell, H.H. *Five Years a Cavalryman.* Jacksboro, Tex.: J.N. Rogers & Co., 1889.

Mackenzie, Ranald Slidell. "Letterbook." Original in the Thomas Gilcrease Institute, Tulsa, Okla.; typescript in possession of the author.

Marcum, Richard T. "Fort Brown, Texas: The History of a Border Post." PhD. diss., Texas Tech University, 1964.

Meltzer, Milton. *Bound for the Rio Grande, The Mexican Struggle, 1845-1850.* New York: Alfred A. Knopf, 1974.

Miller, Nathan. *The U.S. Navy: An Illustrated History.* New York: Simon & Schuster, 1977.

Morison, Samuel Eliot. *John Paul Jones, A Sailor's Biography.* Boston: Little, Brown and Company, 1959.

Muir, Andrew Forest, ed. *Texas in 1837, an Anonymous Contemporary Narrative.* 1958. Reprint. Austin: University of Texas Press, 1988.

Myers, James Will. Papers. Panhandle-Plains Historical Society, Canyon, Texas.

Nielsen, Soren W. "Ranald S. Mackenzie: The Man and His Battle." *West Texas Historical Association Year Book* 64 (1988): 140-52.

Nevin, David, and the Editors of Time-Life Books. *The Old West—The Soldiers.* New York: Time-Life Books, 1973.

Nohl, Lessing. "Bad Hand: The Military Career of Ranald Slidell Mackenzie, 1871-1889." PhD. diss., University of New Mexico, 1962.

North, Luther. *Man of the Plains: Recollections of Luther North, 1856-1882.* Lincoln: University of Nebraska Press, 1961.

Nye, Wilbur S. *Carbine and Lance: The Story of Old Fort Sill.* 1937. Reprint. Norman: University of Oklahoma Press, 1969.

O'Neal, Bill. *Fighting Men of the Indian Wars.* Stillwater, Okla.: Barbed Wire Press, 1991.

Parker, James. *The Old Army Memories 1872-1918.* Philadelphia: Dorrance and Company, 1929.

Pate, J'Nell Laverne. "Colonel Ranald Slidell Mackenzie's First Four Years with the Fourth Cavalry in Texas, 1871-1874." MA Thesis, Texas Christian University, 1963.

Pohanka, Brian C., ed. *Nelson A. Miles: A Documentary Biography of His Military Career 1861-1903.* Glendale, Calif.: Arthur H. Clark Co., 1985.

Porter, Horace. *Campaigning with Grant.* 1887. Reprint. Alexandria, Va.: Time-Life Books, 1981.

Pratt, Richard Henry. *Battlefield and Classroom: Four Decades with the American Indian, 1867-1904.* New Haven: Yale University Press, 1964.

Richardson, Rupert N. "The Comanche Indians and the Fight at Adobe Walls." *Panhandle-Plains Historical Review.* Vol. 4 (1931).

Riddle, Jack, P. "Besieged on Milk Creek." *Great Western Indian Fights.* Potomac Corral of the Westerners, comps. Lincoln: University of Nebraska Press, 1966.

Rister, C.C., ed. "Documents Relating to General W.T. Sherman['s] Southern Plains Indian Policy 1871-1875." *Panhandle-Plains Historical Review.* Vol. 9 (1936).

Robinson, Charles M. III. *Frontier Forts of Texas.* Houston: Gulf Publishing Co., 1986.

_____. "New Ideas on Brig. Gen. Ranald S. Mackenzie's Insanity and Death." Paper presented at the annual meeting of the Texas State Historical Association, Austin, March 4, 1988.

_____. *The Frontier World of Fort Griffin: The Life and Death of a Frontier Town*. Spokane: The Arthur H. Clark Company, 1992.

Roehl, Marjorie. "Looking Back: John Slidell, Ever Slick, Ever Controversial." Clipping provided by Greater Slidell Area Chamber of Commerce, Slidell, Louisiana, n.d.

Roscoe, Theodore, and Fred Freeman. *Picture History of the U.S. Navy*. New York: Charles Scribner's Sons, 1966.

Schaff, Morris. *The Spirit of Old West Point 1858-1862*. Boston: Houghton, Mifflin and Company, 1897.

Schmitt, Martin F., ed. *General George Crook, His Autobiography*. 1946. Reprint. Norman: University of Oklahoma Press, 1986.

Sears, Louis Martin. *John Slidell*. Durham, N.C.: Duke University Press, 1925.

Sides, Joseph C. *Fort Brown Historical*. San Antonio: The Naylor Company, 1942.

Sheridan, P.H. *Personal Memoirs*. New York: Charles L. Webster & Co., 1888.

Sherman, W.T. Unofficial Papers. Library of Congress, Washington, D.C.

Smith, James Weldon. "Colonel Ranald Slidell Mackenzie and the Apache Problem, 1881-1883." MA Thesis, Texas Tech University, 1973.

Smith, Sherry L., ed. *Sagebrush Soldier: Private William Earl Smith's View of the Sioux War of 1876*. Norman: University of Oklahoma Press, 1989.

Spring, Leverett Wilson. *A History of Williams College*. New York and Boston: Houghton Mifflin Co., 1917.

Strong, Henry W. *My Frontier Days and Indian Fights*. Dallas, 1926.

Sullivan, Jerry M. "Fort McKavett: A Texas Frontier Post." Vol. 20, *The Museum Journal*. Lubbock: West Texas Museum Association, 1981.

Tatum, Lawrie. *Our Red Brothers and the Peace Policy of President Ulysses S. Grant*. 1899. Reprint. Lincoln: University of Nebraska Press, 1970.

Thompson, Richard A. *Crossing the Border with the 4th Cavalry: Mackenzie's Raid into Mexico—1873*. Waco: Texian Press, 1986.

Thompson, W.A. "Scouting with Mackenzie." *Journal of the United States Cavalry Association*. Vol. 10, No. 36 (March, 1897):429-33.

Thrapp, Dan L. *The Conquest of Apacheria*. Norman: University of Oklahoma Press, 1967.

Time-Life Books, eds. *The Civil War—The Blockade: Runners and Raiders*. Alexandria, Va.: Time-Life Books, 1983.

Tudor, William G. "Was Carter with Mackenzie at the Palo Duro in 1874?" Paper presented at the annual meeting of the West Texas Historical Association, Sul Ross State University, Alpine, Tex., April 4, 1992.

Utley, Robert M. *Cavalier in Buckskin: George Armstrong Custer and the Western Military Frontier*. Norman: University of Oklahoma Press, 1988.

Utley, Robert M., and Wilcomb E. Washburn. *The American Heritage History of the Indian Wars*. New York: American Heritage/Bonanza Books, 1982.

van de Water, Frederic. "Panic Rides the High Seas." *American Heritage*. Vol. 12, No. 4 (June, 1961).

Wallace, Edward S. "Border Warrior." *American Heritage*. Vol. 9, No. 4 (June, 1958).

Wallace, Ernest. *Ranald S. Mackenzie on the Texas Frontier*. *The Museum Journal*. Vol. 7-8. Lubbock: West Texas Museum Association, 1964.

———. "The Mackenzie Raid." *The Westerners New York Posse Brand Book* 4, no. 4 (1958): 73-90.

———, ed. "Ranald S. Mackenzie's Official Correspondence Relating to Texas, 1871-1873." Vol. 9, *The Museum Journal*. Lubbock: West Texas Museum Association, 1967.

———. "Ranald S. Mackenzie's Official Correspondence Relating to Texas, 1873-1879." Vol. 10, *The Museum Journal*. Lubbock: West Texas Museum Association, 1968.

Wellman, Paul I. *Death in the Desert: The Fifty Years' War for the Great Southwest.* 1935. Reprint. Lincoln: University of Nebraska Press, 1987.

Wheeler, Homer W. *Buffalo Days: The Personal Narrative of a Cattleman, Indian Fighter and Army Officer.* 1923. Reprint. Lincoln: University of Nebraska Press, 1990.

Wilbarger, J.W. *Indian Depredations in Texas.* 1889. Reprint. Austin: Eakin Press and State House Books, 1985.

Williams College, Class of 1859. Williamstown, Mass.: Williams College, Report for January 1, 1863, July 23, 1877, and 1884.

Wooster, Robert. "The Army and the Politics of Expansion: Texas and the Southwestern Borderlands, 1870-1886." *Southwestern Historical Quarterly* 93, no. 2 (October 1989): 151-67.

GOVERNMENT DOCUMENTS

Department of Records and Information Service, City of New York, New York, Records of Death, Town of Castleton, Richmond, Staten Island, Register No. 2568, Ronald *[sic]* Slidell Mackenzie, January 19, 1889.

District Clerk's Office, Jacksboro, Jack County, Texas. Minutes of the District Court, Cause No. 224, the State of Texas vs. Satanta and Big Tree, 1871.

Kiowa Agency, Federal, State and Local Court Relations, Trial of Satanta and Big Tree, 1871-1878. Original in the Indian Archives Division, Oklahoma Historical Society, Oklahoma City. Microfilm copy in possession of the author.

United States Department of War. Office of the Adjutant General. Fourth Cavalry Expedition Records, Letters and endorsements sent and orders issued, 1871-1881, RG 391, Series 757. Microfilm copy in possession of the author.

_____. Letters Received, Main Series, 1871-1880. RG 94 AGO. Arranged as received by AGO, rather then chonologically. Microfilm copy in possession of the author.

_____. Letters Received, 1881, Department of Arizona. RG 393 AGO.

BIBLIOGRAPHY

_____. Letters Received, 1882, Department of the Missouri, District of New Mexico. RG 393 AGO.

_____. Mackenzie, Ranald Slidell. RG 94 3877 ACP 1873. Microfiche copy in the possession of the author.

_____. Military Division of the Missouri, Ute War. RG 393, Special File. Microfilm copy in possession of the author.

_____. Post Medical Reports, Old Records Division of the Adjutant General's Office, National Archives, as follows:

_____.Fort Brown, Texas. Microfilm copy in Arnulfo Oliveira Library, Fort Brown, Brownsville, Texas.

_____.Fort Concho, Texas. Reprint. San Angelo, Texas: Fort Concho Preservation and Museum, 1974.

_____.Fort Griffin, Texas. Microfilm copy in Arnulfo Oliveira Library, Fort Brown, Brownsville, Texas.

_____.Returns of U.S. Military Posts, 1800-1916. RG 94 Microcopy 617, as follows:

_____.Fort Brown, Texas, June 1866-December 1886. Microfilm copy in possession of the author.

_____.Fort McKavett, Texas, March 1852-December 1872. Microfilm copy in possession of the author.

_____.Fort Richardson, Texas, June 1866-May 1878. Microfilm copy in possession of the author.

_____. *War of the Rebellion: A Compilation of the Official Records of the Union and Confederate Armies.* 130 vols. Washington: U.S. Government Printing Office, 1891-1898.

United States Military Academy, West Point, New York, *Official Register of the Officers and Cadets of the U.S. Military Academy,* June, 1862.

Washington, D.C.: Bureau of National Literature and Art. *A Compilation of the Messages and Papers of the Presidents.* 11 volumes with supplements. James D. Richardson, comp. 1910-1929.

PERIODICALS

Albuquerque *Daily Review,* March 15, 1882; April 25, 1882; May 9, 1882; May 16, 1882; May 19, 1882.

Albuquerque *Evening Review,* March 18, 1882; March 30, 1882; April 6, 1882; October 27, 1882; November 3, 1882.

Army and Navy Journal 7, no. 43 (June 10, 1871): 675; 15, no. 52 (August 3, 1876): 842; 25, no. 22 (January 26, 1889): 423-424.

Austin *Daily State Journal,* December 29, 1870.

Brownsville *Daily Ranchero* June 28, 1867; various issues, summer, 1867.

Cheyenne *Leader,* October 24, 1876.

Chicago *Tribune,* April 23, 1877.

Frontier Times, vol. 15, no. 7 (April 1933); vol. 15, no. 9 (June 1938) article "Fort McKavett was a Frontier Post" reprinted from San Angelo *Times.*

Galveston *News,* March 7, 1873; October 16, 1874.

The Nation, January 3, 1884.

New York *Times,* October 30, 1867; November 4, 1867; May 20, 1873; May 23, 1873; June 2, 1873; July 12, 1873; July 20, 1873; July 24, 1873; May 4, 1875; June 12, 1875; April 7, 1876; April 28, 1876; May 27, 1876; January 21, 1889.

New York *Tribune,* April 23, 1877.

San Antonio *Daily Express,* June 11, 1873.

Santa Fe *New Mexican Review,* July 7, 1883; April 1, 1884.

Index

Richards, H.J., 127
Richards, Jonathan, 189
Ringgold Barracks, Tex., 47
Robinson, Catherine (Mrs.
    Alexander S. Mackenzie,
    mother), 6-9, 11, 17, 309,
    310
Robinson, Henrietta Elizabeth
    Duer, 6
Robinson, Joshua D., 52
Robinson, Morris, 6
Rodgers, Alexander, 319-20
Rodgers, C.R.P., 320
Roosevelt, Franklin D., 336
Rothe, Augustus, 127
Royall, William B., 309
Russell, J.J., 276

Sagotal (Apache), 304
Sanford, G.B., 287, 288, 290,
    294
Santa Anna, Antonio López de, 6
Sapanovero (Ute chief), 278-79
Satank (Kiowa chief), 59-60,
    81-83, 91
Satanta (Kiowa chief), 58-60,
    81-86, 88, 91, 122, 160
Schofield, G.W., 122
Schofield, John M., 273, 311,
    317-19
Schuhardt, William, 128, 145,
    148-50
Schurz, Carl, 260, 263, 264,
    266, 276, 278
Schuyler, Walter, 217, 218
Sergeant Dandy Jim (scout),
    295, 298
Sergeant Dead Shot (scout),
    295, 298
Shafter, William R., 42-44, 48,
    115-17, 119, 147-48, 150,
    157, 242-43, 246-51, 330,
    337

Sharp Nose (Arapahoe chief),
    216
Sharp, John, 214
Sharpe, Florida. See Tunstall,
    Florida
Sharpe, Redford, 49, 53
Sheldon, L.A., 307
Sheridan Philip H., xiv, 21,
    23-26, 32-39, 82, 107,
    114-15, 130-32, 135,
    145-46, 148-49, 151, 153,
    155, 162, 172, 182,
    183-84, 198, 202, 212,
    214, 228-29, 232, 238,
    239, 245, 255, 261-63,
    265, 266, 270, 272, 273,
    275, 283, 285-87, 292,
    305, 311, 318-21, 330
Sherman, William T., 31, 39,
    74-83, 88, 91, 92-93,
    106-7, 125-26, 151, 155,
    157, 165, 192-94, 201-2,
    228, 239, 260, 261-63,
    266, 268, 271, 281,
    283-89, 292-93, 297, 302,
    306-7, 310, 311
Sitting Bear (Cheyenne), 214
Sitting Bull (Sioux chief), 201,
    207
Skiles, J.W., 254-55
Slidell, Alexander Mackenzie
    (father). See Mackenzie,
    Alexander Slidell, Sr.
Slidell, Jane (Mrs. Matthew C.
    Perry), 2
Slidell, John (grandfather), 2
Slidell, John (uncle), 2-3, 11-13
Slidell, Julia (Mrs. Raymond
    Rogers), 2
Slidell, Thomas, 2
Small, Elisha, 6
Smith, Captain, 203
Smith, Charles H., 37

CPSIA information can be obtained at www.ICGtesting.com
Printed in the USA
LVOW06s0340041115

460959LV00001B/3/P